Energies of Love

Energies of Love

SEXUALITY RE-VISIONED

JUNE SINGER

ANCHOR PRESS/DOUBLEDAY

Garden City, New York

1983

HQ
21
S55
1983

Copyright © 1983 by June Singer

Library of Congress Cataloging in Publication Data

Singer, June.
  Energies of love.

  Includes index.
  1. Sex. 2. Sex (Psychology)   I. Title.
HQ21.S55   1983   155.3

ISBN: 0-385-17022-X
Library of Congress Catalog Card Number: 81-43658

To all those souls
alive in this dimension
or another
who knowingly or unknowingly
have taught me
what love is,
and is not,
and who, for discretion's sake,
must remain unnamed,
I dedicate this book.

CONTENTS

Some day, after mastering the winds, the waves, the tides, and gravity, we will harness for God the energies of love. And then, for the second time in the history of the world, man will have discovered fire.

TEILHARD DE CHARDIN

Energies of Love

1

Great Knowledge and Small Knowledge

While in timeless time
  we embrace
  bodies bursting with energy
Arms legs hands fingers tuned to touch
  draw each to each closer and closer
No I exists
  no You
  only the We is present
Patterns of movement form and change
  undulating thrusting
  exploding releasing
  sinking into the oceanic silence of becoming
One
  with all there is

Two human beings who come together in the act of love express the totality of their selves. This event crystallizes all they feel and all they know. Each person opens to receive the fullness of the other in this unguarded moment. Not that all they share is consciously given, for many are the secrets that lovers keep from one another. Yet the body does not lie. The regard in which one person holds the other, or the lack of it, is embodied in the sexual act. Often the body proclaims what reason does not intend to convey. For sexuality, whatever else it does, communicates.

The phone rings. I, the writer, am jarred out of my reflections. An anxious young woman is on the line. She recently began her internship as a psychotherapist and I'm supervising her. She tells me that one of her clients just called to say that her two daughters have been sexually molested by their uncle. The client, a single woman, is paralyzed with fright. She doesn't know what to do. Confront the man? Call the police? Do nothing and let it blow over? I ask the therapist to tell me exactly what happened. The children said that he got on top of them, first one and then the other, with his pants open and "rubbed his thing against their peepee." They didn't like it, they said, got scared and told their mother.

I'm reminded, right at the outset, that sexual energy refers not only to the "energies of love," in Teilhard de Chardin's best sense, but that this energy can get horribly warped and twisted, that the energy we so often crave can also be turned into the most unloving of acts. Perhaps we should read Teilhard in his deeper meaning—that those powerful energies of love, like those of nature, are fully capable of overwhelming the human spirit, of degrading it as well as lifting it up. Like the gift Prometheus stole from the gods for his love of mortals, the second fire may bring light and warmth. Or, it may bring a curse, ravenously devouring everything in its path, leaving charred remains of fawn and rabbit on the smoking field.

Sexuality gains power by employing all the senses. Touch, taste, smell, vision, and hearing, and all the finer senses unnamed perceive the gross and subtle shifts and variations in the intimate encounter. In this human interaction nonverbal communication counts for far more than anything that can be said. Words follow words in orderly procession, but sexuality comes in waves and swirls, rising and falling, and in the beat of the heart and the pulsing of the loins. What is unspeakable and hence remains unspoken falls into two categories, as we conceptualize it: the preverbal and the transverbal.

Preverbal communication is powerful, strong, primordial, and uninhibited—the sound of the infant's feelings before it can form words or understand meanings. This language expresses basic needs and desires in unmistakable ways, with grunts and cries, smiles and sighs, loving and shoving. During sexual intercourse people fall back into these elemental expressions that exist at the opposite pole from ordinary rational discourse. They belong to the language of the body and of the soul. The language is prelogical, holistic and childlike, and sometimes frenzied. It is the impulse toward life, seeking its voice.

Transverbal communication, a pole apart, encompasses the look of understanding, the touch of empathy, and an awareness of tenderness that goes beyond words. Neither preverbal nor transverbal communication can be studied by the usual methods of science. What is the average length of a sigh? Does a deep kiss increase the heart rate more than a superficial one? What is the pressure per square inch of an embrace? Perhaps because of the tendency of these modes of communication to resist precise definition, they fail to attract scientists working in traditional ways. Since they cannot be quantified, they are not easily accessible to laboratory experiments or statistical studies. Nor is it possible to take into account the infinite numbers of variables that might contribute to their continually changing patterns. Preverbal communication is close to human instinctive behavior, where mankind interfaces with the primate ancestors. Transverbal communication, like the mystical experience, moves ahead of and outside of words, and cannot be contained in words.

When we human beings participate in an ongoing creative process, we are functioning to a large extent in the extraverbal realms. As we respond to our world, individuals vary in degree of awareness. This variation depends upon the complex interactions among many factors, including biological constitution, what we have learned, and how we relate to what we perceive as "other" or distinct from our own selves.

Most of us experience ourselves most of the time as separate beings encased in our skin. We feel alone; thoughts and feelings surge up in us wordlessly and we respond to them. Our bodies stretch and strain and move about to accommodate what we sense to be the movement of energy in us and through us. When another being enters our space and intimacy develops between us, the lines of separation blur. Communication takes place on many levels. You come into the room and my brain is assailed by millions of impressions transmitted by my sensory apparatus. Light enters my eye through the pupil, is focused by the lens, and an image falls on the retina. This is transmitted to the brain, which perceives it, gives meaning to it, and projects an image outward in your direction. What I become aware of is not a collection of neural impulses or chemical alterations. Through a miraculous transformation I see you reconstituted before me, an individual like no other, who can move me to anger, affection, or tears.

My attention is concentrated upon what I see as your being in this moment. What I see is only a small part of what you are in your totality. Because I am I, what I see will be different from what someone else looking at you would see. Yet there is far more that I observe than I could possibly express in words. Along with some detailed impressions, I take in the total gestalt, a configuration in time and space and involving a multitude of associations. Alfred Korzybski's famous statement, "The map is not the territory and the name is not the thing named," applies here. So much of every experience defies verbal expression, yet the meaning of the extraverbal must be extracted if we are to deal with it at all. Nowhere is this more true than when we deal with the subtle exchanges that come about as we experience sexuality. When we attempt to transpose these extraverbal perceptions into words and put them into linear sequence on a page, we produce an expectation that ideas will follow one another in a certain logical progression. But this is at variance with the way we actually experience life, as William Blake well knew when he wrote:

> Can Wisdom be put in a silver rod?
> Or Love in a golden bowl?[1]

These lines present the paradox in symbolic form which, when addressed, issues an imperative to re-vision sexuality. Although sexuality is a powerful form of communication, to set forth and properly illuminate its essence within the pages of a book is an impossible undertaking. The living experience of sexuality defies communication in rational terms. Only if the words are used symbolically can they begin to evoke even a proximate vision. Symbolic language leads us into imaginal realms where we find ourselves suffused with energy we did not know could move us so much. Symbols make us aware of our participation in an unbounded mystery. People who live "the symbolic life" are aware of the presence of many layers of meaning in quite ordinary events. The language of science is no less symbolic than that of religious mysticism. To decode information received from stars in distant space using numerical symbols is as strange and wonderful as discerning the messages our own bodies and senses make available to us.

Consider the striking similarity between subjective experiences of mystic union and those of deep and encompassing sexual union. Religious mystics, when describing their feelings during the profound ecstasy of communion with the divine, have often chosen to express them in terms of a spiritual union with God. Other mystics have found that same sense of unity and at-one-ness with the universe in the feeling of being themselves nature incarnate within the realm of the natural. Similarly, in sexual love there may be a sense of losing one's own personal identity and becoming one with the other. Then both persons are joined in the fullest sense—as one body, one consciousness—if only for a moment.

A biological interpretation of these experiences of union has been suggested by Alexander Maven.[2] He makes the observation that each of the ways of describing the experience is analogous to a description of the union of sperm and ovum. In that biological union, when the sperm penetrates the ovum and is absorbed by it, or dissolves into it, its protoplasm merges into that of the host and its chromosomes pair off with the like parts of the ovum. From a gamete, the mature germ cell that is capable of initiating the formation of a new individual only through fusion with another gamete, the ovum is transformed into a zygote, which is able to produce a developing individual. The sperm now ceases to exist as a separate entity, but continues to exist as an integral part of the zygote. The language used by some mystics communicates a similar experience but with different imagery. Some say the Divine Spirit enters the soul and, uniting with it, transforms and immortalizes it. Others say that the soul or Self enters into the Divine like a drop of dew slipping into the ocean, and therein dissolves and merges with the ocean. But these are only words striving for the meaning of the union between human and human, and between the individual and the Godhead.

C. G. Jung, in his essay "Psychology of Transference,"[3] draws a
parallel between the intimacy that occurs in the experience of psychological analysis and the mystical experience as described in an
alchemical manuscript of the fifteenth century, the *Rosarium Phi-
losophorum*. In the latter, the union of soul and body is presented
in sexual terms as a union of "king" and "queen" or royal brother
and sister. When we read of this inner marriage, and particularly
when we view the accompanying woodcut, we are able to discern
the same biological analogy:

THE CONJUNCTION

The sea has closed over the king and queen, and they have gone
back to the chaotic beginnings, the *massa confusa*. Physis has
wrapped the "man of light" in a passionate embrace. As the
text says: "Then Beya [the maternal sea] rose up over Gabricus
and enclosed him in her womb, so that nothing more of him
was to be seen. And she embraced Gabricus with so much love
that she absorbed him completely into her own nature, and dissolved him into atoms."[4]

The literature of mysticism contains many similar descriptions
of the experience of mystic union which are obvious and close
analogies to the union of sperm and ovum.

Maven makes an intuitive speculation that "the experience of
the mystic union in its various forms may be a 'play-back' of the
record of the mystic's biological conception as it might have been
experienced, respectively, by the ovum, by the sperm, and by both
together." He notes that laboratory experiments have brought to
light evidence of memory in unicellular organisms. "And if,"
Maven continues, "as we must assume, the unicellular organism is
capable of recording its experiences somehow so that they can be
'played back,' it may well be that the record would be duplicated
in every cell of the multicellular organism that develops from the
zygote. That duplication might account for the felt immediacy of
a 'play-back' which has led some mystics to say that they felt the
experience 'in the very marrow of their bones.'"[5]

When mystics try to talk about their experiences they are nearly
unanimous in expressing that their deepest, most ecstatic feelings

extend beyond words. Nevertheless, these men and women reflect in calmer moments, and finally are able to say a great deal about the experience of mystic union which was "ineffable" at the time. We may ask, why were there no words for this most immediate and most powerful of experiences? Maven suggests a possible reason. If the mystical experience is a "play-back" of the experience of the mystic's conception, the reexperiencing would be ineffable, beyond words, because the *original experience* of conception occurred before the mystic had learned a language, hence it had no verbal component. But the "play-back," unlike the original experience, could be described when it was remembered later.

There is an exceedingly dangerous aspect to the preverbal primal encounter which results in conception. For conception follows a war to the death, in which only one of the thousands of spermatozoa that fight their way up the vaginal passage toward the uterus will survive to be accepted by the ovum. The failure of the gamete to unite with the ovum means death. The violent emotions that later will come to be associated with sexuality may have their beginnings here in this fear. The counterpoint to this is the intense joy of a spiritual nature which is possible with the initiation of a new life. If the union does occur and is viable, the resulting zygote carries the potential for immortality, in the sense that the spark of life it ignites may be passed on to subsequent generations.

Not in words, but in a mysterious kind of knowing that precedes words, we possess some awareness of how we experienced our own beginnings—or at least this is what some people believe. Beyond the barriers of memory may lie a history more ancient than we can possibly imagine, the genetic history of all beings who were incarnated or reincarnated in the burst of sperm and the embrace of ovum. We embody that age-old heritage and we may pass it on through the exercise of our sexuality. It appears that at least one purpose of our existence on this planet is to carry forward the life principle, which depends upon living beings for continuity. Wordsworth understands this as an unconscious remembering of our immortality:

> Our birth is but a sleep and a forgetting:
> The Soul that rises with us, our life's Star,

Hath had elsewhere its setting,
And cometh from afar . . .[6]

The poet writes out of a nonlinear consciousness. He does not perceive events in a logical order, but they burst upon his senses as though from many levels of awareness all operating simultaneously. It is as though the highly focused quality of mind that our society cultivates had departed from him, leaving him with images and emotions that are not bound by time or space. The poetic dimension is a nonordinary reality—it is the world of the artist, out of which creation comes. Creation has little to do with linear memory, but much to do with this other, stranger memory, in which insights suddenly appear or wherein one hears an entire piece of music whole. The mystical experience is of this quality also. Like art, it is not dependent upon linear time. It changes little over the centuries; it always has to do with the seeking and sometimes the finding of an intimate relationship between the human and the divine.

This is one level of reality. Contemporary brain research has associated this sort of consciousness with the right hemisphere of the brain, which is thought to be more holistically organized than the left hemisphere, more tuned for music and art, and for seeing things in their entirety rather than detail by detail. Being less addicted to the rational, the right hemisphere can play with images and ideas and, above all, is able to maintain a sense of mystery and wonder. For this hemisphere, it is not important to offer proofs, but rather to experience reality as it presents itself to the individual.

Our culture in the Western world has placed a higher premium on the so-called left-brain productions than on those of the right. Accustomed as we are to the linear, one-at-a-time character of speech and writing, we tend to view our lives as event following event in endless succession. We report about what happens to us in the same way. We see ourselves as standing on this long road, somewhere between antecedent cause and subsequent event. We look backward in order to see how we have come to this place, and forward to project how our current behavior will affect what happens in the future. So much for our reasoned process.

But we do not experience life in this cumbersome linear fashion. How could we live for even one moment if we had to operate our bodies consciously by taking command of every breath, every beat of the heart, every neural impulse? Fortunately, these matters proceed independently of conscious will and intention. We need only attend directly to the events occurring in a focal area of consciousness, taking care of one small area after another. Meanwhile, our peripheral vision scans a wider area and, either consciously or unconsciously, perceives immediate things in a wider context. We can expand that context indefinitely, being limited only by our sensory capacity and the capability of our brains, and of the machines we devise to record, store, process, and retrieve information.

Sexuality is surely an area of life that escapes confinement by the centrally focused vision which characterizes our more rational activities most of the time. The power of sexuality is just that it can transcend the superficial layers of consciousness and strike hard at the core of one's being. This power can shake one out of time and space, can instantaneously alter one's mood, one's desires, and one's capacity to function in the everyday world. Even when people have seasoned and matured to a degree that they believe their impulses are under control, and the desire to possess the lover has been mitigated by the realization that no one can rightly "possess" another person, the power of sexuality can reach with a swift hand and wipe away everything learned from past relationships, however painfully. The lessons of experience are not entirely wiped away and surely not forever, for the body experiences the pain in the chest as real when, for example, you suddenly learn that your lover has been sexually intimate with another person. Even though you had offered each other complete freedom, the pain stuns. Self-torture, self-doubt, fear, and dread come in its wake. Even suicide may loom as a real possibility when the meaning you counted on in your life seems to disappear. Or an urge to murder may come upon you, because you feel betrayed, set up, your place invaded, your valuables ransacked. Emotions spill over you. You see no limit to the misery. Nothing else matters right now. It doesn't count that you have done the same thing to your lover, or other lovers, in the past. It doesn't count that you have made no claims upon each other. It doesn't add up. Conventional wisdom does not apply. The power of emotion has catapulted you from one sphere to another: from the time-bound linear-sequential ego consciousness where you felt in charge of yourself, to another, timeless dimension of reality. Here you feel helpless against forces that defy your attempts at understanding.

More often than not, sexual relations are carried out without full appreciation of the power of sexuality. Just because this power is potentially so overwhelming, it is denied, its expression trivialized. It is like those little pink statues of the Virgin that people hang up in their cars to dangle from the rear-view mirror—as though they needed to know that the power was present but did not want to admit how important it was to them. If we could only believe that we have some control over this power, then it would not appear so fearsome. Sooner or later we invoke the power of reason against emotion, as we have been taught to do in the socializing process of our times. We firmly believe that everything has a cause and an explanation. We remind ourselves that discovering these will somehow set us free.

Most ideas we hold today about the origins of sexual feeling and the developmental patterns of human sexuality still reflect scientific views that were current during the last part of the nineteenth century and the beginning of the twentieth. In response to rapidly changing social, political, and environmental conditions since 1900, and especially since the end of the Second World War, behavioral patterns in every area, and particularly in the area of sexuality, have undergone radical alteration. Morals and mores, practice and parlance, differ markedly from what they were when behavior was being described, analyzed, and predicted by Freud and the early psychoanalysts and by John B. Watson and the early behaviorists. Child development studies incorporating one or another of the earlier models have proliferated under two or three generations of investigators. The principles established by the early schools continue to influence some of the recent explorations in the field. Developmental studies originally addressed themselves to charting the progress of individuals but moved quickly into the area of interpersonal development, studying group behavior on an increasingly inclusive scale. Social scientists have been extrapolating from the findings drawn from individual and small group studies, and applying what they have learned to community structures and broader issues. Students of cross-cultural behavior have helped to bring into perspective how people differ behaviorally from group to group, and how they are similar. Their work provides a basis for differentiating basic human tendencies that are inborn and are archetypal in nature, from culturally acquired patterns, if indeed these distinctions can be made with certainty.

Despite all this valuable work, I sense a great void in the study of human psychosexual development. This void I see as the absence of an encompassing world view that could provide a setting within which to discuss recent trends in sexual interaction. If a new world view is in the making, as I believe it is, sexuality has not yet been incorporated into that vision. Current sexual practice can no longer be explained by the old theories and we do not yet understand it in the light of the new ones. Racing ahead of history, we now find ourselves in a new territory. We may as well begin drawing some new maps. This is the first step in the process of re-visioning sexuality, a step which I believe is necessary to our personal growth and collective evolution.

When I began to consider how much has been written about sexuality recently, not to mention the vast literature over the years dating back to the beginning of our century, even back to the Bible, and before that in ancient Greece, the Near East, and the Orient, I realized the awesomeness of the undertaking. It would be far simpler to carve out a small area from this limitless subject and concentrate on that, as any sensible scholar would do. Some workable hypothesis could be proposed, and the necessary data generated to validate or disprove it could be gathered. At this time, however, concentrating upon the minute particulars would draw our attention away from the sweep of the whole. The subject is incredibly complicated, and the complexities threaten to lead us away from the broader considerations. During the past half century, behavioral scientists, biologists, and physicians have carried on research into the many varied areas of human sexuality. Without their detailed studies and careful reporting, there would be little empirical data available to support a broader view. At the risk of being incomplete and imprecise, I want to bring a more generalized broader perspective to a subject that is often viewed symptomatically and partially.

I want to look at sexuality with "soft eyes,"[7] with a diffused gaze, sensing the feelings and textures of events in their context, in the large sweeps of time and space that blur details but shape attitudes. My spiritual mentor, C. G. Jung, often spoke of the need to regard phenomena *sub specie aeternitatis*, under the eye of eternity. As a Jungian analyst, I am accustomed to meeting with the total person in a total situation, and to accepting that unity. I want to bring to this person a fresh and innocent eye, not a piercing eye but a receptive one. I want to envision the person, and that person's life story, both as individual experience and as integral part of a dynamic universe. Sexuality belongs to both aspects: it is a matter of personal intimacy, and it is a key to how the individual participates in life in response to patterns in nature that are only imperfectly understood.

Ordinarily, we concern ourselves with problems of everyday living and their solutions. These are the "ten thousand things" of the Chinese philosophers. Rarely do we see how they take their place in the larger systems, or even how they relate to each other. Were we to step out of our Western tradition and attend to the words of Chuang Tzu, the ancient and wise philosopher, we would gain insight as to how we might proceed toward a widening vision of our subject:

GREAT KNOWLEDGE

Great knowledge sees all in one.
Small knowledge breaks down into the many.

When the body sleeps, the soul is enfolded in One.
When the body wakes, the openings begin to function.
They resound with every encounter
With all the varied business of life, the strivings of the heart;
Men are blocked, perplexed, lost in doubt.
Little fears eat away their peace of heart.
Great fears swallow them whole.
Arrows shot at a target: hit and miss, right and wrong.
This is what men call judgment, decision.

Their pronouncements are as final
As treaties between emperors.
O, they make their point!
Yet their arguments fall faster and feebler
Than dead leaves in autumn and winter.
Their talk flows out like piss,
Never to be recovered.
They stand at last, blocked, bound, and gagged,
Choked up like old drain pipes.
The mind fails. It shall not see light again.

Pleasure and rage
Sadness and joy
Hopes and regrets
Change and stability
Weakness and decision
Impatience and sloth:
All are sounds from the same flute,
All mushrooms from the same wet mould.
Day and night follow one another and come upon us
Without our seeing how they sprout!

Enough! Enough!
Early and late we meet the "that"
From which "these" all grow!

If there were no "that"
There would be no "this."
If there were no "this"
There would be nothing for all these winds to play on.
So far can we go.
But how shall we understand
What brings it about?

One may well suppose the True Governor
To be behind it all. That such a Power works
I can believe. I cannot see his form.

He acts, but has no form.[8]

Although I was reared in a traditional Western religion and trained in the social sciences, the image of the "True Governor" and the recognition "That such a Power works" resonates with me. The orderly progressions of nature confirm my conviction that my being here in just the way I am here in this moment is not a matter of pure chance but the inevitable outcome of many converging events. I do not find it too difficult to surrender my acquired skepticism to the likelihood that this order is governed according to natural rhythms. I do not need to imagine that the True Governor is outside of the order, any more than the "governor" of an automobile is outside the automobile. A True Governor is implied in the order of systems within systems, and systems encompassing systems; all functioning so effectively and so smoothly that robins consistently lay pale blue eggs, and hyacinth bulbs turn earth, water, and sunshine into marvelously fragrant clusters of purple blooms, and spring arrives on schedule.

I do not find it necessary to know the name or shape of the True Governor. All that is needed is to know that the True Governor exists, and is embodied in energy which we sometimes call power, and that such a power works. The Chinese call this subtle property of energy *ch'i*, the Hindus call it *prāna*. It is the *pneuma* of the Greeks, the *ruach* of the Hebrews. No one has seen it, yet many know of its existence. It works in the multitude of ways that Chuang Tzu suggested, and more. The forms of its manifestations are numerous also—the faces of the serene Buddhas and smiling bodhisattvas, of dancing Shiva and the soulful-eyed Kwan-Yin, of Krishna playing his flute in flowery meadows, of Zeus hurling thunderbolts and of Dionysius dismembered, of Persephone deflowered and of Mary pregnant with her holy child, of Jesus suffering on the cross and of Muhammad ascending toward heaven from the Holy Mount in the city of Jerusalem. Seen from the perspective of the many, every god is a separate entity; each has followers and worshippers and each is a focus of ritual and belief. But seen from the standpoint of the One, the many array themselves against one another, dividing themselves from each other and their adherents from each other. Their adherents do not observe that while the many deities appear to have their own powers, all these derive from One, the power that works through energy, *ch'i*. There is only One, acting through a multitude of manifestations, but the One is Itself without form.

Nevertheless, Great Knowledge acts through small knowledge, even in matters between individuals. In sexuality, small and great knowledge meet. Sexuality engages us in personal encounters; it also responds to the energetic force that quickens the life process on our planet Earth. It keeps consciousness alive, although the vessels (ourselves) which temporarily give form and shape to consciousness may crumble or break. Nature uses sexuality to ensure the continuation of Life.

How we observe, understand, and experience our sexuality affects not only our personal lives and personal history, but also the vast interconnecting network of relationships which forms the context for all of Life. These observations and insights appear to us to be part of our conscious orientation as we have been taught and as it has grown out of our personal experience. On another level, the way in which we see our world and the sense we make of it—including our standards and values and belief systems—are products of the collective unconscious. We assimilate them without realizing it out of a commonly held world view that may never be articulated explicitly but is nevertheless a part of the current mindset in a particular time and place. The German expression *Zeitgeist*, spirit of the times, describes our superficial experience of this world view very well. Underlying this experience, however, is a complex conceptual and behavioral framework that is accepted by an entire society. This framework is not a single theory but a meta-theory composed of many theories bearing on different aspects of reality and welded together by some overarching principles.

Such a framework is called a *paradigm*. Every organized society operates under a ruling paradigm, whether its members are aware of it or not. For most people, the paradigm is unconscious, which is to say that it is not seen as a particular model of reality. Rather, their world view tends to be regarded as the "truth." In its fundamentals, a paradigm is based upon the state of scientific knowledge, out of which is constructed a physical and materialistic view. Physics not only tells us the way things are supposed to be in the physical world, but it is also the basis for models of the world that lies outside of the physical realm, what has been called the world of spirit, of mind, or of consciousness.

By the time paradigms are officially formulated, they generally characterize the culmination of long-term cultural developments. Paradigms emerge slowly, out of fundamental changes in relationships between individuals, nature, and society. Customs and mores undergo alteration and after a while people begin to notice that the principles and rules by which they believed themselves to be governed no longer exert the influence they did in the past. The principles remain in effect, but people pay less and less attention to them. Rules remain rigid but behavior shrugs them off. People experience cognitive dissonance between what they say they believe in and what, in fact, they do.

In the early stages of a shift in patterns of morality, people may feel unsettled, deviant, sinful, or out of tempo with what they had formerly assumed to be true and appropriate. Such a sense of inner discord affects that part of the ego personality we know as the "self." Ego psychologists use "self" to refer to the sense we have of being complete and coherent individuals. Self-esteem arises from the regard in which each person holds this self. When the self-image is depreciated by others or injured by failure and defeat, then self-esteem falls. When individuals become self-absorbed and consumed with concern about themselves, at the expense of relating in a mature and mutual way to other people, they are said to be suffering from a "narcissistic personality disorder." If we can believe the trend in psychological literature, narcissism is the illness of our times. Its symptoms include persistent demands for immediate gratification, concern with one's own comfort and amusement, indifference to the wider environment except insofar as it serves one's own desires, and the exploitation of other people to secure one's own ends. A one-sided introversion and preoccupation with personal concerns characterize the narcissistic personality. In order to experience the self as coherent, a certain consistency is needed between one's perceived self-image and one's idealized self-image, both in terms of what one believes in, and in one's behavior. Serious inconsistencies here can bring about a crisis of conscience resulting in a degraded self-image. This self that suffers is personal, in the sense that it is ours alone.

Also, it is engaged in relationships with other people. All this occurs in the world of the particular, the world of small knowledge.

There is another Self with which we will be concerned throughout this work. This will be spelled with a capital "S" to indicate that it belongs to the realm of Great Knowledge. Borrowed from the Hindu *Atman/Self* concept, "Self," as used by Jung, refers to the central moving force of the universe. All images of the Godhead are fashioned after the Self, and all approximate it but none encompasses it. The Self is the central archetype, according to Jung. As the all-inclusive creative aspect of the universe, the Self manifests within each individual and is recognized by some persons as the divine spark within. Focused, it is the central reference point of the psyche; diffused, it encompasses the totality of its conscious and unconscious aspects. This is why it is referred to as "smaller than small and bigger than big." The individual self, the reflexive aspect of consciousness, is subsumed under the wider Self, and self relates to Self as part to whole. If we could imagine an axis which connects the personal self with the archetypal or transpersonal Self, we would have the image of a finite individual consciousness embedded in the conscious/unconscious totality that extends beyond the boundaries of our ordinary awareness.

On one level, the personal self perceives the paradigm to which it has been acculturated. Those of us who have grown up during the first half or the first two-thirds of the twentieth century have become acculturated to the paradigm of "modernity." This paradigm was conceived during the period of the Enlightenment in seventeenth-century France and England, was born in the Industrial Revolution of England and Western Europe, and is now in the process of decay. Modernity began when science was breaking out of the constrictions imposed upon her earlier by the Church, and science rapidly became the "new religion." Under the paradigm of modernity, faith in miracles was transferred to science which, it was believed, held the key to total comprehension of the mysteries of the universe. Faith in science was faith in the future. But, since so much of science was difficult if not impossible for laypersons to understand, it was left to scientists to mediate between nature's secrets and their utilization by human beings. The new hierarchies of the sciences performed their feats in laboratories instead of churches, used the language of statistics instead of Latin, and were served by graduate students instead of acolytes. Like their theological predecessors, they often took it upon themselves to tell the world what was true and what was false.

On another level, the transpersonal Self perceives the limitations of that paradigm, and offers us the challenge to consider what goes on beyond the boundaries of accepted ideas and approved ways of doing things. The Self is mercurial by nature, instigating the random, the new, the unexpected, while the self is busily attempting to make its adaptations to what it has been informed is the "real world." The Self is mischief-maker, trickster, the one who throws in the mercurial substance that creates the mutation, just when the process of evolution was proceeding nicely according to plan. The self wonders how things came to be as they are, why they don't always conform to its expectations, why it feels uncomfortable at times, why it feels the urge to break the rules and disturb its well-disciplined patterns.

Along the self-Self axis the tendency arises in people to examine their patterns of behavior, as well as the more abstract patterns of science and philosophy, and to wonder whether those latter too are subject to change and, if so, how to change them. Along this self-Self axis, intuitions arise which produce new hypotheses, or impulses to test out assumptions that have long been accepted because everybody believed them true instead of merely truisms. Along this self-Self axis, our inquiry into sexuality arises out of our awareness of our own discomfort at recognizing how little relationship there is between the moral stance our culture proclaims and the sexual behavior of its members.

An individual tends to construct the self in such a way as to conform to the shape of reality that is transmitted by our culture. What is that shape of reality? How do we perceive it? These two questions are actually one, because the shape of reality *depends* on how we perceive it. As our perceptions of reality change, so reality changes for us.

I must make it clear that when I talk about *reality* here, I do not mean *ultimate reality*. Ultimate reality belongs to a different logical order than reality as we commonly use the word. We cannot view ultimate reality directly because of the limitations of the human organism. Our senses, our intellects, our bodies, and all the various mechanical and electronic prostheses we attach to them, are able to probe only a little way into the infinite depths of the universe. Ultimate reality encompasses all we know, and can know, and more. It is coexistent with all of it. Finite human beings can hardly do more than beam their small searchlights into the great yawning darkness. So, when we speak about reality, we can only speak about the portion of reality we perceive, given our experience and the information that is passed to us by the agencies of our culture. We often err, in taking *our* reality to be *the* reality, and *our* images of the gods to be coexistent with the ultimate mystery of the Godhead.

Because we are still conditioned to some extent by the paradigm of modernity, with its reliance upon scientific method and the establishment of proofs, we may find this relativism difficult to accept. In our concerns with counting and weighing and measuring, with precise description and careful evaluation, we sometimes fail to recognize or give credit to values that do not fit these criteria. Or, when we do recognize that such values exist, we split them off from the consciousness of the marketplace and relegate them to the categories of religion or the arts. The age of modernity reached its climax with a tendency to polarize concepts and think in pairs of opposites: rational/emotional, scientific/religious, privileged/disadvantaged, masculine/feminine. Most significantly, we have widened the chasm between the sacred and the profane. What began with good intentions by our founding fathers as "separation of Church and State" has degenerated in latter days to a separation between the divine and the human. In the process, the chasm has widened between our individual selves and the universal Self.

2
Moving Toward Modernity

The sense of the sacred was present and active in the everyday lives of people of the Middle Ages, whether they belonged to the landed aristocracy, the peasantry, the artisan classes, or the military. A sensibility prevailed in which one's destiny was acceptable because it was divinely ordained. Progress was associated more with continuity than completion. Nowhere was this more clearly expressed than in the construction of the great Gothic cathedrals. Those lovers of God who laid the foundations deep in the earth never saw the spires rise, and those who carved the delicate angels and fantastic gargoyles on intricate façades and rooftops had never known what stonemasons had placed the huge blocks of marble in the floor of the nave. Yet all of it was one offering, reaching back in time and soaring toward a mystery behind the skies—beyond perception, but not beyond belief.

The spiritual glory of the Middle Ages was accompanied by much physical discomfort and suffering, by plagues and wars, and by extreme simplicity of life-style for those in the lower ranks of the social structure. Yet even those who were poorest in material goods trusted that their entry into heaven would recompense them for their trials on earth, and so they did not need, in T. S. Eliot's phrase, to wait without hope. They lived under the paradigm of a spiritually oriented existence, where the hierarchy of the heavens manifested in the hierarchies on earth to which they were subjected, and the royal personages who ruled the earth took their rights from the Ruler in heaven, and governed in His name. Thus an authoritarian society met the needs of an untutored populace to be protected by a father-lord, and his people willingly paid him homage. Women served as vessels for spiritual power. Women of good family were highly romanticized. Yet with few exceptions they were politically invisible, except as objects controlled by men.

Around the end of the thirteenth century, the Church of the High Middle Ages had attained its zenith. With tremendous power accruing to the papacy and the clergy, corruption now began to set in and many of the proclaimed ideals of the Church came gradually under suspicion. The spirituality of the age of chivalry, with its reverence for women and its Mariolatry, began to lose its fascination. Nevertheless, the great institutions that had their beginnings in the Middle Ages remained as the framework of collective action far into the modern centuries. But during the next two centuries voices were beginning to be heard outside the Church, demanding that some power and some authority be extended to the common people, the craftsmen and merchants, the travelers and townsfolk. Gradually and not without periodic violence, the feudal economic system dissolved, and along with it most of the associated political and ecclesiastical networks.

The sixteenth and seventeenth centuries saw the rise of capitalism in England and Western Europe. In its early stages, many religious, educational, and commercial activities were centered in the home. Often women became de facto partners of their men, both in parenting and in working to provide economic support for their families. Power and authority were still concentrated in husband and father, but in everyday life there was a great deal of sharing and camaraderie between men and women. What women lost in distinctiveness and autonomy, they gained in respect from men—and this was in marked contrast to their earlier idealized position on a pedestal. The home became the center of work and family life. Father, mother, and several children would share the family bedroom, and sometimes the family bed. Sexual behavior, loving behavior, was part of everyday life. There was no need to be secretive and mysterious about it. Living in such close quarters, the physical bodies of members of the opposite sex were taken for granted as being mostly the same as one's own, give or take a few inches here or there; and of the differences, no one made much fuss over them. The "primal scene" was no big trauma, making love was just something one's parents did from time to time. Even the Church recognized the importance of encouraging the pleasurable relations of marital sex for their own sake as well as for purposes of procreation.

The middle class in the English-speaking capitalist nations initiated some important socioeconomic movements which have affected the sexual lives of men and women in the Western world from that time until today. They expanded and centralized commerce and industry, taking business outside of the home and severely restricting men's daily intimate contact with their families. The Protestant Reformation emphasized patriarchal authority in the home, with the father/husband assuming the judgmental, Old Testament authority inherent in the God-image presented there. Protestants no longer prayed to women saints, as Catholics continued to do. Some Protestants even objected to the Catholic portrayal of the Christ Child in his mother's arms, on the grounds that this would make him appear as an underling to a woman. The abolition of celibate orders within Protestantism removed from women the possibility of a separate and sacred status.

The new literacy that came into being with the Protestant Reformation was extended to women as well as to men. With the invention of movable type and the translation of the Bible into the vernacular, everyone was expected to learn to read, even lower-class men, and women of all stations. Both men and women were now privileged to have individual relationships with God, unmediated by a male clergy. The very powerful maleness of that stern image of God portrayed by the Protestants encouraged both men and women to relate to him in a mode of submission. This, also, tended to diminish the sexual distinctions. Men and women began to see each other in more human terms, and some of the most oppressive aspects of sexual inequality were discouraged. The Protestants placed more and more emphasis on the reciprocal responsibility within the marriage for love and companionship. In the older tradition, women had been thought more volatile and emotional than men, but slowly the image of women as vulnerable to irrational behavior began to fade. Occasionally shadows of the past erupted in regressive practices, as in the burning of witches in the sixteenth and seventeenth centuries. But, on the whole, the relationship of men and women in the conjugal setting was bonded with love and respect, predicated, of course, on woman's duty to obey her husband.

This shift in the role and function of women can clearly be seen as it was reflected in the architecture, arts, and crafts of the sixteenth and seventeenth centuries. The vigorous art of the Middle Ages created under the stimulus and patronage of the Church gave way to a secular form of art which, if not as lofty as its predecessor, was surely more human and utilitarian. Great manor houses were built. They had spacious gardens, and a love of detail showed there as well as in the woodwork, textiles, and furniture. Among the middle classes this careful craftsmanship was carried out on a smaller scale. In painting, idealized images were no longer in vogue but realistic portraiture came into its own, with women as subjects as often as men. Men and women were represented as active and robust, often engaging in playful occupations of a romantic or adventurous nature. The lady of the house was portrayed with dignity and a certain sturdy beauty, a far cry from the earlier images of ethereal virgins or saints. Women appeared warm and charming, as the sort of people you could talk to and enjoy being with, rather than as remote and archetypal beings. Especially in the paintings of Holland and southern Germany, scenes teemed with the life of the populace and the women and children and dogs were no less important in the general schema than the head of the family.

As the economic stability of the times increased, some of the more austere religious and social traditions gave way to a tendency for individuals to seek a more sensually oriented life. People realized that they could set about to improve their material conditions through their own efforts. Utilitarian concerns increased in importance. Secular achievements were rewarded with more money and higher status. Individualism became a secret objective as talented citizens decided to try to make the most of themselves. Clearly, the virtues of humility and obedience had lost their appeal for a growing number of enterprising individuals.

With more energy directed toward materialistic values, many people rejected their spiritual values outright. Others gave them relatively perfunctory expression on the special occasions set aside for church attendance, in this way avoiding a direct confrontation between matters of the world and spiritual commitment. Beyond any personal considerations, this avoidance of confrontation served the needs of Church and State, two institutions whose interests as a rule had been so arranged as to serve one another with mutual effectiveness. But the compatibility of Church and State was to be unsettled by developments from another quarter.

Continuing advances in the natural sciences that had begun in the sixteenth and seventeenth centuries brought about a development of philosophical ideas that were closely connected with the fundamental tenets of science. Descartes had made a clear differentiation between mental processes and the material world, and thus became an important influence in initiating a widespread change of attitude. Cartesian philosophy extended and developed the new humanism that had earlier made its appearance during the Renaissance in Italy and the Reformation in the North. Religion became more personal and subjective, inspiring art and music and devotion to the life of the spirit. At the same time, natural science became more "objective." The world of the mind/emotions/spirit and the natural world were not seen to act upon each other, since they seemed so different in their essence. The systems were not interdependent, but parallel. People began to believe that the mind and its activities were determined by laws that were different from, but parallel to, the laws of chemistry and physics.

The effects of this parallelism on the modern understanding of sexuality is especially problematical. It is clear enough that physiology and mental imagery are inextricably interwoven when sexuality is being experienced. What every poet, playwright, novelist, and lover knows about sexuality's way of merging the subtle emotions and the involvement of the body has managed to escape those theoreticians who deal with sexual issues either solely from the physiological or solely from the psychological perspective. Ideas and feelings arise in their specific contexts. Unless they are re-visioned from time to time, they tend to continue to exert their influence long after the context has altered and there is no longer any need for them.

The separation of the natural sciences from matters of the soul worked successfully for several centuries. It had its profound effect on the nature of human relationships. Where sex differences had been receiving minimal emphasis in the sixteenth and seventeenth centuries, by the eighteenth and nineteenth our concepts of what is manly and what is womanly had once more diverged in significant ways. With the separation of the rational aspects from the affective aspects of life, masculine imagery began to be associated with everything rational, linear, logical, and powerful, and female imagery with everything affective, cyclic, impulsive, irrational, and vulnerable. As ever in the past, now again sex roles conformed to adapt to the sweeping cultural changes in process.

Scientific progress advanced rapidly as scientists committed themselves to careful observation and study of the natural world. Classical Newtonian physics demonstrated that a model of the natural world could be produced without reference either to God or to the scientist who was doing the observing. The natural world was believed to operate like a machine, the functions of which could be described by an observer. The laws by which it operated could be formulated. Indeed, Newton succeeded in abstracting the information derived from his mathematical observations and restating it in mathematical language as laws with their corollaries and propositions, which explained how the world worked.[1] Newton's conception of the universe was fundamental to the paradigm of modernity. Newton's universe comfortably contained all physical phenomena. He based his descriptions of the universe on the three-dimensional space of classical Euclidean geometry, where space is absolute, always at rest and unchangeable. He saw time as flowing from the past through the present to the future. "Absolute, true, and mathematical time," said Newton, "of itself and by its own nature, flows uniformly, without regard to anything external."[2] For a long time it was believed that the laws derived from Newton's work and the later extensions of it would remain an inclusive description of the functioning of the natural physical world. Newton's conceptualization of the workings of the physical universe was fundamental to the formation of the world view that was to mature as "the paradigm of modernity."

Michael Faraday and James C. Maxwell were the first to extend Newtonian physics when they replaced the concept of a force with that of a force field. This eventuated in a profound change in our view of physical reality. While their work did not invalidate Newton's theories, it placed beside them a theory that applied to different phenomena, which Newton's mechanics had not taken into consideration. By the beginning of the twentieth century, there were two successful theories which physicists could apply to different phenomena, Newton's mechanics and Maxwell's electrodynamics. Although the mechanical model of Newton had ceased to be the basis of all physics, where it was applicable it influenced profoundly the modern world view.

During the early scientific era of the sixteenth and seventeenth centuries, knowledge had derived from observation and deduction. Later on, modern scientific method came to rely far more upon experimentation and measurement. When more exact ways were found to describe and explain phenomena, scientists could better predict what would be likely to occur in the future on the basis of information at hand. Theoretically, by deliberately altering certain conditions, it would be possible to predict correspondingly different outcomes. Science had begun its methodical attempts to manipulate and control nature and natural processes.

Another trend in the development of science was the striving of a certain group of scientists, or philosophers of science, to unify human knowledge. They believed that there is only one science, encompassing a single world view, and that all its disciplines stem from this common source and therefore must be able to function in relationship with one another. Since science is all-inclusive, there can be no legitimate extra-scientific teaching. In principle this may have some basis, but in practice the idea was limiting. Only the normative sciences were recognized. The "paranormal" was suspect, because it could not be accessible to manipulation in laboratory experiments.

The mechanistic approach that characterized science addressed itself to the human condition as well. Medicine was the branch of science that dealt with human illness, both physical and psychological. Psychiatry was the subdivision of medicine that specialized in psychological concerns, and psychotherapy was a further specialization of psychiatry and a technical application of it. Other specialties within medicine dealt with other aspects of human illness. The person came to be viewed not as the person as he knew himself, but as a collection of organs and functions, some of which become dysfunctional and have to be repaired like parts of a machine.

The progress brought about by industrialization, technological advance, urbanization, and other aspects of modernization emancipated people from the necessity of producing everything by hard physical labor. To be sure, many still sweated in factories and mills, but a rising middle class began to know a new freedom that had not been experienced a couple of generations earlier. More and more people now owned real property. As they became landowners and householders, their values shifted. What they were able to accumulate in material goods took on a greater importance to them. When a man's home became his castle, his interest in the kingdom of the spirit waned. The home became the central focus of the family; family members were the reason for the home's existence, and they used the home in part for pleasure and serviceability, and in part it signified their social rank and status. It fell to the woman to maintain the home so that it could provide continuity for her family, which centered about it. Household and family became more closely connected. It was expected that the home would be passed on to the next generation. All of this served to stabilize the middle-class family.

By the end of the nineteenth century, the division of labor between men and women was more marked than ever. This had a decided effect upon sexual mores and sexual practices. Not since the knights of the Middle Ages had gone off to fight their battles, leaving their pristine ladies behind them, had such a dichotomy existed between the masculine and feminine approach to sexuality. The importance of the biological differences between men and women was emphasized by the social order, which prescribed sharply defined sex-role behavior. Men working away from their homes in a rapidly growing and changing industrial society faced increasing competition for jobs, for status, and for positions of power. You had to be aggressive to survive, even more aggressive and manipulative in order to succeed. Economic success came to those who were clever in their dealings and quick to seize advantage.

Wives and other female relatives were badly needed as a sup-

port system for men in the middle classes, who were engaged
mostly in business and commerce. Responsibility for the manage-
ment of the home and the rearing of children fell almost exclusively upon the woman. The task did not require the pressure that
was expected of men, but a woman had to meet expectations also.
No matter how many household problems she had to solve, and
no matter how many children to bear and nurture, she was expected to retain her helpful and submissive character in the presence of her husband and other adult males. The arrangement was
that the wife would provide a setting for her husband in which he
could relax and restore his energies. She was to provide the sexual
partnership he needed, when he needed it. She had little expectation that her own sexual rhythms would define the nature of the
marital relationship.

If these middle-class women were unhappy in their sex lives and
unable to ask for the tenderness and time they required, they did
not often feel in a position to bring this to the attention of their
men. Their lives offered little that could satisfy an urge toward
creativity or toward testing their mettle in the world outside the
home, so that frustration of one kind or another was common
among many women at the turn of the century. While they held
back their complaints as well as they could, their anger and loneliness retreated into the deeper, less-conscious recesses of the
psyche. Their sexual energy remained bound up in repressions, almost as though they knew that there would be little hope of receiving help were they to exhibit symptoms of a clearly psychological nature. Having no other socially acceptable outlet, the
neurotic process often transformed their anger into physical symptoms. As Freud was to discover, the prevailing symptom of the
middle-class mid-European woman at the end of the nineteenth
century was the classical conversion hysteria. Women's bodies
spoke out in a language that their lips refused to form. As to the
poorer women, many of whom worked in the factories and the
mills, they were as devoid of power as their working-class husbands and neither sex had much opportunity to affect the social
system.

The paradigm of modernity had reached its peak by the beginning of the twentieth century. The roles of the sexes had been

thoroughly polarized in the prominent and socially dominant middle class. The working lives of men and women were of distinctly different orders. There was greater disparity than ever between the images of ideal man and ideal woman. In the industrial-technological institutions the dominating principle was masculine and patriarchal, while the feminine principle was secondary and supportive. Each sex was essential to the other; neither could exist and feel whole alone. The differences were accepted and respected, and even valued. But finally masculinity and femininity became stereotyped, and the patriarchal-masculine vision assumed precedence over the less clearly articulated feminine vision. Working-class men and women, even where they performed similar work, tended to imitate the middle class when it came to social and sexual conventions.

As the separation of men and women in the everyday business of life increased, sexuality became more discreet, more often hidden behind closed doors, less fit as a topic for open and frank discussion, and certainly to be concealed from the children. Proper men and women did not discuss such things together except, perhaps, in hushed tones in the bedroom. When the sexes were segregated, each told its little embarrassed jokes about sex and the sexual parts of the body. Sexuality became something special and separate from the everyday occurrences of life. Legs became "limbs," penis and vulva became "privates," and people did not urinate or defecate, they "went to the bathroom." The repression of a free and open attitude toward sexuality drove this part of life into the dark corners of existence. Sexual repression's shadow side expressed itself furtively through pornography, obscenity, prostitution (mostly for the men); and for women, a vast passionate romantic literature where love and violence jostled with each other in one breathless situation after another. How pallid the sex life of the decent Victorian women must have seemed, in contrast to the voluptuous fantasies that engaged them!

Men acquired technical and scientific education that social pressure denied to women. That members of the male sex were the physicists, biologists, physicians, designers, and makers of machinery and houses, of schools and churches, determined the nature of modern sciences and technologies. Now buildings were designed for efficiency and cost effectiveness rather than for beauty. Architecture was based on the principle that "form follows function." The stateliness of Gothic spires served only as reminders of the past. In the first decade of the twentieth century, the gentle swirls of Art Nouveau gave way to the straight and severe linear designs of Art Déco.

Business and industry grew ever more hierarchical. Yet unlike earlier hierarchies, in which people knew where they belonged and stayed in their places, the new industrial hierarchies that arose were made up of striving and struggling men, competing fiercely for prestige and fortune. Those who were successful in rising to the top organized social and political structures to support themselves and their status there, and to exclude those who had not made it.

The collective syndrome paralleled the individual syndrome in that everything had to be bigger and better this year than last. Corporations expected to earn more money, to increase their dividends, to expand their production, to enlarge their buildings. Men found themselves oppressed by the excessive demands of the American dream. America was to supply the whole world with industrial and technological knowledge, and she was to receive in return the rich natural resources of undeveloped countries. America would help these countries to develop and in due time they would become a market for the goods America would produce, providing her with sufficient profits to make it all worthwhile. Men engaged eagerly in this less than altruistic system, and perhaps the women suspected the exploitation of the poorer countries. Yet they also stood to enjoy the abundance. At any rate, they had little chance to say anything about it since for the most part women were kept out of the marketplace by tradition, by social pressure, by lack of education, and by the important fact that to a large extent they were still being regarded as severely limited by their anatomy.

Advances in science and technology and the tendency toward change produced its reaction in the reinforcement of the established religious institutions. Not surprisingly, the power of the churches stood behind patterns of traditional morality. Small fissures began to appear in that bulwark, however. Some political activists distrusted the conservatism of the churches. Radical intellectuals, following Marx and Engels, saw the churches as condoning and even furthering class distinctions. Debates in the universities raged around philosophical issues that had newly broken out about the heads of students. Young people—mostly men—who were being exposed for the first time in their lives to classical studies, saw challenges to values that they had not even known existed: the gods were seen to have many faces, and morality could be variously interpreted. Students in the sciences adopted highly rational postures. They extolled the scientific method as the *only* sure way to salvation, which they called "the truth." The young scions of orthodox or traditionally oriented religious families underwent nothing less than conversion experiences when they embarked upon university life. However, these conversions led them away from the God of their fathers, and not toward him. When the students rejected traditional religion, they deified freedom. Where religious dogma lost its hold on them, their yearning for answers inspired another kind of adherence—to any disciplines that helped convince a man that he could be in charge of his own destiny if only he could learn enough about the way things worked in the mechanistic world he had come to believe in.

In the early years of the twentieth century, very few American women participated in this kind of clitist education, either in the humanities or in the hard sciences. A college education was not considered necessary for women, even for those from the "best families." Finishing schools prepared young women to take their places as socially adept wives who could manage home and family in ways that would further the ambitions and careers of their husbands. The few women who attended coeducational universities often did so to find a husband, or to acquire "insurance" in case they did not marry or might be widowed. A few prestigious women's colleges provided intellectual challenge in an environment where young women would not feel that it was necessary to inhibit their curiosity or creativity for fear of frightening off potential mates. Those who wanted to get married could become appropriately vacuous on weekends, while the others prepared for professions in which celibacy (the only proper alternative to marriage) was a virtue. Often professions such as teaching were barred to married women.

The social convention of marriage that permitted a man and woman to live together acknowledged only superficially the great differences between the life-styles of the two sexes. The roles of male and female continued to diverge until it came to pass that at dinner parties the sexes could only tolerate each other's company until dessert was over; then the men would retire for smoking and weighty conversation, while the women could chat about their troubles with the servants, their children, or their church activities. Although their formal education had prepared them for responsibilities as wives, mothers, and homemakers in a world their husbands scarcely knew, they brought to their men an important viewpoint just because it derived from a different perspective. Women kept alive the values that even today we continue to associate with the feminine gender: devotion to spiritual values, concern for others, especially those less fortunate, nurturance of children, care and sympathy for the mate, and gentleness and forbearance whenever these were needed. These "feminine" virtues were rewarded with security and status according to the husband's position. Personal autonomy for women was not explicit. If a woman wanted to have personal power (in the sense of potency or effectiveness), she would have to manipulate herself into a position of strength. Inheriting a fortune or a husband's business was one way of achieving that autonomy, and there must have been some other ways as well.

In affluent times, wives of working-class men were not usually employed outside their homes. When they did hold jobs out of economic necessity, the conditions of labor were usually deplorable. Women's wages were significantly lower than those of men and their jobs were for the most part incredibly tedious. Nor did their employment exempt them from full responsibility for their households. Because they had so little else to support their self-esteem, most of them held on to faith in a God who loved them and concerned himself about them.

The "common man" at the beginning of the twentieth century typically found himself experiencing rootlessness and alienation in a world of work where his activities were prescribed and where there was little opportunity for the development of individuality. The old traditional values held less weight for him than they had for his parents. There was nothing to take their place except, perhaps, the hope for a new vision to emerge in the changing times that were being predicted for the new century. Sexual mores were as rigid as ever, but now they were not supported by currently held religious values so much as by the values imparted, on an unconscious level, by the parents—to whose generation they had more appropriately belonged. When one or the other marital partner breached the conventional morality and found another intimate relationship on the outside, the one who felt betrayed suffered great pain while the other was usually beset with guilt and shame. Yet these feelings were seldom brought out into the open between husband and wife. It was more common for the emotions to build as great silent blocks separating them in their relationship, but not accessible to anything approaching shared awareness. It seemed that there was either silence and withdrawal or else rage and conflict. This alienation could occur even in the absence of an extramarital relationship, for the energy and attention of one of the mates could as well be diverted from the other by the man's absorption in his work or the woman's complete devotion to domesticity and serving the needs of a growing family. Through many circumstances, communication that should have reached its fulfillment in warm sexual feelings and relatedness, often grew cool and perfunctory, and the worst part of it was that so little was said or done about it.

For this and other reasons, just when it appeared to be working successfully, the nineteenth-century social and sexual patterns associated with the paradigm of modernity began to break down. Middle-class women may have been a significant factor in its deterioration. When they began to be affluent enough to enjoy some leisure, when technological aids like washing machines and sewing machines and refrigerators relieved them from many of the tasks of caring for home and family, they had time to discover that their lives were not personally as enriching as they hoped. Suspecting that there might be other ways to use their skills and ideas, women began to organize in groups of various kinds. At first these centered around the churches or social welfare activities. Women would meet outside their homes where they were able to establish close relationships with female friends. They exchanged confidences and began to share their images of themselves in ways that helped each woman to understand that her sense of powerlessness was not a unique experience but one common to many women. It wasn't really that women had no power. They knew they had a great deal of power in terms of their influence upon their men. The way they functioned might either support or undermine their husbands' sense of security and consequently their capacity to be successful in the world. A woman was expected to reinforce her man's potency. She could take some satisfaction from this. But mostly, men and women were worlds apart.

The ways in which the culture collectively viewed masculinity and femininity were also worlds apart. Ideally, the male was the exemplar of *logos*. His world was a measured one, and life was a linear-sequential experience where one could start at the beginning and plan through to the end. A man of action made things happen. He kept his emotions under control. His sexuality had become as utilitarian as the rest of his life.

Women, as a rule, entered into marriage with little or no preparation for sexual intimacy. Their husbands were supposed to teach them all they needed to know. The young woman who had been taught by her mother to withhold herself sexually and to repress any sexual feelings was expected suddenly at the moment she was pronounced married to drop all her reserves and willingly submit to her mate. Though given little introduction to sexuality itself, she was informed as to what her sex role would be and how it would determine the patterns of her married life. She would conform to women's roles as they had existed for the last two centuries. These were the stories our mothers told us.

The marriage relationship allowed sexual relations to occur within a socially prescribed context. Sexuality conformed to the patterns of the conventional marriage or, when it did not, the deviations occurred mostly in secret with a cloud over them. How then was woman to imagine, as she approached the beginning of the twentieth century, that she would participate in radical changes that were already brewing in the unconscious, changes that eventually would be instrumental in bringing down the paradigm of modernity?

3
Models of Psyche

When the twentieth century was new, Britannia ruled the waves in its imperial peace, America's nouveaux riches wielded tremendous economic power, and Science reigned as queen of the intellect in the Western world. All three glorious monarchs have since fallen upon hard times, and we wonder what has happened to the promises made to us when we agreed to serve our masters. We were bedazzled by the realization that we'd welcomed the final century of the millennium. Millenarian times are numinous, for it is said that then heaven and earth conspire to work great change. Rumblings of unrest inevitably precede the arrival of the thousandth year. Something stirs ominously beneath the ground of consciousness. Is it chaos, readying to break forth? Will a Redeemer come in time and, if so, in what form or forms? Between the great millenarian tides, the centuries mount in waves. Ebbing, they sweep away much of what the past has imprinted and leave a cleaner beach upon which the people of a new century may press their mark.

The final century is likely to be the most crucial one, for the changes that occur within its brackets are understood to cast their shadows on the future. There is no doubt that the twentieth century has seen the texture of human life alter more profoundly and more rapidly than any century before. The year 1900 was especially eventful. In the field of physics Max Planck published the quantum hypothesis that revolutionized the way we would look at the composition of the universe. Einstein was working on his special theory of relativity in a Swiss patent office. Edison, having already invented the incandescent lamp and stock ticker, was developing dynamos, electric railways, electric motors, motion pictures, and the phonograph. John B. Watson, who would become the "father of behaviorism," in that year received the first doctorate in psychology given by the University of Chicago. His dissertation was on maze learning by rats.

Freud's investigations of his own inner life came to light with the completion of his *Interpretation of Dreams* in 1899. Significantly, he wanted the date 1900 to appear on the title page. He had not yet heard of Carl Jung, the young psychiatrist who was to become his most problematic colleague and who simultaneously and independently was uncovering the mechanism of repression through his research on word association at Burghölzli Klinik in Zürich.

At this time Freud's thinking was being strongly influenced by the work of Ernst Haeckel, distinguished German physician, zoologist, professor of comparative anatomy, and author of numerous scientific works. An ardent supporter of Darwin's theory of evolution, Haeckel dismissed traditional religions as being based on superstitious beliefs. He published *Die Welträtsel* (The Riddle of the Universe) in 1899, a book in which he adopted an uncompromising monistic attitude by asserting the essential unity of organic and inorganic nature. He regarded psychology as merely a branch of physiology, and mental activity as depending solely on physiological actions and material changes taking place in the protoplasm of organisms. As a consequence of these beliefs, Haeckel denied the immortality of the individual soul (as distinct from the body), the freedom of the will, and the existence of a personal God. He envisioned the appearance of a new religion, the Monistic Church, and he, himself, was its prophet. The "faith" was to be placed in science, but the worshippers would perform aesthetic rites reminiscent of ancient religious ceremonies. In this church, the altar would be replaced by a celestial globe showing the movements of the stars and planets. Thus the universe would be understood as the manifestation of the divine power inherent in all of nature.[1] This vision, understandably, was far from being acceptable to the rationalistic mind so characteristic of modernity in the Western world.

Freud must have been intrigued with Haeckel's view of the nature of man, that man has no soul distinct from the body, and that the human organism can be understood totally in biological and physiological terms. That this provided a rationale for denying validity to traditional religions corresponded nicely with Freud's eagerness to establish a clearly scientific basis for the theories he was beginning to formulate. But Freud did not accord recognition to the unitive principle behind monism. Had he done so perhaps his own creation, psychoanalysis, might have been instrumental in lifting the spiritual awareness of people to a higher level of consciousness, based on the overriding unity that is the ground of all phenomena. Instead, he adopted only those aspects of Haeckel's approach that corresponded with his own vision. Freud was not oblivious to the mood of the times, in which scientific research was a prestigious occupation and the highest status in the intellectual world was being conferred upon the natural scientist. Then as now, social scientists often gained credibility for their work by borrowing from the terminology of the natural sciences and then applying it more or less metaphorically to their own disciplines. I say "metaphorically" because it is not altogether clear whether they referred to their work in the language of physics, for example, because they believed that language was applicable, or because they saw a parallel between the laws of their own discipline and those of the natural sciences.

This raises the question as to whether the use of such terminology for describing the structure and dynamics of the psyche led Freud and other investigators to believe that they actually had to do with a "science of the soul." For "psyche," the Greek root of the word psychology, means *breath*, which ancient peoples considered to be the principle of life, or *soul*. There is a paradox here, that science would seem too small a container for soul, if science is understood as commonly defined: "knowledge that has been systematized and formulated with reference to the discovery of general truths or the operation of general laws . . . especially knowledge obtained and tested through use of the scientific method."[2] Even so, wearing the ill-fitting mantle of science, the new psychodynamic psychology exerted a profound influence on cultural attitudes toward sexuality as it traveled westward all the

way from Vienna to San Francisco. The United States, lacking
the ballast of a long cultural tradition of morals and mores, experienced the new doctrine and the ensuing changes as a dramatic
shift in consciousness, rather than as still another link in a chain
of cultural developments.

Yet the coming of the new century offered hope in the area of
sexual awareness as in every other area of human concern. Already, new approaches to psychological ills were being tested. Dynamic psychiatry moved forward from its early days when it had
relied upon hypnosis, suggestion, and magnetizing as approaches
to psychotherapy. Neuropsychiatry was building on nineteenth-
century advances in physiological chemistry, embryology, bacteri-
ology, and clinical medicine to create a physiological approach to
mental illness. Ivan Pavlov was working on his theory of conditioned reflexes. His experiments laid the basis for much of the
later work of behaviorist psychologists, not only in Russia but also
in the United States.[3]

Both Freud and Pavlov had their difficulties with the collectives
to which they belonged. Freud was severely criticized, especially
by the Zürich school of psychoanalysis, for supporting Haeckel in
his synthesis of the spiritual and physiological aspects of man.
After Freud proclaimed his atheism, he adopted a more mechanistic approach to the psyche, and he made it clear that he was
unwilling to espouse monism and its spokesman. Similarly, Pavlov
had early expressed opposition to Lenin, but later in his life he
too modified his political viewpoint and entered into a harmonious relationship with the government.[4]

We are all the products of our time to a greater degree than we
are inclined to realize. The psychological approaches to sexuality
that set the stage during the early decades of the century reveal
the guiding principles we have assimilated and that have brought
us to our current position. At least three general approaches have
made crucial contributions to the present context: psychoanalysis,
learning-theory, and cognitive developmental theory. Each school
offers models which lead us to view sexuality in specific ways,
based on the theoretical positions of the schools. It is necessary to
consider these models, since our models to a large extent determine our behavior.

The psychoanalytic model emphasizes the role of unconscious factors, and their interaction with the conscious aspect of the individual that belongs to the province of the ego. Since the roots of mental illness are mostly unconscious, according to this model, treatment requires the intervention of a person highly skilled in evoking unconscious contents and interpreting them in the light of the psychodynamic theory. This model is hierarchical in nature, with the psychoanalyst structuring the situation in which the patient reveals himself or herself, and the analyst interprets the material that comes forth. Since behavior is reduced to the product of all past experiences, behavior is seen as "nothing but" the effect of something else.

The learning-theory model assumes that nearly all patterns of behavior are acquired. Behaviorists, whose psychological approach is based on learning theory, are interested in observing and studying the learning process itself with a view toward understanding how people learn to behave in the ways that they do. Again, an expert is needed to analyze the conditioning factors that form behavior patterns, and to determine how to extinguish undesirable patterns and generate new ones. Thus this model is also hierarchical, notwithstanding the fact that the client participates in goal-setting. This model looks to prior causes of present symptoms. It is also future-directed, in that it moves in measured steps toward goals that have been set.

The model of cognitive development tends to be less authority-centered, since it requires a participatory atmosphere in which its researchers can observe how people develop and grow. The participant-observer type of research is often used, since what is studied is the interaction between the innate patterns of development in the person and the environmental influences. Depending upon the orientation of the psychological researcher in this model, the way in which observations are interpreted may be affected by the psychoanalytic school or by learning-theory or by both.

The implications derived from each of these models depend to a considerable degree upon the basic assumptions held by those who constructed the models. The models have in common that each has its origin in the manners and mores of the past. By the time a theoretical position is well established, the conditions that gave rise to it have already altered. We still believe what we learned yesterday, while we often behave as though we were preparing for tomorrow. This is because science is basically causally oriented, while the human psyche appears to have a dynamic, purposive orientation of its own. More than only the result of its past experiences, the psyche seems also to be geared toward the future, toward telos, toward goals. The scientific method looks backward, from its observations of phenomena to a hypothesis about the phenomena, to an exploration that will establish the prior cause of the phenomena. Science, essentially, is asking what has happened. Nature seems to work in the opposite fashion. The chicken is already implied in the egg, the egg is programmed for it; the egg hatches to fulfill its plan for the future. Of course, it may also be argued that the egg is there because it was produced by the chicken, to which we can only answer, "toward what purpose?" It is no accident that chickens are produced from hens' eggs rather than from any other kind of egg. Each seed carries the potential of becoming a plant of its own species. Resolutely, all nature moves toward its foreordained end as determined in its genetic code: moving through embryonic, youthful, and mature stages, reproducing itself, and passing from the scene to make way for succeeding generations. This is not to deny the dependence of nature upon causality, but rather to show that living things are pulled along by the future at least as much as they are pushed from behind by the past.

The psyche, as part of nature, is no less purposive. The purposes toward which we move are not always under our conscious direction; on the contrary, there are in us certain potentialities which move us in specific ways and toward specific goals—some refer to these as "fate" or "desire" or "talent" or the "creative spirit." Whatever these directing forces may be, we have all experienced that they make their demands upon us and we either give assent to those demands or resist them. This is what is meant by feeling drawn toward a certain behavior or a way of life as though from within ourselves. This is a forward-looking impulse, which is scarcely dealt with by those traditional psychologies that seek to repair the damage of the past or to help the individual make peace with the present.

Both psychoanalysis and learning theory were formulated in response to the conditions of modern man, "mass man." (I am using these terms with full awareness of their sexist implications because it was exactly that level of consciousness that provided the context in which this psychological development took place.) These approaches recognized a need to explore the human condition in ways differing from those which had led to the feeling of loss of autonomy that had been so widespread early in our century. The genius of Freud was that he sensed in modern man the need for self-examination. As prototype of man struggling under that urgent necessity, he began his own major life work with a personal and painstakingly detailed process of looking within himself. To call Freud the father of "psychological man" is to give him credit for the seminal ideas which offered to mass man a way out of the oceanic womb of unconsciousness.

Through such efforts, "psychological man" came into being. He looked about himself and began to realize the extent to which he was being ruled by collective standards and the strictures of traditional religion. Now he began the shift to finding his direction from the present. In David Riesman's words, he became either "other directed," that is, influenced by his peers, or else "inner directed," or reflective. From his former rigid morality, psychological man moved to a relative morality. From being fixed in a specific role, he learned to take on a protean character which allowed him to meet situations spontaneously and individually. If mass man had felt most comfortable when he conformed to social norms, psychological man was willing to risk nonconformity for the sake of understanding himself better. When psychological man was dissatisfied with the status quo, he questioned himself as to how *he* might be responsible, and how he might change *himself* and so alter his situation. Much of the impetus for the willingness of people to begin looking within themselves came through the influence of psychoanalysis, as its principles slowly filtered down from its esoteric beginnings to the wider public by way of the popular press, books, stage and screen, and the many derivative psychotherapies that took their inspiration from Freud and those who followed him.

THE PSYCHOANALYTIC MODEL

Freud's fundamental hypothesis dealt with the nature of libido, or psychosexual energy. He drew his concept of libido from his background in human physiology, coupled with his understanding of the operation of the physical world, that is, the world as described by the science of physics. Freud had studied the work of Hermann Helmholtz, the German physicist, anatomist, and physiologist who had mathematically formulated the law of the conservation of energy. Helmholtz was "one of my idols," Freud wrote.[5] Freud had worked for physiologist Ernst Brücke, a leading member of the Helmholtz school, for six of his formative years. When Freud came to formulating his own clinical model, he based it on psychophysicalist assumptions suggesting that the mind operates through "forces" and "energies" and is capable of "increase, diminution, displacement and discharge, and which is spread over the memory-traces of ideas somewhat as an electric charge is spread over the surface of a body. This hypothesis . . . can be applied in the same sense as physicists apply the hypothesis of a flow of electric fluid."[6]

The parallel between Freud's "psychic energy" or "libido" and the electrical energy that the science of physics concerns itself with is obvious. But not so apparent is the possibility that libido could also be related to the archetypal concept of a mysterious energy that I referred to earlier, and which may be nonphysical in nature. This was the "subtle energy" well known in esoteric philosophies and Eastern spiritual traditions for its capacity to potentiate the human organism in ways that cannot be explained in purely objective terms. Freud, given his background, was more comfortable with a physicalist description of the mental energies or life forces he perceived as sources of the dynamism effecting movement and change. He rejected any explanation of the life force that might be construed as mystical or religious. Though later in his life he extended and transcended the narrowly physicalist model, he never abandoned it.[7] The libido theory remained within the system of Newtonian mechanics.

Libido, Freud stated, was primarily if not entirely sexual in nature. Insisting on this, he gave to sexuality a central position in psychic life. Sexuality, in the broadest sense of the word, was the dynamic factor that moved people psychologically. Sexual tensions innervated the organism, and directed it toward seeking pleasure through the discharge of those tensions and a restoration of a state of calm and balance. Pain resulted from the frustration of the sexual impulses, from the repression of the libido, or from sublimation, that is, forcing the libido into channels other than those which would have been the natural outlets for its expression.

For Freud, human development centered on the growth and differentiation of the ego. When the ego begins to form, it is tentative and dependent, getting its strength from unconscious biological instincts or drives of a primitive nature. The "id" is the undifferentiated reservoir of the instinctual energy. When Freud considered the area of infantile sexuality, he theorized that the newborn child comes into the world with germs of the sexual instinct already present. These germs continue to develop by stages, and are countered by frustration, repression, sublimation, and other mechanisms. Much of what inhibits this natural development derives from limitations imposed by the parent on the infant or child, and later from the influences produced by the culture in which the young person grows up. These inhibiting and shaping influences, which are at first external to the child, become internalized as he accepts them as part of his own mode of being. They become incorporated as a "superego," and continue to exert important limitations on the flow of the libido.

The emergent ego is reality-oriented. It tries to satisfy the demands of the id within the limits imposed by the superego and by external circumstances. The sexualized life force, libido, focuses on different erogenous zones during the first three or four years, or until the oedipal stage develops. This involves an erotic attachment to the parent of the opposite sex. The psychosexual divergence that occurs during this time forms some of the bases for what Freud saw as the dramatic differences between the sexes.

His idea that infantile sexuality plays an important, even crucial, role in later sexual development revolutionized our thinking about ourselves as sexual beings. Freud showed the importance of unconscious factors in structuring the ways in which we experi-

ence our sexuality. If we derive our self-image, the sense of who
we are, out of early experiences around sexuality which we then
forget or repress, then the archetypal dramas we enacted in early
childhood may continue to rule us without our realizing it.

The myth of the Divine Child is told in many cultures. Such a
child is usually born under some unusual circumstances, and there
comes an ominous warning that something terrible will happen if
the child is not destroyed. He is put out to die, or left with
strangers and forgotten, yet he inevitably returns to fulfill the destiny that was foretold. Freud selected a single archetypal tale of
this genre to use as a model or illustration of how males and females arrive at their gender identities. The familiar tale of the ill-
starred Oedipus who killed his father and (unwittingly) married,
or possessed, his mother, is only one of many possible scenarios he
might have chosen from the many examples of son-lover relationships in ancient lore. Jung objected to Freud's reliance on this
single legend to build his prototype of human sexual development. He felt that, like so many of Freud's unequivocal propositions, the model might have described the particularities of development in some individuals, but surely not in *all*. Nevertheless,
the theory seemed so plausible and was so well orchestrated that it
became a dominant recurrent theme in the developmental history
of psychological man, and woman.

Briefly, the familiar extrapolation runs like this: For the first
three years or so, both boys and girls are emotionally attached to
their mothers. Boys are supposed to experience a desire for a generalized possession of their mother. Around the age of four or five
this may become a desire to have a child by the mother. Such a
desire may be triggered by the arrival of a sibling. The girl reacts
more in terms of wondering what it will be like for her to be a
mother some day. Freud seemed not to take into account that in
his time, as even in our own, most children of this age did not really understand the relationship between sexual intercourse and
childbirth.

Freud ascribes perceptions to children that may or may not be
real. A boy is assumed to perceive the father as rival for the
mother's love. His aroused sexual feelings seek expression through
masturbation. Someone catches him at it and threatens to cut off

his penis. These threats acquire a horrific reality for him when he first sees female genitalia. He reacts to the female as a mutilated creature. Holding her in triumphant contempt, he is, at the same time, tortured by castration anxiety. Finally the hopelessness of his desire for his mother and the fear of punishment convinces the boy that he may as well give up hope for the mother and cast in his lot with the father as the model for future behavior. The superego as arbiter of right and wrong begins to take shape in this process as a part of the child's personality and the male gender identity solidifies. The boy goes on to mature and want a wife of his own.[8]

Freud presents a variation on this theme for the female child, but complicated by an additional factor. The girl's original love object, like the boy's, is the mother, and the girl too abandons it and becomes emotionally attached to the father. The first step in the girl's "phallic" phase is the discovery that boys have penises. Somewhere she gets the message that this is a superior organ, and she envies its possessor. She experiences the lack of such an organ as a wound to her self-image and consequently she develops a sense of inferiority. This feeling persists, even after her envy has been displaced from the literal penis and is transformed into a generalized jealousy of the male sex. The girl's masturbatory experience is with the clitoris, an activity which loses its appeal when she discovers that the clitoris is inferior in size to the penis. Between her humiliation and her envy, she realizes that she cannot compete with boys and should give up. Her recognition of the anatomical difference between herself and males leads her to give up her "masculinity" and to pattern herself after the mother by developing her "femininity." For Freud, male and female gender identity is established during this oedipal stage. It goes almost without saying that a legitimate goal of the developmental process is the individual's adaptation to the sex role defined by the society in which he or she is a member.

When a researcher approaches a subject, or a psychiatrist approaches a patient, with a preconceived notion of the dynamics that are operating, they tend to interpret their findings in accordance with their presuppositions. They usually find what they are looking for, the more so in dealing with human material which cannot easily be quantified or replicated by other observers. Evidence is highly subjective. Freud's conviction of the rightness of his theories, the precision and clarity with which he presented them, and his capacity to gather about him a circle of people who would support his ideas and help to disseminate them had much to do with the rapid spread of his audacious concepts. Furthermore, his assumptions may have been correct at least some of the time. The difficulty came when he insisted on the universal applicability of theories he developed on the bases of a limited number of cases. Remember, this "expert" on infantile sexuality did not even work with children directly, but only with the memories of childhood as recalled by adults or, in the famous case of "Little Hans,"[9] he treated the boy's phobia by analyzing the child's father.

Statements based largely on generalizations from the particular, like articles of faith, are either accepted or they are not, and for a long time Freud's view of early childhood development was widely accepted in certain circles. For one thing, the constructs were elegant and complex, and it required much study and application to grasp the totality of the system. By the time the neophyte psychoanalysts had completed the task of assimilating Freud's theories, they had made a considerable psychic investment. Also, since the premises were based upon anecdotal records of individual cases, there was no effective way to disprove them. However, if one viewed the development of infantile sexuality from a different perspective, one could make different interpretations of the child's fantasies and experiences. Or, as Jung did, one could try out the theories by working independently and adhering strictly to psychoanalytic techniques, without making any *a priori* assumptions about their validity. Several of those who had worked closely with Freud without sharing his conviction that his theories were universally applicable discovered, in their own patients' material, data that failed to confirm Freud's assumptions. These differences led to confrontations with Freud, and eventually to estrangement from the psychoanalytic circle. Those who remained supported Freud's arguments, while those who left developed independent theoretical positions, adapting what they had found valid in

Freud's work to the evidence gained from their own observations and praxis.

Had there been more "liberated" female psychoanalysts among Freud's early followers, certain specific issues might have arisen earlier, for example, the question as to the superiority of the penis over the clitoris. Naturally, the idea that "big is beautiful" when applied to the penis was a concept that could appeal to men. But, a woman who had a nonsexist rearing might have concluded that a big penis is not necessarily more attractive than a small one, any more than a big nose is superior to a small one. The nose, like the penis, is highly attuned to sensation, gives pleasure, and produces eager anticipation. Everyone knows that a big nose is not necessarily more efficient than a small one—but noses are common to both men and women—therefore why would either sex assert the superiority of the big nose? It would give no one an advantage. Yet the big penis was valued by men over the small clitoris. The early psychoanalytic establishment which was predominantly male managed to sell its adherents and followers on the superiority of the male organ and, by inference, on the superiority of the male body and the male person. This one-sided view is by no means universally held.

I can recall that before I ever heard of Freud, I was convinced that the female body was, if anything, superior to that of the male. Perhaps this had something to do with my mother's vanity and my father's reticence. From early childhood, I had enjoyed looking at art books showing graceful female nudes, and I liked what appealed to Renoir and Degas and Raphael and Rubens. I do not recall having seen as many male nudes, which suggests that, Freud notwithstanding, artists found the female body more attractive, appealing, and beautiful than the male body. I recall that the first time I ever saw a real penis, I was not even remotely desirous of having one. By that time I had been taught by my protofeminist mother that the way to fulfillment was through the brain, not through the penis. I was encouraged early in my life to learn various competencies, if I expected to be able to function successfully in the world. The possibility that any opportunities would be withheld from me because I possessed a clitoris and not a penis never occurred to me until I began to study psychology.

I believe that where the girl, as she approaches puberty, is taught to value her femininity, she will respect her womb as the place where a child may be conceived and brought to readiness for birth. She will regard her reproductive system as being of great importance, both for herself and for society. She will be aware of the consequences of allowing herself to engage in sexual relations before she is emotionally ready, and she will be less likely to allow herself to be exposed to contamination by disease. Yet today so many girls are encouraged to practice sexuality freely, almost as soon as they reach an age when they become interested in the male sex. In my psychological work, over and over again I meet young women who have postponed childbearing until their middle thirties, only to find that they cannot conceive when they want to because of obstruction or scar tissue in the Fallopian tubes due to acquiring in their teens a venereal disease of which they may never have been aware. It is hard to know how much of this misery may be the end result of the girl's or woman's devaluation of her femininity.

Sexologist John Money is reported to have asked his students whether they would take a magic pill, if offered, that would instantly change their sex. Out of curiosity, I have posed this question to several groups of my own. In any group where I have tried the question, none of the participants was willing to state that he or she would want a permanent reversal of their sex—although some indicated that they might have considered it at an earlier time in their lives. Facing the question in the immediate present, every individual answered in the negative. So much for penis envy, or for the projected "inferiority feelings" of the feminine sex.

Neo-Freudian Karen Horney asserts that the intense envy of motherhood that males develop is much stronger than female penis envy. She believes that some of the efforts of the male toward worldly achievements may be, in part, compensatory for his inability to bear children, and that the depreciation of women by men may be an expression of the same need to compensate.[10] Another neo-Freudian, Ruth Moulton, challenges the "passive" connotation of the receptiveness of the vagina. "Receptive aims do not imply inertness: the truly receptive vagina is grasping, secreting, and pleasure-giving through its own functions rather than just through the eroticization of pain."[11]

Psychoanalysis had advanced the notion that little girls have a hard time establishing their gender identity because the girl cannot observe her vagina as well as the clitoris. But the experience of many females is that the vagina is well known to them as the outlet through which babies are born, while the clitoris itself is often undiscovered for a long time because sexual excitement may be felt as generally distributed over the entire vulvar area. Psychoanalysis insists on the necessity of shifting from clitoral to vaginal orgasm in the course of female development and maturation. I could only wish that this issue had never been raised, for what a great loss of spontaneity and freedom there must be in the sex act when the woman has consciously to center the locus of her excitement to the precise point where Freud decreed it should be. What women want, Dr. Freud, is sexual fulfillment and, finally, this is experienced by the whole person functioning in total harmony.

More and more neo-Freudians have been insisting that the concept of male superiority and penis envy is not to be taken literally, but rather symbolically, with penis meaning the power and economic superiority of the male sex vis-à-vis the female sex. It is surely true that the powerless envy the powerful, the poor envy the rich, the dependent envy the independent; but in my view this does not, and need not, necessarily break down along sex lines. All individuals, both sexes, desire that which appears to them to be superior to what they individually possess. The sexual connotation placed upon this natural emotion, it seems to me, has been blown far out of proportion.

The psychoanalytic movement has spawned a host of contemporary psychotherapies, from Primal Scream to Transactional Analysis. All are retreaded versions of the archetype of Oedipus; all strive toward resolving infantile objections to the demands of the social order and, finally, they seek adaptation to the sex-role stereotypes engendered by that social order. Consequently, there is no hope of transcending sex-role stereotypes in this model. Therapists who recognize this are looking for new approaches which contain the possibility of transcending models of behavior that are no longer viable and, for many people, never were.

SOCIAL LEARNING THEORY

Another model that has long been used to understand human behavior and treat its dysfunctions is that of social learning theory. The basis of this system is the concept that the way we think, feel, and act is largely determined by our interaction with the environment in the process of socialization. Sexuality, like other kinds of human behavior, is learned. This approach to human problems is a product of our cultural orientation to rationalism and the scientific method at the beginning of the twentieth century.

Social learning theory was the basis for the principle that the educator's role was to promote learning through environmental manipulation. The term "behavior modification" was first used to describe this approach in 1932.[12] Behavior therapy, an application of behavior modification, entered into the period of its most rapid growth around midcentury. It grew partly out of dissatisfaction with the predominant psychoanalytic model of psychotherapy and its reliance on unconscious factors, and partly out of a reaction against the difficulty in psychoanalysis of making precise evaluations as to its success or failure. Hans Eysenck characterized the differences between behavior therapy and psychotherapy along several dimensions:

1) behavior therapy is founded on consistent, testable theory while psychotherapy is theoretically inconsistent;
2) behavior therapy derives from experimental studies, while psychotherapy is based on clinical observations;
3) behavior therapy sees symptoms as arising from learning and conditioning, while psychotherapy posits defense mechanisms;
4) behavior therapy does not rely on interpretation as psychotherapy does;
5) behavior therapy sees the relationship between clients and

therapist as relatively unimportant, while psychotherapy places great value on that relationship.[13]

In summary, the learning-theory approach and its applications are based on tangible, measurable bits of behavior that may be modified by controlling the environment, while psychotherapy posits unconscious factors which cannot readily be measured or controlled, if at all, but which must be approached with an eye toward insight and understanding. Behavior therapy is outer-directed, psychotherapy is inner-directed.

Some general principles of learning theory are: children tend to imitate their parents and others; when behavior is rewarded, it tends to be repeated in similar situations; behavior is shaped as patterns of reward and punishment from parents and society change; behavior that is learned later tends to take precedence over earlier behavior; when more mature behavior is not rewarded, people tend to regress to less mature forms of behavior; and once a specific behavior is learned, people tend to generalize it to situations that are similar to the original one.

Seen from the viewpoint of the social learning theorists, male and female sex roles are learned early in life. The imitation of adults plays an important part in the process. Children are keen observers and will practice behaviors that they see enacted before them, even to inflections of voice and styles of walking. Whether they see affectionate, loving behavior or cool, detached behavior in their parents will affect their own sexual development and the expectations they will have for a future partner. Behavior patterns are formed as children are rewarded for certain acts, and tend not to be repeated when there is either no reward or a negative response. These positive and negative reinforcements are not necessarily given consciously, but the messages are nevertheless effectively transmitted by a subtle intonation of voice, a more attentive look, concern shown, a frown—as well as by the more obvious expressions. The child learns to discriminate what kinds of behavior will meet with approval and what will meet with disapproval from the powerful persons that parents seem to be. The child makes choices, which result in learning and performance. Boys and girls first learn to conform to the expectations for their particular sex

that their parents hold and then to those held by a larger portion
of society. That girls will fulfill the familiar feminine stereotype
and that boys will follow the masculine route is anticipated by
most of society, since these stereotypes correspond to cultural
norms. Conformity is usually rewarded. Consequently, children
acquire "sex-typed behaviors," which are behaviors that typically
elicit different rewards for one sex than the other. Aggressive behavior is fine for the male; it is "bitchy" for the female. A sensitive girl is fine, a sensitive boy is a "sissy."

The environment exerts a none too subtle influence on the development of sex-role awareness. Clearly, mass media's models are
highly influential, especially since many children today spend
more hours of their formative years before a television set than
they do in the school classroom. The stereotypical and often cari-
catured television or movie portrayals of each sex lead to an easy
acceptance of sharply defined and role-specific behavior on the
part of young people. Rock and country music with their strong
sexual orientation accent the demand for freedom in sexual expression with little thought for the consequences in human costs.
Viewers are encouraged to spend huge sums on appearing sexually
attractive in the current season's fashions as widely advertised.
Seductive appeals assault eyes and ears and nostrils with every variety of emotion. And raw emotion is a far more powerful impetus
to learning than intellect or the thinking process, just because
emotion works on a more immediate, instinctive level.

Learning theorists in their experiments attempt to break down
behavior into small bits or events in order to discover how certain
behaviors are learned and how they may be altered. They believe
that the human organism, as complex as it is, cannot be approached in its totality. Their approach is to isolate a specific pattern or even a specific event, and then to alter one single variable
at a time, noting its effect on the behavior under question. When
sexual therapy, for example, is based primarily on learning theory,
the focus of attention tends to be upon specific aspects of sexual
behavior that are viewed as "symptoms." The idea seems to be
that if the behavior can be changed, a change in attitude will follow. By gradually introducing sexual techniques designed to extinguish undesirable patterns and to encourage the development of

those behaviors that are considered desirable, more positive behavior is expected to replace that which was frustrating or otherwise unsatisfactory.

What seems to be taken insufficiently into account by this approach is that learning does not take place in a vacuum, but rather in the complex biochemical-neurological structures of the body and especially of the brain. Whatever bit of information one learns affects the biochemical structure of the whole organism. The organism is not quite the same after having learned or experienced something as it was before. Learning is not like writing something on a slate that can be erased at some later date. We now know that learning profoundly alters the organization of consciousness, and that unlearning is really not possible. If by learning we mean increasing the capability of consciousness, then what is required is a true transformation. This comes about not by "unlearning," but by understanding what has been learned within a different context, which gives new meaning to the content of the learning.

It is next to impossible to isolate the forms of behavior from emotional responses that the behaviors have caused to become habitual. Nowhere is this more true than in therapy for so-called sexual dysfunction. If therapists proceed from the belief that certain unsatisfactory modes of sexual behavior have been acquired through a learning process that can be reversed, they soon discover that it is no easy matter to unlearn those behaviors. Repeated patterns of sexual disharmony or sexual inadequacy over the years have led to resentment, frustration, distance, and misunderstanding between sexual partners. These feelings destroy the quality of the entire relationship between the partners and lead to actions that are far more destructive than were the sexual problems originally. To deal with the specific behavior patterns that people blame for a breakdown of relationship is not likely to be helpful in the long run. Only when the difficulties are short-lived, based on misinformation, or relatively superficial can simple learning theory be productive. Or, it may be useful as one element in a more inclusive program. But if the real underlying issues were confronted in depth, it might very well be that the accompanying negative behavior would correct itself.

Nevertheless, society continues to place emphasis on the value of behavior modification, with its hopes of being able to predict and control behavior by careful attention to specific goals and measured progress in the direction of those goals. People like to believe that they are "accomplishing something," that they are achieving what they have set out to do. It is part of the American dream, that everything can be accomplished if only we can work out the method and account for all the variables. It is part of that dream, too, that since how individuals learn to think, feel, act, and behave is largely determined by the socialization process, it makes sense to expend our efforts toward changing society so as to make a better learning environment. Speaking for society, as he so often does, B. F. Skinner says: ". . . our task is not to encourage moral struggle or to build or demonstrate inner virtues. It is to make life less punishing and in doing so to release for more reinforcing activities the time and energy consumed in the avoidance of punishment. Up to a point the literatures of freedom and dignity have played a part in the slow and erratic alleviation of aversive features of the human environment, including the aversive features used in intentional control. But they have formulated the task in such a way that they cannot now accept the fact that all control is exerted by the environment and proceed to the design of better environments rather than of better men."[14]

My own contention is that, yes, we need to design better environments, but it will require better human beings to create them, for those who today seem bent upon "making life less punishing" often are doing so by despoiling the natural environment in order to supply increasingly gargantuan human appetites. Without moral struggles or inner virtues, what kind of control will be exerted by that abstract entity that Skinner calls "environment"? Who will pull the strings?

COGNITIVE DEVELOPMENTAL THEORY

We have seen how the prevailing attitudes toward sexuality in the age of modernity were shaped by two major psychological models: psychoanalysis and learning theory. More recently, a third model, that of cognitive development, has been receiving a great deal of attention. Its wide acceptance may be due, in part, to the fact that it incorporates some of the more useful features of the other two models within its own conceptual framework. In the early days of the twentieth century, when modernity was at its zenith, psychologists expressed their interest in character development in tones which tended to be philosophical and moral, and many "wise essays" were written on the subject. The authors saw, as an important task of child development, the furthering of children's natural tendencies toward emotional and social growth by setting before them the values to which this particular culture of twentieth-century America—in precept if not in deed—was committed.

During the heyday of the learning-theory period, values were determined in terms of psychometrics; which is to say that nothing was regarded as important unless it could be weighed, measured, and replicated by others in experiments. The philosophical approach to child development fell out of vogue. Only a few writers focused on issues of character formation; for example, Erik Erikson, whose basic training had been in anthropology, and not primarily in psychology or education. Erikson formulated a series of eight successive stages in human development, each with its own developmental task to fulfill before the person could move successfully on to the next stage. These stages proceeded from infancy to old age, with each incorporating the achievement of a certain level of maturity represented by the previous stage as a precondition to the individual's continuing on to another stage with its greater demands and greater complexity. While Erikson established a whole-life scheme in his writing,[15] other contemporary writers have turned their attention to studies of one or the other sex and a particular age group; for example, Lillian Rubin and Gail Sheehey have been interested in middle-aged women, while Daniel Levinson and his colleagues have written on men in midlife transitions. These writers are indebted to the pioneer in the field of human development, psychologist and epistemologist Jean Piaget, who carefully and creatively observed children as they slowly constructed their knowledge of the physical world. Piaget devised experiments for children of various ages that made it possible to discern the typical age at which certain kinds of knowledge, skill, and judgment could be expected to emerge. His early empirical work differed from that of the psychoanalysts in that it depended not upon a prior theory, but upon the evidence of the senses in the process of keen observation. It differed, too, from the work of the learning theorists in that Piaget stressed the importance of the biological inheritance and innate developmental potentials which infants bring into the world with them. For Piaget, the infant's and child's intelligence proceeds through the mutual influence of biological maturation and the child's own efforts. In the process of interacting with people and objects in the environment, the child's innate patterns of relationship emerge and take form. Piaget delineated four major stages from birth to adolescence, which described the child's growing ability to cope with the environment by utilizing his or her own developing mental powers. Thus expectations were formulated as to how children would or should develop, according to chronological age.

Implicit in the development of concepts that enable children to deal with their world are those having to do with themselves and others as sexual beings. Not too surprisingly in our contemporary American society, the development of sex-role concepts and sexual behavior has been linked to the development of morality and social behavior. These developments have been formulated into stages in which "maturity" is defined in terms of the level of moral awareness attained. Lawrence Kohlberg, who is well known for his work on the development of moral character and moral ideology,[16] has applied the cognitive-developmental approach of Piaget to the process by which children become aware of themselves as sexual beings. He uses stage theory to describe how children arrive at a more or less fixed concept of sexual identity and discover how they are supposed to behave, that is, to adopt a moral position consistent with the cultural imperatives as to how individuals of their sex ought to live out their sexuality.

Kohlberg asserts that children learn about human bodies just as Piaget showed that they learn about inanimate worlds. This learning is quite natural, and rarely traumatic as Freud would have had us believe. Between the ages of two and four, the child usually learns about the unchangeable nature of the inanimate world—that a table today will be the same table tomorrow and the bed that awaits the child at night is the same bed in which he or she will awaken in the morning. But the child also learns that some objects are not constant. At a picnic recently, I watched a little boy of about three in the process of developing a sense of object constancy. It was delightful and intriguing to observe the child encountering rainbow bubbles from another child's soap-bubble pipe and trying to catch them, only to have them vanish at his touch. I saw the mystified delight of this little boy occupying himself in the play for over an hour, testing between what was "real" and constant, and what was ephemeral.

Somewhere during this age of wondrous discovery, the child learns about the unchangeability of sex; that once you are a boy you will always be a boy and eventually a man, and once you are a girl you will be a girl and then a woman for as long as you live. Perhaps a trace of the belief in the ephemeral nature of sex still exists in the transsexual. I can still recall from my own preschool days that I once asked my mother if she would take me to the barber and have my curls cut off, and then get me a pair of short pants and a shirt, because I would like to try being a boy for a while. I now understand that gender constancy had not yet been established. My mother helped it along by showing me the impressive sculpture of Rodin's Adam.

Usually by the age of four, children have learned that people are either male or female and will remain so. They understand that they will always be of one gender and they begin to value the objects and characteristics that go with that gender. The environment imposes its concepts of what is expected of males and what of females, in the form of playthings presented as sex-appropriate or tasks that the child is asked to do. To the extent that these are different for males and females, they become fixed as "gender-appropriate." Appearance, clothing, and relative physical strength are all part of the formation of the *idea* of what is male and what is female. Much of gender identity, or the sense of who one is, is already established before the genital differences are noticed, says Kohlberg. But by age six or seven, when as a rule the child knows about genital differences, the genitals take on added importance.

The impact of the first awareness of the genital difference between the sexes surely varies greatly from one individual to an-

other. Undoubtedly one possibility is the image so graphically portrayed by Freud: the small boy's terror at seeing the little girl as
the castrated freak which he himself could become. The image of
male as the norm, and female as a deviation from the norm, is a
less emotionally charged version of the same idea, and this is probably more widely accepted today as a social and political construct
than the Freudian view. Kohlberg suggests that when children do
note anatomical sex differences they may think it strange, as they
do with so many initial observations in the world of childhood,
but that there are no feelings of inferiority/superiority attached to
them, unless these were imposed by the parents early on. Nor does
he believe that the early childhood fantasies of boys losing the
penis, or of girls acquiring one, are based on sexual urges of an
oedipal nature. He would say, rather, that if children around four
or five show concern about this difference it is because they don't
yet understand that their genitals are not going to change; and
this is an expression of the child's general uncertainty about the
constancy of objects, including parts of the body.

Nevertheless, the familiar sex stereotypes do typically emerge in
the child by the age of six or seven. Kohlberg points to "practically universal" cross-cultural patterns of social roles in which
males are likely to engage in aggressive and dangerous activities
outside the home, while females tend to engage in nurturant activities inside the home. We may well ask what motivates the
child to conform to these stereotypes. Most likely, the behavior
corresponds to the self-concept of the child, which is based on
gender identity. But even here, it works out differently for boys
than it does for girls. The boy perceives the masculine stereotype
and begins to value it for the strength, power, and prestige that
are associated with it. He begins to imitate the adults in his personal life and those he observes on television and in the movies
who fit the stereotypes. His attachment to his father comes partly
out of his own gender identity, and partly from the pleasure he
takes in joining in with sex-typed interests which the father en-
courages. But the paternal warmth does not *cause* the boy's
identification with the father, since the cause is seen to stem from
the boy's own thought processes. Kohlberg says that the feeling of

the father for his son only *augments* the boy's "natural" gender identification.

The girl's development of gender identity is not quite so clear-cut, according to his view. It begins in much the same way as that of the boy, with the recognition that she is and always will be female. She wants to do "female things," that is, things that are related to the female body image, including nurturance and child care and involving a relative lack of activity, power, and aggression. By the age of six or seven, the girl thinks that being female is best, because she is female, and seeks self-consistency. However, she sees that power and prestige are also desirable, and that these are part of the male stereotype. Therefore, an ambivalence develops between her need for self-consistency and her desire for power and prestige. She is torn between these two kinds of behavior as exemplified by her two parents. She is most likely to resolve, or try to resolve, this ambivalence by imitating her mother while seeking approval from her father through accommodating behavior, as she may see her mother do.

The cognitive developmental approach to an understanding of sex typed behavior is primarily descriptive. Careful observations are made as to *what happens* in the course of the child's development, and at what stage various developments are likely to occur. Less attention is paid to the unconscious aspects of personality development as children are learning to adapt and please, while at the same time repressing or extinguishing or resentfully remembering those kinds of behavior which do not correspond to what they believe society expects. Social expectations depend in part on morals and mores, and in part on the theory that children are biologically programmed to develop certain kinds of thought processes at certain ages. Consequently, cognitive-developmental psychologists are more interested in discovering universal principles of thought than they are in studying social and cultural influences or individual differences.[17]

Other theoreticians in this field have worked out their own systems of "developmental stages." A good example is Jane Loevinger's model, which she arrived at on the basis of conclusions derived from interpretations of her sentence-completion test. The person's responses to the incomplete statements indicate the level of ego development attained. For Loevinger, the various life-stages are not necessarily age-bound, but since some degree of maturity is implied as one moves from one stage to another, there is some relationship to chronological age. She sees ego development as encompassing moral development, character development, and cognitive development. She does not limit cognitive development to the thinking process but includes other ways of knowing as well, and especially the learning that comes through feeling and sensation. She understands the ego as the "master-personality trait" which describes the development of the "self-system," and which organizes and integrates all other aspects of the personality.[18] She differentiates between ego development and the development of sexual expression but recognizes that there is some relationship between the two, as, for example, between height and weight—although these are really two very separate things. If one can estimate the development of one, it is possible to guess that of the other, but in actual, careful measurement there may be considerable variation.

Loevinger's stage theory of ego development considers the child from birth to what is called "maturity." As we review the stages she has delineated, we may recognize what seems to us a basic limitation of ego psychology—its principles being confined to the personal and interpersonal dimensions of experience. Successful adaptation in these areas constitutes maturity. Ego psychology, which in some sense includes all the schools I have been discussing in this chapter, is primarily concerned with individuals moving through levels of consciousness which enable them to cope with their environment in an adaptive way. To be imaginative and creative is valued, to be sure, but it is made clear enough that it is better not to make too much commotion or to indulge in radical or innovative behavior to the extent that one might be called eccentric. "Mastery" is the key idea of ego psychology. This means both self-mastery and mastery over the environment.

From the ego psychology point of view, the sequence of stages may be accurate enough, but if we are to look beyond ego for the fuller development of the person it is incomplete. Ego psychology turns away from the challenge of dealing with the soul's mysteries, which border on Great Knowledge, for these cannot be mastered by the human intellect. When we begin to concern ourselves (in the next chapter) with psychological approaches that cross the barrier between the ego and the unconscious, giving greater weight to unconscious processes than to the processes that the ego is able to master, we will see more clearly the limitations of the "well-developed ego."

How, in the view of Loevinger, does maturity develop? In reviewing her schema briefly, I will conjecture freely as to what sexual patterning might be taking place during the various stages of ego development.

The first stage in Loevinger's system is the *presocial-symbiotic* stage. At birth the infant is autistic, that is, self-absorbed and unable to differentiate itself from its surroundings. When the infant begins to recognize the difference between self and not-self, it relates to the other in that symbiotic way that sees the other person as existing to meet one's own needs. From birth on, the infant probably experiences sexual or at least presexual feelings, even while it has not yet become aware that it is a being separate from the mother. Pleasure at the breast, it seems to me, must be closely akin to sexual pleasure, for it pleasurably involves the stimulation of the mouth and digestive system and skin. There is more than a need for nourishment here, there is a need for nurturance—which means warmth, loving, physical contact, special sounds and smells —and nurturance belongs to the realm of erotic experience.

Then follows the *impulse-ridden* stage of early childhood, in which the child is attempting to establish his or her separate identity. Other people are seen in terms of what they can give to the child, who wants what he wants when he wants it. Failure to control impulses leads to punishment and, consequently, to pain. This overwhelming desire "to get" was described by Freud as the psychosexual stage of orality. Surely the anticipation of the satisfaction that comes from having desires fulfilled is not unrelated to what will later develop as explicit sexual demands and for the willingness to see the partner primarily as "sex object."

As the child becomes a little wiser, he or she progresses to the *opportunistic* stage. By this time the child has learned some self-protective mechanisms, for example, to anticipate rewards and punishments over the short term. The older child learns what the rules are, and finds out that it is important not to get caught. If this development is not transcended, the child could develop into a sociopath, or criminal. In Freudian terms, the child is at the anal stage of psychosexuality and is instinctively using manipulation to get what is desired, through giving or withholding the behavior that the parents expect. The techniques, first employed here, develop in later life into manipulative sexual behavior, particularly through using sexual responses to reward or punish the partner. To the degree that this stage is incompletely resolved, the sexual life of the adult is dedicated to the desire to gain maximum pleasure for oneself while avoiding pain as much as possible.

Loevinger's *conformist* stage is most typically seen in adolescents and people of college age, although in many individuals it persists far beyond those years. The beginnings of conformity may correspond to some extent with Freud's phallic stage, in that the ideal of conformity is a step toward acquiring power at a time of life when gender-identity and the power-sex link are becoming established. At the conformist stage, people obey the rules because they identify their welfare with that of the family or peer group to which they belong. They are very much concerned with such externals as appearance, social acceptance, and reputation. Sexual behavior follows peer patterns, and the hope of "being popular" seduces many people into sexual behavior they do not really desire.

The transitional stage of *self-awareness* follows the conformist stage. It is here that, according to Loevinger, the average adult in our society begins to form a unique self-concept. With increasing self-awareness, the individual learns to appreciate the multiplicity of possibilities within a given situation. As a prerequisite to this development it will be necessary for a person to begin to replace the values of the group with his or her own personal values. Without this, no choices can be made that are valid for the individual. With self-awareness, the individual's personal sexual style begins to develop. In this postpubertal period of exploration and discovery, the person begins to learn what is possible as sexuality develops. What are the rewards and what are the punishments if certain types of behavior are engaged in? Experimentation is a part of growing self-awareness. At this stage, people often find their first loves. If they do, it is likely that the union will be based on attractions that are in large measure unconscious. The sense of the self is not yet fully known, much less integrated, so there is the risk that sexual relationships of significance may be initiated because the loved person embodies, literally, elements missing from the conscious personality of the lover. What people do not recognize as a part of their own nature, they tend to project onto the other and there they find a shining mirror of the undiscovered self.

The *conscientious* stage follows upon the earlier stages as defined by Loevinger. By now the "rules" have become internalized and the individuals view them as self-understood. An adult consciousness marks this stage, with self-criticism an important element in it. These people evaluate their long-term goals in terms of some "objective" value system. They have a long time-perspective on events. Mutuality is the keynote in personal relationships. When they seek and find life partners, they are concerned with their own sexual style of relating and with the assignment of sex roles along traditional lines. At this stage, people tend to want the partner to fulfill the appropriate sex role as defined by the particular social group to which the couple belongs. Toward this end, the inner "ideal partner" may be projected onto the mate, but people seem to be able to become more conscious about this than they were in the previous stage. When marriage and family are embarked upon by people at this stage of development, the prognosis for stability is probably higher than at any other stage. This stage would represent mature adulthood as envisioned in the psychoanalytic model or the learning-theory model. The "right stuff" has been inculcated and assimilated. These people are well adjusted.

But people do not necessarily remain static, even though the situation in which they find themselves may appear to be comfortable and satisfying. Among some individuals bonded in a relationship, a new transitional stage may arise. Loevinger calls this the *individualistic* stage, with its hallmark a heightened sense of individuality and a strong desire for emotional independence. Here people experience conflict between their own needs and those of others. It is at this point that individuals may rebel against the constrictions of being "well adjusted" in their fixed roles. As a society, this has been and still is being experienced in the women's liberation movement, and in other struggles for the freedom to be who we are regardless of the categories of appropriateness spread out before us by the social order. In the next chapter, I will deal with the wider implications of this stage as it turned into large-scale rebellion against the mores of the paradigm of modernity. But here we need only be concerned with this particular stage of cognitive development where the eyes of the dutiful and conscientious people are opened and they see how bored they are. We are economically and socially successful, they say, but is this all there is? It is at this stage that many illusions are shattered, and especially those attached to the sexual partner. It is now possible to see how this person really is, and not as a useful or troublesome appendage to one's own being. It is now that many relationships fall apart because the person one believed in did not manage to live up to the expectations one had for that person. Adaptation begins to break down as one sees the status quo as less desirable than before.

The struggles of this transitional stage, if negotiated successfully, lead to the *autonomous* stage. These people have by now developed the capacity to recognize conflicts and to handle them realistically and with good humor. Sexually, they can transcend the polarities that defined sex roles for them at earlier stages. Now they are more concerned with the needs of each person in a relationship than they are with fulfilling their earlier images of what should constitute the ideal relationship. They are able to tolerate ambiguity and to deal with paradoxes in their personal lives and their views of the world. The autonomous stage is likely to be a time of reflection, review, and reorganization of the person's entire life. This stage tends to occur at midlife or later. Youthful rebellion does not belong to this stage, for true autonomy cannot occur until the individual has first made peace with the collective which is society and has learned to abide by its rules and to meet its demands. Only when this first half of the life-task has been accomplished can the need for conformity and conscientiousness be placed in a position secondary to the goal of self-fulfillment. Once those adaptive tasks are accomplished, a person may seize the freedom to shift roles in relationships, to change occupations, and often to replace a primary relationship that may have been outgrown with another, or others, more consonant with this stage of development. Sexual life can take on a new dimension. It can become at once freer and more responsible: freer in that it is no longer so responsive to societal patterns, and more responsible in that sexuality is viewed as a component of one's total being. The autonomous person realizes that there is no difference between what one does and what one is.

The highest stage which Loevinger identifies is the *integrated* stage. Here, she says, "the person proceeds beyond coping with conflict to reconciliation of conflicting demands, and, where necessary, to renunciation of the unattainable, beyond toleration to the cherishing of individual differences, beyond role differentiation to the achievement of a sense of integrated identity."[19] She believes that such persons rarely appear in "normal groups," so new insights are hard to confirm. And she cites Abraham Maslow's early work, in which he began to identify self-actualizing persons and to describe some of their unusual experiences.[20]

The publication of Loevinger's major paper on the subject in 1966 was preceded by years of research which led to the conceptualization of these stages. One might regard this paper as a milestone which appeared just before a sharp turn in the course of human psychosexual development. In the middle of the sixties, when universities were torn by ideological strife, when feeling was high about social inequities, and the life-styles of members of the affluent society imitated their less well-off colleagues, when the flower children were still starry-eyed and only a few had tried psychedelics, "normal groups" did not know much about experiences that could transcend autonomy. Yet there were a few people who did know, or at least they had an inkling, and that inkling led them to search out the spaces within themselves which the psychologies of the Western world had left largely unexplored.

Maslow's "self-actualized persons," to whom Loevinger referred, were the ones who had successfully negotiated the *individualistic* stage and who were moving on. The inner need to assert independence was no longer such a driving force, for they had proved to themselves that they had successfully survived those acts of personal rebellion which mark the adolescence of consciousness. They had been able to say no to many of the behavior patterns that had been explicitly transmitted to them by their parents. This gave them the space to break out of the constricted roles in which they had been taught to function. The *autonomous* stage they were now entering held new challenges. Most of these had to do with discovering that the psyche has its own purposes beyond anything that one may be taught. The mysteries hidden in the seeds of one's own potential could be discovered only by recognizing the possibilities and the limitations of the developing ego which, the self-actualizing person believed, was able to stand on its own. Finally, in Loevinger's schema, the stage of *integration* is reached. The person who comes to this level of achievement can experience a sense of individual identity that is firm enough to transcend conflict, flexible enough to respect individual differences, and knowledgeable enough to have a sense of how to function in the world. Loevinger's essential objectives, after all, are not so very different from those of psychoanalysis or behavioral psychology. All would assist the individual in achieving a creative adaptation to society as it has been defined under the ruling paradigm of modernity.

The last three stages of Loevinger's schema carry ego development to its very highest level. A peak is reached, after a long climb upward. But mountaineers do not necessarily stop at the peak. There is the long look over to a new vista, and there is a descent which may, or may not, be a return in the same direction from which the climber has come. In this sense, the transpersonal vision cannot be seen in its full sweep until the personal has been attained, and finally the transpersonal cannot be fully entered into until the personal or ego realm is able to be transcended. This is not to say that we give up our attachment to ego and the ego world when we move into a transpersonal level of consciousness. On the contrary, the achievement of a strong ego and a clear sense of personal identity is the *sine qua non* for the next step. That step is into the realm of consciousness that is beyond ego, beyond the limits and goals of the "personality." It becomes necessary, before this transition can be made, for the individual to relinquish the supremacy of the ego, the sense that "I can do it if only I try hard enough, or want it enough, or if the conditions can be manipulated or if, if, if . . ." This sense of personal or ego importance needs to be subordinated to the awareness of the transpersonal Self, in the embrace of which we all live and have our being. One must be able to say, "*Thy* will be done."

The chief tools for functioning in the ego realm are *logos* and *eros*, reasoned intellect and passionate feeling. In the realm of the transpersonal Self, the chief tools are *intuition*, which means direct knowing, and *a suspension of the habit of uncritically accepting "received knowledge,"* which is passed on through custom or tradition or consensual agreement.

The *transpersonal* realm of development cannot be divided into so many hierarchical stages, for the world view that is considered to be transpersonal allows a multitude of images and symbols to be considered valid, approaching as they do the ineffable wisdom that cannot be fully apprehended by humans. And so each culture, each religious or philosophical or scientific discipline which is able to describe reality in its own terms without falling into the error that theirs is the only truth, or even the truth entire, can partake of the transpersonal vision. If the *integrated* ego state means that the person feels secure in a particular perspective or world view, then the *transpersonal* state admits a certain amount of disintegration, or a loosening of ego boundaries. No longer is one fully attached to a particular "truth" even though tolerating divergent views; the difference is in the transpersonal awareness that every view takes its value from the subjective stance of the observer in interaction with what is observed. To take this a step further, the transpersonal perspective is that there is no observer without an "observed" and that nothing is observed without the observer—hence these concepts "observer" and "observed phenomena" are part and parcel of each other.

The transpersonal re-vision of the relative values of ego and Self implies that we trust the orderly processes of the universe enough to allow ourselves to move in harmony with them and not in opposition to them. Personal power needs are put aside in favor of a sense of wonder. The naïve wonder of the child is not called for here, rather the wonder of one who sees people no longer as fully separate entities operating under their own power, but as integral parts of dynamic systems within larger and larger systems. Transpersonal awareness goes beyond thinking that we can and do make our own world or, conversely, that the environment fashions those who inhabit it. It sees that person and environment are truly inseparable.

In the process of coming to a transpersonal perspective, the ego must first release itself from all those internalized authorities, from the parents to those in the wider world. As these have an inhibitory function, they need to be allowed to ebb away, leaving a space for something new to enter. At this point, the Self may appear as a rebel, devaluing the past and casting about among the infinite possibilities for new ways to reveal itself. Between the fitful and tentative rebellions against more or less stultifying concepts, the quality of consciousness goes through successive transformations. Some seem like regressive actions, some seem too unrealistic, some expect too much too fast. The movement toward the transpersonal is experienced as a series of shifts and changes in consciousness, usually with the uneasy feelings that accompany disturbances of equilibrium. These shifts and changes have been occurring not alone in individuals, but within the general culture as well. The clear message of the transpersonal perspective is that, in the evolution of consciousness, individual and collective are inextricably involved.

4
Rebellion of the Self

World War Two began, and ended, with catastrophic explosions of power. In each instance, the carefully engineered products of the intellect rained down destruction upon the innocent, the naïve, and the unprepared. The scientifically trained minds of two countries created the means—for the Japanese attack on Pearl Harbor and for the American atomic bombings of Hiroshima and Nagasaki. In the interval between the two rounds of devastation, the American character underwent a series of drastic alterations. The events following the war brought about even more change. Lives of almost all of the young people in the country were uprooted in one way or another, whether they went off to fight, or whether they lost the stability of a predictable existence even while they remained at home. The war was necessary, we told ourselves, and patriotism and honor did not permit us to question our moral position. In gearing up ourselves psychologically for the war effort it seemed necessary to fall in with the collective lockstep. The individual human experience of intimacy with another human being had to be subordinated to the need for survival under the powerful impact of the events that threatened people's existence, their families, their homes, their land. In time of war the tender feelings must be cut off from consciousness. The deeper injuries to the soul were reflected in the ways in which people experienced their sexuality. Here was mirrored the bruising of human sensitivity, the crushing of individuality, and the elevation of the instinct to preserve one's own self at any cost. In an increase of violent, kinky, and promiscuous sex, the symptoms of a sick society found expression. Soldiers soon learned to suppress the gentle and vulnerable aspects of their humanity lest those aspects be taken for weakness.

The far-reaching and varied effects of the War cannot be described in ways that would make them seem other than impersonal. I would rather attempt a microcosmic view by describing some of what I saw from my own perspective in that time, inasmuch as every drop of water contains, in some measure, the ocean. I remember how it was in 1938–40, when we would hear on the radio that the German Army was marching into one country after another, taking it over militarily, and thereby gaining in strength and power. At first it was the Sudetenland. Well, they are *almost* Germans, we thought. Then Austria, Czechoslovakia, Poland, Denmark, Norway, Luxembourg, Belgium, Holland, France . . . These countries put up little struggle against the Wehrmacht, or so it seemed to us. That was Germany's business, or Europe's business, not ours. Peace was the highest value. We would support peace, here on our safe continent. Let Europe blow itself to bits, or come under the heel of the German. We would provide an example of democracy and, in the process, mind our own affairs.

But then it began to dawn on some of us that the America First organization which so ardently espoused American isolationism was, in reality, a front organization of Nazi sympathizers who exploited America's desire for peace to keep us from interfering with German ambitions for conquest. And then the stories of the persecution of Jews and others began to trickle through, and we heard reports of concentration camps with rumored gas chambers where wholesale extermination of human beings was carried on. We didn't want to believe it. We heard about the Jews wanting the war, wanting to push the United States into attacking Germany because of their own stake in getting rid of Nazism. As an American Jew, I found myself doing some investigative reporting, covering meetings which inflamed American citizens with anti-Semitic bigotry and hate. These soon convinced me to abandon my pacifist position and join the Fight for Freedom organization, which was formed to unmask the America First Committee and to alert Americans to the dangers of German, Italian, and Japanese totalitarianism. Most people, however, refused to listen, and said we were alarmists. They closed their ears to the cries of the subjugated people of Europe, to the moans from the concentration camps. How little compassion was felt or expressed, how little action called forth, until our own skins were in jeopardy! We woke up on December 7, 1941.

The men who left home to join the armed forces had to become soldiers in a hurry. They were not like European youths, who had been disciplined for military life throughout their adolescence. A sudden and radical transformation was needed. They were subjected to rigorous and often brutal experiences in basic training. These experiences were meant to make men tough, and in some ways they did. Bayonet practice, long grueling marches in the hot sun, living in cramped barracks, all created the psychological pressure-cooker atmosphere. Letting off steam had to be as intense as the training itself. Hard drinking, wild parties, casual and promiscuous sex, all were part of a desensitization process that would allow people to look upon other human beings as enemies, and to be able to kill as many of them as possible with hardly any remorse or guilt.

I was a young bride of a few months when the announcement of the bombing of Pearl Harbor came over the radio on that Sunday afternoon. There was no television yet, but no picture could have been more compelling than the intensity in President Franklin D. Roosevelt's voice when he called that Sunday "the day that shall live in infamy." Within hours, thousands of men of military age were lining up at recruiting stations all over the nation, eager to go off to fight on distant shores. They did not ask what jobs they would be assigned to, or what the pay would be, or what the benefits. They made themselves available because their country needed them, and they stood there angry, muttering about "getting even with those slanty-eyed sons-of-bitches."

My husband enlisted. When his basic training was over I followed him, like so many other service wives, as the Army moved him from one post to another within the United States. By the time he was shipped over to the China-Burma-India theater, we had an infant daughter. There was a severe shortage of the sort of housing that could be afforded on a soldier's pay, so the baby and

I went to live with my in-laws, and later I moved in with my own
parents. It wasn't easy for us women who had been living in our
own homes suddenly to be crowded in with relatives. Many
women took jobs that had been vacated by the soldiers. They
worked in factories; they built airplanes and guns; they got their
hands greasy, developed their muscles and grew strong. Their female anatomy presented no hindrance when their country was
eager for their services.

Some of us, especially those with small children, did not need
or want to take a job. We met in the parks and watched our children together. We'd sit there endlessly knitting sweaters and socks
for the soldiers out of the coarse olive drab yarn provided by the
Red Cross. We read our letters aloud sometimes and sometimes
shared the grief of one or another of our group whose husband
was killed, or who was declared missing in action after his plane
failed to return from a mission over enemy territory. The women
were frightened, lonely, longing, frustrated and, as far as I know,
faithful to their husbands. That wasn't too difficult since there
were hardly any healthy able-bodied men around. Those who remained were mostly too guilt-ridden to approach war wives, however lonely or frustrated the latter might be. The women felt
strongly that their part of the war effort required that they be loyal
and steadfast. Looking back from the eighties, one might think
that many lesbian relationships would have developed at that
time, but if they did I never heard about them. I suspect that
they were rare and covert if they did exist, because the overwhelming spirit of the time was one of patriotic sacrifice, and sex was one
of the things that women sacrificed. Some had married in haste before their husbands shipped out, and some had only promised. But
they were committed to their men. Sometimes a woman discovered that a relationship she had hoped would be permanent could
not possibly survive. She felt honor bound to write her man a
"Dear John" letter and tell him honestly how things stood. Everything was open and aboveboard.

I remember well my feelings that ghastly morning in August
1945 when we heard about Hiroshima, and then, three days later,
Nagasaki. I shuddered in disbelief. I recognized the enormity of

the act we had perpetrated, long before I understood how and why we did it.

O my God, how unspeakable!

Our country had committed the ultimate sin, in its unforgivable righteousness. Loyalty, patriotism, all hope of love or tenderness lay broken and lifeless like a flower trampled by wild horses. Our own love and tenderness retreated within us in the moment that we learned of a holocaust we dared not name, our holocaust, that wreaked as much destruction in minutes as the Nazis had accomplished in years. We were not able to transform the soul-sickness that afflicted us into an outspoken guilt that might have brought about repentance and atonement. We were pacified with words. "It was done to end the war quickly." "It saved many thousands of American lives." Since our husbands and lovers were among those who were saved, we wanted to accept this rationalization. We wanted to be happy when the war ended. So we cheered and waved our flags in the streets when the Japanese surrendered. We rejoiced that our men were coming home, but our joy was marred by the tacit knowledge that they had not fought the brave fight to the finish—Satan had brought down his atomic rain for their benefit. He had won the war for them in the "dark Satanic mills." The innocents had been ransomed by the devil, who always names his price.

The men came home gladly, their bellies full of war and hard liquor, their minds jaded with promiscuous sex. They were not the same men who had left us. They were high-wired with a lust for travel, and excitement had captured their hearts. They rejoined their wives and children, but not to resume the status quo ante. Most of them were determined, now, to establish homes far away from their parents. Any sense of continuity with the past was gone; in a war in which any moment might be your last, the men had learned to live fully in and for the present moment. Young couples and young families began moving all over the country in search of new jobs and new challenges in different places. After all the loss and sorrow, and before the costs of the war could be measured in the woundedness of soul, men and women clung tightly to each other for comfort and affection. They wanted, more than anything else, to put the war behind them.

Sexuality was frankly addressed to procreation by men and women whose marriages had been interrupted during the war years. The birth rate increased dramatically and our preoccupation with our children did wonders for us emotionally and for our collective self-image. We felt that we were good and wholesome people. We were going to rear our children differently from the way we were reared. No more would we be bamboozled by psychoanalysts, who had laid so much blame at the feet of our mothers that they feared that whatever they might do—breastfeeding or bottle-feeding, toilet training too late or too early, being overprotective or being too objective, dominating their young or submitting to them—would cause infant traumas that their children would carry with them down the long road from the cradle to the couch. None of that for us!

Nor would we try to shape our children's behavior to suit our convenience by making them conform to rigid schedules or rules. Out went the four-hour feedings prescribed for us when we were small, and carried out religiously by our mothers. We read books like *Babies Are Human Beings*,[1] which informed us that infants knew when they were hungry or thirsty or when they needed to empty their bowels or their bladders, and that we should pay attention to their needs, not press them to attend to ours. We were told not only to allow, but also to encourage them to explore the world, beginning with their own bodies and moving outward wherever their curiosity might lead. Dr. Benjamin M. Spock, the mothers' guru, taught us to respond to our children's demands, feeding them when they cried, showing them unconditional love, encouraging their adventures, and limiting our control to matters of safety and health. We understood that it was all right to allow the baby to choose whatever foods it wanted without our worrying about balancing the diet. If the child chooses nothing but peanut butter and Coca-Cola, don't worry, over a period of time things will even out and the child will discover what it needs. Permissiveness was a new buzz word.

We learned also not to pay too much attention to the developmental scales or standards based on age-level studies of "normal" children. Babies were not only human beings, they were individuals as well. If we were to try to fit them into generally accepted

norms of behavior, we could destroy their natural and spontaneous patterns of growth. If we were to see our children fall below
the established norms for this or that behavioral pattern or skill,
our very expectations could lead our child to develop feelings of
inferiority. If, on the other hand, the child ranked higher than average, a feeling of specialness and consequent elitism might follow. We criticized the tendency of psychologists to arrange children in hierarchical categories and to educate differently within
those categories. It did not support the American egalitarian
dream which asserted that all are alike and of equal value, and
that any man can grow up to be President. And of course, in those
times, it never occurred to any of us to suggest that there might
be something sexist in the last statement.

In this fecund society, few concerned themselves with anything
like sex roles or sexually dictated differences in behavior or psychological makeup between men and women. Nearly all those women
who had successfully "manned" assembly lines, and even those
who had taken over their husbands' executive positions or had run
the family business during the war years, were willing enough to
preside at home while their children were growing up. They hap-
pily turned back the job of providing for the family's material
needs to the fathers.

When the young marrieds finally settled down to peacetime, it
was often far from where they had been born and raised. A man
and woman started their nuclear family away from the moral in-
junctions of their parents, the church, and the watchful eyes of
the neighbors. Many people who would not have thought of steal-
ing a towel from the home of a friend did not hesitate to do so in
a motel in a strange town. Psychoanalyst Allen Wheelis, a social
critic of the early fifties, described the change in morals as "the
decline of the superego." If the executive department of the personality is the ego, the internalized judicial department is the
superego. Prior to the formation of the superego, a child may re-
frain from a forbidden act because of the likelihood of being
apprehended and punished; after its formation he or she will re-
frain because the act is "wrong." The superego becomes relatively
autonomous, but it depends to some degree upon the family at
first, and later on the expectations of those around the young per-

son. In a community that continues the way of life in which the superego was formed, the superego continues to receive support and strength. Under such conditions life is orderly and predictable. But the mobility brought about by the war and other changes in man/woman relations resulted in less support from the superego. The conformity that used to be consonant with the precepts of the parents shifted to the expectation of the contemporaries.[2]

During the decade of the fifties, my husband and I owned and operated a summer camp in the Blue Ridge Mountains for children from six to fifteen. We had in our charge postwar babies of the newly affluent middle class, and we watched over them into mid-adolescence. Although admittedly this was a limited segment of the population, it was a significant one, for these children were to be college students in the sixties. They and their peers created the social, political, and sexual revolution, the effects of which are still reverberating throughout our society. These were permissively reared children of upwardly mobile parents. Theirs was the mobility of the socioeconomic scale, where success depends upon power and the appetite for competitiveness. It was an age of conformity, of the man in the gray flannel suit, of the mothers who spent their time transporting their children to music lessons and scouts, to orthodontists and skating classes, and who invested much energy entertaining their husbands' business associates or customers. By the end of June these parents were glad to discharge their children into our care for several weeks so that they could be relieved to travel or otherwise amuse themselves, without benefit of brood.

And no wonder! Many of the children who could be so easily dispensed with were difficult, to say the least, and in serious ways confused. Rearing children permissively tends to become a tug-of-war. When no specified limits are set on behavior, the need of young children to discover where the boundaries really are becomes consuming. They try their parents to the point of desperation; then the parent who has been pushed to wit's end clamps down—with rules and punishments—with a sudden severity that the child is ill prepared to comprehend. The child's startled and pained reactions evoke remorse and guilt on the part of the parent, and memories of Dr. Spock; and once more the restrictions are lifted. So it goes, back and forth between boundaries and freedom, with inconsistency the theme, and insecurity the result. Thus permissiveness, when exercised in the extreme, produces an intolerable situation. It brings about a backlash reaction in which excessive freedom is countered by a renewed demand for conformity. One reason these parents sent their children to us was that they secretly hoped we would be able to bring their offspring back into line.

We saw a lot of depression in these children during the first few days after they came to us. Often this was covered over by a forced boisterousness, a show of will against what they had anticipated would be a rigidly structured situation. These children expected camp to be an institution, like the big corporations their fathers worked for, or the churches or schools they attended. They regarded the rules as challenges to evade or to defy. They made general nuisances of themselves, for example, by deliberately getting "lost," inevitably right around sundown. They greeted with sublime indifference the bells that rang out the schedules. They produced arguments to meet every request, every plan. Their manners were atrocious: they practically stampeded when the dining hall doors were opened. But they knew, and we knew, that in the end they would conform, and feel safe in the knowledge that despite their parents' absence they would be taken care of. The determinism of the institutional structure won out; though in the process of making it work we had to allow for the exercise of as much free will as possible under the limitations that had to be set for reasons of safety, responsibility, and our own conceptions of what was "right" and "moral."

These children grew up unbridled, innocent, and strong-willed, as often happens in protected environments. Their explorations into sexuality around the time of puberty had more to do with curiosity than with intense desire. They would play at sex, but mostly these younger adolescents strictly avoided genital intercourse for fear of pregnancy and consequent social ostracism. Conformity was essential in the peer culture. Self-interest led to self-protectiveness. Girls still believed that virginity was a valuable possession to be guarded, and boys were often encouraged by their buddies, or even by their fathers, to gain their first sexual experiences with prostitutes. In a materialistic and secularized society all pleasures, including sex and sexual initiation, were available at a price. Money determined what something was worth in a society that was becoming increasingly quantified. Spiritual values had reached a low point. Many people had lost interest in a God who allowed gas chambers and atomic bombs. Churches and synagogues now became political platforms, advocating the causes of one group of people over another in the name of "social justice." Yet the social fabric managed to hold together; and perhaps this was because the institutions of Big Business, Big Government, and Big Religion proffered so many rewards to those who, to all appearances, supported the established patterns.

Despite the wider dispersion of the psychologies that had arisen toward the end of the age of modernity, psychological man had not yet found his voice, psychological woman even less. There was a deadly neutrality about psychology. Remember that a stated goal of each of the major psychological schools—psychoanalysis, learning theory, and cognitive development—was to remain "value free." Yet paradoxically, by this very attempt, the goal was bound to be unattainable because objectivity and neutrality are, in themselves, values. In a society that demands conformity, intense pain will occur and neurotic solutions will be found when individuals are unable to adjust to the demands made upon them. Frequently they will seek out psychotherapists for help in achieving a better adaptation, and consequently psychotherapists tend to respond by guiding their clients toward accepting the way things are. So, without passing judgment, most psychotherapists at midcentury assisted the process of adaptation to the status quo. "You can't change the external situation, but you can change your inner attitude toward it," was the watchword of the day. The separation of person from environment was an example of dualistic thinking at its height. We were encouraged to adapt to alien circumstances, manipulating our own minds. We did not see ourselves as part and parcel of the context in which we were, or as cause and agent of our own circumstances.

Under the glossy appearance of middle-class culture at the end of the fifties, under the neat conformity to the careful patterns of society, the caldron of discontent was seething and bubbling. The way I experienced it personally was in my feeling of constriction at home, ministering to a family that gradually needed my services less and less and that presented few opportunities for personal growth or intellectual challenge. I was among those wives who went back to school to complete college or earn advanced degrees before this became the prevailing trend. After finishing my studies, I took my first job away from home since the birth of my daughter. She was by now in her middle teens. Commuting to work over an hour in each direction required me to be gone from home from eight in the morning until six-thirty in the evening. My long day produced one family crisis after another. For instance, it did not occur to any of us, least of all to myself, that there was any possible way that an evening meal could get started in my absence, let alone cooked in its entirety. It appeared to be quite true still, as Esther Harding had written in the thirties, that "if women are to progress further in the man's world of work, they must recognize it is a case of 'This ought ye to have done and not to have left the other undone.' "[3]

Because I held a job, it was made clear that I was no longer adequate as wife or mother. I was selfish. I forced everybody to readjust to my schedule. Nobody considered that for the past fifteen years I had been adjusting to the needs and schedules of other people. An atmosphere of anger and reproach settled about the house. My husband felt neglected and disparaged (wives don't work when their husbands can provide for all their needs). My daughter was caught in the middle of domestic quarrels and she was confused. As for me, it was all I could do to get off to work in the morning because I felt compelled to complete the tiring household routine first. But, once the commuter train pulled into the station, Cinderella entered the magic coach and the mice turned into white horses. How luxurious it felt to sit on a velvet couch and watch the squalid city speed by! When I reached my destination I found my handsome prince, too. Only he was a starving poet in the disguise of an editor. With him I could share some fantasies and dreams and our common dislike of the mundane aspects of the work situation. When I began to feel myself becoming emotionally involved, I studiously took care to avoid him, even to taking the long way round to my office cubicle so that I would not pass his. I was frightened of entering into a sexual relationship with him for fear of disastrous consequences to my marriage. I did not yet think of myself as a woman who could possibly manage alone. My marriage, unsteady though it was, provided a sort of equilibrium for me. I knew how to adapt to it, and in some significant ways I felt supported by it. To be fully independent as woman was a situation I did not dare to risk at that time.

I was far from unique. How many women, at the beginning of the sixties, with their children no longer dependent on them, their husbands absorbed in chasing after Success, suffered from loneliness and depression, and sought some way out! We started, tentatively enough, taking a course here and there, initiating a new relationship, joining an activist group, taking a part-time job. How cold so many marriages had become, how isolated husband and wife from one another. How little energy was available to direct toward furthering the closeness of the family. Meanwhile, the children who had been so well trained to be self-sufficient were moving off on their own, deeply involved with their friends and taking their standards from their peers in a world where traditional values were becoming less and less visible.

I could not resolve the family tensions in which I was personally embedded, but transferred them to Zürich, Switzerland. The year was 1960. My husband was to undergo training there to become a Jungian analyst. A short time later, I also joined the training program at the C. G. Jung Institute for Analytical Psychology. While we had been in the United States neither one of us had ever seriously considered entering psychotherapy for ourselves, much less analysis, despite the problems that confronted us. We still believed that psychotherapy was for the emotionally disturbed, and that entering into analysis was tantamount to a public admission that there was something radically wrong with you. Such an admission would not correspond to the self-image held by either one of us. But in Zürich, as in every analytic training program that I know, each candidate is *required* to undergo an intensive personal analysis. Among its other potential values, this requirement provided the needed face-saving device for two people who had "absolutely nothing wrong" with them to spend a number of years sorting out the labyrinthine ways of their individual psyches. And since the Jungian training institute was in another country, we were able to do this outside and away from the society out of which our own individuality had emerged. We were able to gain some perspective on the cultural setting from which we had emerged as well as on its collective unconscious base, the repository of those least understood, possibly archaic or mythic forces that motivate the human organism to behave as it does. We spent our time and energy delving into the backgrounds of our own experiences, both as individuals and as members of a contemporary society.

When we returned four years later, either the United States was a very different country from the one we left, or we brought back to it a very different sensibility. We perceived that pressures that had been building up when we left had now broken through their containers. Depending upon how you looked at it, the abscesses of society were bursting and spilling their foul-smelling pus all around, or cocoons were being torn open by winged creatures emerging from their dark protected places. Whatever metaphor was fitting, it was clear that important changes were coming out into the open for all to see. A new breed of young people were singing of a "new age." They were living communally, sharing whatever they had with one another; and this sharing included rooms, beds, love and sex, filth and venereal disease, food and music and laughter, psychedelics, disdain for the work ethic, mistrust of their parents and their parents' generation, and a boundless hope for a better world that would miraculously spring into being at some future time, after the present "system" was destroyed.

Even before I left Zürich, there had been portents of things to come. One by one they cast shadows over the bright image of America with which I had come away—or at least the image I remembered in my nostalgic moments. One day I was sitting with a group of Jung Institute students in the bar of a ski hotel at Kleine Scheidegg, partway up the Jungfrau, when a man came over to our table to join us. He had overheard our conversation and recognized us as Americans and "Jungians." He introduced himself as Albert Hofmann, the chemist who had inadvertently discovered LSD while experimenting at Sandoz Laboratories. He told us how he had fallen into a highly disoriented state which he described as swinging between heaven and hell. This was after he had unknowingly ingested the substance. Hofmann expressed his concern to us about the reports he had been receiving from Harvard University about the experimentation with psychedelics currently being carried on by Professors Timothy Leary and Richard Alpert, and a graduate student, Ralph Metzner. Hofmann said he had the impression (which later proved to be accurate) that the three were in some difficulty with the University because the drug had gotten out of the controlled setting of the classroom and laboratory and was being used irresponsibly by people who did not understand the implications of what they were doing. As well as I can recall, Hofmann stated, "In Switzerland this would never happen. The University would exercise strict control. But you Americans like to take things into your own hands. It is important that you Jungians, who understand the powerful nature of the unconscious with all its archetypes, go back and warn your countrymen to treat this substance with caution and respect. It shouldn't be around for just anyone to get hold of. It could be dangerous, even life-threatening. Great caution must be exercised."

The second portent was the advent of the birth control pill. Here for the first time was a contraceptive a woman could take without her mate being aware of it. This was heralded as the woman's key to freedom from her role of subordination to the male sex. The newfound ability of any woman who so desired to regulate her own reproductive functioning provided the impetus for the women's liberation movement to begin on a mass scale. Women found themselves facing a whole new set of options for which many felt unprepared. Not every woman was so eager to be answerable for her choices. To say that women were of two minds on the subject would be a gross understatement. There were many different views as to the advantages and penalties that might be in store for the emerging New Woman.

The third portent was the assassination of President John F. Kennedy, followed by those of Martin Luther King and Robert Kennedy. Grieving and disillusioned, we ceased to look for heroic models. The American Dream became blurred with the tears shed by ordinary Americans. Everyone, from schoolchildren to the elderly, gazed at their television sets in dismay and disbelief, and finally in resignation.

The ground was cut out from under us, spiritually, ideologically, and materially. Leaving the States had meant to me selling a tree-shaded home with a vegetable garden in back and leaving old friends behind. I returned to the twenty-second floor of an air-conditioned and hermetically sealed concrete blockhouse, and to strangers. I remembered that when I was a little girl the futurologists kept predicting a population explosion, and I couldn't imagine what that would be like. In those early days the kids on the block used to play baseball in the street of our middle-sized suburb. When an occasional car would come along, we would pause in our game and step up onto the curb to let it pass, then resume the game. Now, I looked down from the window of my high-rise apartment upon patterns of red taillights streaming along four lanes of traffic heading north and white headlights coming down the four lanes heading south. My socioeconomic status had not changed appreciably, only the world had changed. Cities, suburbs, homes, apartments, schools, churches, bars and sports arenas, colleges and universities were crowded with people jostling against each other. A gaseous haze hung over industrial areas. To get out, to get some fresh air, people were taking to their automobiles, the biggest and best they could afford. They jammed the streets and highways. Competition for goods and services heightened in intensity and prices were up. It seemed to us, when we returned from Zürich, that you had to be tough-minded to survive.

What happens to the tender-minded in a tough-minded world? What happens to the young and idealistic in a pragmatic society where a person's effectiveness is gauged by the ability to manipulate other people? What happens to those who orient themselves to their environment through feeling and intuition, in a world where a higher value is placed upon hard thinking in the realm of the practical as defined by the senses? What happens to the possibility of living out sexuality in trust and openness, in a world which treats sex as a commodity, where love is "made," and sexual attractiveness is bottled and boxed and advertised in every medium? What happens to those young people who cannot meet the academic demands to achieve that "excellence" which, by its very definition, is accomplished only by the few who reach the top?

They could kill themselves trying to adapt. Many did. The suicide rate among older adolescents and college-age adults rose alarmingly in the sixties. They could become psychotic and create a situation which made it impossible for their parents to deal with them, so that they had to be sent to psychiatrists or placed in mental hospitals. Or, if they were only "troublesome," they could be sent off to Europe or India with backpacks and a little cash for an indefinite stay. There, living in conditions of freedom beyond any they had ever imagined, young people managed to survive by their wits and wiles, or through friendships and relationships that were loving and supportive. Those were the fortunate ones. Others even survived relationships that were exploitative and destructive. On their return, many joined the counter-culture, a movement that was rapidly becoming an extremely vocal element within the total youth culture. Its members learned to recognize the processes by which an established culture enacts its enterprises as a "game" in the sense in which one of their chief gurus, Timothy Leary, observed: "*Games* are behavioral sequences defined by roles, rituals, goals, strategies, values, language, characteristic space-time locations and characteristic patterns of movement."[4] Such an attitude denied moral responsibility. Skill in winning over your adversary, or undermining him, were the major objectives. The established culture itself was often seen as the adversary.

Youthful members of the counter-culture separated themselves ideologically from their parents as much as their own World War Two parents had separated geographically from their own families of origin. The young people of the sixties formed their own solid groups to which no one of their parents' generation except a few wise fools and gurus had access. If you were over thirty you were as good as dead. In these new youth-centered settings there were no parental eyes to watch and judge, to give the perspective of time or the gentle guidance born of tolerance long practiced. As the superego gave up its ground, the youthful ego found itself afloat without much of a support system. Ego building, which is clearly an important task during the first part of life, involves the process of finding one's place in society, of learning to function productively in everyday practical reality situations, of acting with conviction, determination, and focused energy. Many young people now rejected such ego tasks, or at least they called these tasks into question. Some who were in this situation came to my consulting room in the late sixties seeking guidance as they tried to discover how to live in a world that had grown too difficult for them and for which their permissive rearing had inadequately prepared them. Paradoxically, they feared the power of the social system within which they had been reared, feeling helpless to deal with it, while at the same time claiming they were capable of functioning independently of it. Looking for alternate values, they might have taken William Blake's words from his prophetic work *Jerusalem* for their slogan:

I must Create a System, or be enslav'd by another Mans
I will not Reason & Compare: my business is to Create.[5]

What was happening, it seems to me, is that in a rather primitive and unconscious way, these young people were experiencing a rebellion of the Self. I use the word *Self* here in Jung's sense, as the archetypal principle of wholeness. When a one-sided development occurs on the side of the ego's personal strivings, the psyche becomes overbalanced in the extreme. Then the compensatory function of the Self seeks to restore the balance. The Self, as a function of the world of nature to which the ego must be subordinated, may induce a swing of the pendulum in the opposite direction.

A Taoist metaphor, taken from the *I Ching*, is appropriate here: "The primal powers never come to a standstill; the cycle of becoming continues uninterruptedly. The reason is that between the two primal powers there arises again and again a state of tension, a potential that keeps the powers in motion and causes them to unite, whereby they are constantly regenerated. Tao brings this about without ever becoming manifest. The power of tao to maintain the world by constant renewal of a state of tension between the polar forces, is designated as good."[6]

The demands that were being placed upon young people to

enter the great arms race, which started with the appearance of Sputnik in the Russian skies, had left many with the feeling of having been violated. The culture that they had experienced as children in an immediate and personal way now seemed bent upon turning students into scientists and engineers in the service of a vast war machine, euphemistically designated as a system of national defense. Education, which in the past had provided room for the study of the humanities, now seemed to be taken over by a model of abstract thinking in which language, digital calculations, and algebra served to combine and rearrange a few symbols in logical, scientific ways. In this one-sided world, the stern, calculating, objective mind was highly valued. Subjective feeling and the finer points of human relationship were of little account in the marketplace. In such a world, sexuality was far from central in consciousness. It served more as something tangential to the earnestness of life, available as a means of escaping from the pressures to which people were being subjected day by day. Through the exercise of sexuality, one could slip into a world of sensual abundance, of dominance and submission games. Sexual relationships did not have to be taken too seriously now that we had The Pill. The complications resulting from the sex act could be viewed as inconsequential. Even where sexual feelings ran deep, even when they propelled people in the direction of emotional commitment, the actual expression of those feelings tended to be relatively shallow in the context of a social order that undervalued the entire affective side of the person.

Among many of those people who had become disenchanted with that abstract mode of reality, there arose an urgent desire for its opposite: a more tangible model based on a world you could touch and see and feel, a world full of song and dance and celebration of the human body. This other world had to do with shapes and forms. It would be geometric rather than algebraic in concept. Vision and imagery would take on renewed respect, and analogical thinking would be at least as acceptable as analytical thinking. The mind, or that aspect of the mind that encompassed body and human relationships as well as thought, rebelled against the thin, attenuated model of society that was being proffered by most educational institutions. It sought, instead, a more joyous, carefree, and practical way of dealing with life and art and feelings.

The dispersion of psychedelic drugs had begun in a cautious and responsible way, with research into the properties of several mind-altering substances, under the guidance of faculty members in the Department of Social Relations at Harvard University. Other institutions were also involved in the research, but it was at Harvard that it became evident beyond doubt that the experimenters and the experiments could not be separated. It is hard to say whether the outcome of the experiments was affected more by the persons of the experimenters, or the experimenters were more profoundly changed by the nature of the experiments. In any case, there was mutual interaction. Everyone who became involved as participant-experimenters underwent shaking psychological experiences that affected whatever equilibrium they might have possessed prior to the work. These experiences called for, even demanded, far-reaching restructuring of the personalities of those involved, so that the new perceptions that came flooding in could somehow be assimilated.

I talked recently with Ralph Metzner about those experiments with psilocybin and lysergic acid diethylamide at Harvard of some twenty years ago, which he had helped to conduct. He reminded me that psychedelic substances such as peyote, hashish, and mescaline had been in use for many centuries, but that it was only in the early sixties that the possibility of psychedelic experience became available to anyone who wanted it. He told me that members of the psychology faculty and others who became interested in the search expressed fear and concern to the experimenters from the beginning. Philosopher Gerald Heard, for one, had said, "You shouldn't make it public." I asked Metzner what had been his understanding of the intent behind the project. He responded that the researchers were trying to develop a framework for further exploration of the mind-expanding properties of the drug, and they were working in professional, middle-class circles, with mature responsible people in psychology, psychiatry, the clergy, and the arts. "The Ken Kesey, *Electric Kool-Aid Acid* crowd was horrific to us. We wanted a supportive, benign, and open structure in which to work. It was important that the experience be guided by persons who themselves had experienced the drug and its effects. The principle was that the doctor should take the medicine before giving it to others. At Harvard some graduate students became interested in helping us with the experiments. We were serious in our work; we did pre- and post-testing. Many creative people were involved."

Talking with Metzner, I had the sense that here was a sensitive, introverted person who combined clinical acuity, personal warmth, and an adventurous nature, and at the same time I felt his concern for the protection of others. He said that he had wanted to keep the work contained among the small group of responsible people who had been involved with it from the beginning, but that Leary, that Irish Revolutionary with his extraverted intuition, wanted to turn the world on, as he said, "for the first time since the Eleusinian Mysteries."[7]

From my own limited experience with psychedelics, I can say that afterward the world was never the same for me as it had been before. The first time, in a sterile clinical setting, I saw chaotic shapes and flowing colors gradually resolve themselves into orderly patterns like the mosaic floor of a cathedral, and I knew that in the place of God there was an underlying order that dissolved itself and reappeared, only to dissolve again, but that the order was *implicate* even in its dissolution. The second time, I sat in a garden and saw that the colors of flowers were truly vibrating waves of light, alive and pulsing, and that everything that I could see participated in that vibrating light which gave to it its particular quality of being. After that I knew beyond any doubt that matter *is* energy, and that it can be transmitted backward and forward in an instant by a shift in consciousness. The third time, I wandered through the caverns of the underworld like Eurydice and, finding myself insubstantial in an insubstantial world, I found my beautiful daughter there, and she became my guide. I felt so joyful that I was reluctant to return, but a gentle blonde shaman brought me back. Since then I have had no fear of death. I discovered what I needed to learn about my world in that most personal experiential way, and since then I have had no further desire to pursue eternity with that particular method.

I had been preparing myself psychologically for my experience and was fortunate to have had individuals with me who could provide support without interfering in my inner process. I can understand and appreciate how difficult, disturbing, even devastating such experiences can be for people whose explorations of the farther reaches occurred under less favorable circumstances, or who did not approach the voyage with adequate foreknowledge and guidance. I have often recalled how, on that Swiss mountaintop, Dr. Hofmann had voiced his fears about what could happen if the method of producing LSD were to become widely known and the drug became available to large numbers of people. But even Hofmann did not foresee the tremendous social change that would be ushered in by a part of a generation of young people in the transition between youth and adulthood, suddenly exposed to perceptual input that they were ill prepared to assimilate. Here was a substance that could evoke a vast range of reactions, all the way from boundless terror to blissful ecstasy. Boundlessness, the pervasive quality of the experience, countered everything these people had been taught in their process of acculturation. Many were drowned in the excess of stimulation. Many were able to flow with the immediacy of the experience and to let its wider implications slide off, so that the sensual pleasure or excitement was the main thing. They could open themselves up to the enjoyment of that. Nor had Hofmann spoken about the potential for releasing blocks to creative production, a by-product of the process of blasting through inhibiting preconceptions. The characteristic of the drug that made the impossible appear to be possible enabled some talented people to frame and present what had been locked away in the province of the unconscious heretofore. Others, less gifted, took senseless risks and lost.

William Blake's famous lines became the slogan of the movement: "If the doors of perception were cleansed every thing would appear to man as it is: infinite."[8] The question Blake, and Leary too, forgot to ask of those crowding at the gate to the unconscious was, "Are you ready for this?" For the new drug had the capacity to alter consciousness so as to dissolve the ordinary boundaries of awareness and transcend what most people imagined to be the limitations of human awareness. To "tune in" was as though someone were seated before a silent stereo receiver and suddenly discovered that it could be turned on and tuned in, and in place of silence received an endless variety and flow of music. After a lifetime of existence in chiaroscuro, you were suddenly flooded with a shower of brilliant, vibrating rainbow colors. Not that it was all beauty or harmony by any means, for much was horrible or grotesque; but the doors *were* breached, and every fool could look and see what lay behind them. Whether they could deal with the astounding revelations was quite another matter.

I do not mean to suggest that the tumultuous changes of the sixties all flowed from the proliferation of mind-expanding drugs. However, the use of these substances profoundly affected perception. People entered into altered states of consciousness, experiencing what Kabbalists have called "the breaking of the vessels," in which the contents of the upper (transcendent) worlds escape to the lower one, which is the world of material reality. One of my premises in this writing is that in every area of our lives we behave as we do because of the perceptions we hold. The perceiving organ looks both outward and inward: out upon the world which appears as "objective" and in to the soul, or psyche, which appears "subjective." Our analytical minds tell us that these are two worlds, and that there is a barrier of skin between them; but our analogical minds tell us that what is within is without, what is above is below, and that psyche, or the potentiality for consciousness, is embedded in every cell of our body's "objective reality," just as consciousness is embedded in the ordering process of nature (that some call God).

Awareness of the breakdown of the duality of consciousness/matter or, in the sense of physics, of energy/matter did not dawn upon the general populace all at once. Some do not see it yet. Even those who had participated in the psychedelic adventures of the sixties failed to grasp the full importance of what they had stumbled against, although they may have had some intuitions of the implications of their adventures. Like small children who, upon seeing "monsters in the night," allow themselves to be persuaded that the monsters do not really exist, so these voyagers of the mind tended to put away their visions and get on with the business of living. After a while the strange apparitions they had seen became subsumed into society's approved modes of showing what lies beyond the scope of human accomplishment: science fiction movies, great extravaganzas set in the future, television and film showings of supernatural horrors. And, when the show was over, you walked out of the movie or you switched off the tube, and the world became normal and comprehensible once more.

Nevertheless, the cleansing of the doors effected significant alterations of earlier patterns. A subtle shift in emphasis began to occur. Imagination played an important role. When once the categories of rational thought had been breached, openings for all sorts of new and radical ideas appeared. A few people seemed to understand that anything that can be imagined can be made into a reality, for the brain which conceives ideas is the same brain which constructs artifacts and societies. If it is true, as Blake said, "What is now proved was once, only imagin'd,"⁹ the reverse may also be true: what is now only imagined might once be proved.

What the psychedelic revolution proved, if it did nothing else, was that the unconscious was not an intellectual construct but a hidden kingdom that could be unlocked, and into which one could enter and roam at will if one had the courage and the keys. It had a vast impersonal quality that belonged at once to everyone and to no one. The discovery of the unconscious, not as a theoretical proposition declared by psychologists but as an immediate and intense experience that could be made readily available, forced people into new perspectives. Their own bodies, their relations in a bodily way to other people, changed drastically under these new potentialities.

Sexuality took on new dimensions also. Many people experienced for the first time in their lives the transpersonal aspects of sexuality. In the territory of the unconscious the personal takes on archetypal dimensions. A man becomes Man, and a woman becomes Woman, in the transcendent sense of those words. Each is not only himself or herself, but a carrier of Mankind or Womankind; each is a tiny manifestation of one half of humanity that is meant to unite with the other half, and to participate in the eternal pleasures of joining and separating and coming together and moving apart. All of this may be seen as submission to a larger plan of Nature or of God or of the way the universe works, a plan in which individuals have only limited freedom while they go about fulfilling their destiny. That destiny is perceived as carrying energy and transforming that energy within one's own body into living matter that continues and will continue beyond lifetimes. Each person experiences what it is to be an inseparable part of an evolving universe, and each reacts to it in an individual way. Yet there is a commonality to all of it which comes from being washed over by the collective unconscious, the ocean of unknowing that begins to manifest when inhibitions are dissolved.

The advent of television and its invasion into the living space of almost every American altered profoundly the psychological attitudes abroad in the nation. While psychedelics had opened the door to the inner being, and allowed for voyages into the collective unconscious, now television opened many new doors outward to the nations of the world, to all levels of society—in short, to the collective consciousness. Television was not only an escape into fantasy. It was, as well, a source of information about how people live outside of the community of one's own exposure. People who had been satisfied with relatively little in terms of material comfort, now discovered that other people lived very differently from themselves, and better. Of course, they had read about the "privileged classes" in their books, if they were inclined to read books, but television was different. You entered the magic tube just as Alice had slipped down the rabbit hole, and you found yourself in Wonderland, where everything was different from the way you had always known it. You participated in the living, breathing scene; your adrenaline poured forth when danger threatened, and your sexual desire glowed brightly when your fantasy-partner appeared before your eyes. You saw how people acted to change their lives: the ways were exciting, challenging, amusing, risky, persistent, loving, avenging, all down the range of possibilities. You had models for anything you might conjure up in your fantasy. All this gave you courage and motivated you to try out new ways of being and doing.

The American Dream began to take on new dimensions. No longer was the hard-working and clever individualist the ideal. People began to recognize that in order to combat the established power structures they would have to form their own coalitions and struggle together for change. Intellectualism, the business of *talking about* issues, would have to give way to social action, *doing something* to effect change. Supporters of the Civil Rights movement joined southern blacks and northern liberals in demonstrations that would place living bodies in the way of restrictive practices and they would loudly protest what they regarded as prejudicial laws. Marches on Washington, refusals by blacks to sit in the back of the bus or to accept other real or symbolic indignities, cooperation between racial groups to enforce desegregation— all of these acted not only to catalyze the issues around Civil Rights, but also to bring into closer contact people who might otherwise never have met each other. Given the spirit of energetic cooperation and intense personal interaction that was evident at the time, it is not surprising that some of the energy flowed into sexual relationships of a kind that might have been unthinkable in the past. One way of defying the code of the establishment involved the breaking down of racial barriers to sexual relations. How much can be attributed to politics, and how much to the reality that people were now working closely and living closely with others who had been regarded as forbidden fruit, is impossible to measure, but the fervor and excitement in the movement mingled with the fervor and excitement of new sexual relationships that crossed racial boundaries. Again, that these explorations across boundaries usually took place far from home and outside of people's daily life patterns permitted a sense of freedom and a loosening of ties to the conventional mores.

The power structure was challenged in the universities also, in any of several ways: by dropping out and forming multiple alternative societies based on the new naïveté of the flower children, by joining the drug subculture, by submitting to the attraction of various gurus and cult leaders, by engaging in action such as student strikes and other planned obstructions of the traditional educational process, or by seriously exploring the psychological/spiritual tools of change with the help of a few gifted leaders who were using experiential methods. These tools would come from a revival of ancient spiritual traditions and esoteric practices—for example, there would arise a new interest in astrology, alchemy, various yogic practices, meditation, sacred dance, evocations of altered states of consciousness. In the next chapter we will see how four great leaders appeared on the scene and gave impetus to the "consciousness movement." There were also numerous important spiritual teachers who were less known, and each had his or her own followers. Each of these factions was learning in its own way to reorient its value system by moving from the abstract toward the concrete, from the theoretical toward the experiential, from the impersonal and intellectual toward the personal and passionate. The new approaches sought, even demanded, human connections in depth. Depth is the right word, for these young people and their mentors were leaving the ivory towers of academia to delve into the dark mysteries of earth and human emotion and all things forbidden by those who had written the rules. What they needed most on their journey, their *nekyia,* or their symbolic descent into Hades, was tender companionship, a hand to hold, a body to cling to in time of danger, an embrace, someone with whom to merge, dissolve and, if fate were kind, to emerge anew. When the old inhibitions around sexuality no longer made sense, sexual freedom emerged out of need. People were eager to experience each other in new ways—even if they had first to wrench themselves free of the rigid standards and patterns that bound them to the past.

5

Four Men in Search
of Enlightenment

In those times of confusion shortly after midcentury, when one-sided rationalism left many people feeling cold and empty, it was inevitable that leaders should arise who would express points of view that were heard almost not at all in the dominant culture. These were people who saw the need for a new and vigorous interpretation of the psyche that would include its nonrational aspects. Regarding the ways in which the productions of the psyche were being weighed and measured and counted and rationed, they knew that what mattered most to human beings was exactly what was most lacking: a sense of the meaningfulness of life and of the value of human existence, with all its suffering and its striving.

The generation of those who had been born in the years immediately following the Second World War was ready to hear new voices from the generation of its parents, with messages that were meant for themselves and not for their elders. Coming into manhood and womanhood at the time of the Vietnam War, they felt the war had been thrust upon them by people too old to fight; consequently they questioned the values that they had been taught as children, and which had brought the nation to a crisis of conscience. Universities were continuing to train the extraverted thinking function of students, who were encouraged to become competitive, ambitious, and thorough in finding logical solutions to practical problems. But the curricula left hardly any place for the cultivation of those inner qualities of individuals that are nourished by feeling and intuition and all the gentler sensibilities.

A different sort of teacher was clearly needed, one who could serve as a guide for the sorely neglected soul.

There were those of the parental generation who had been struggling with the fundamental issues underlying the disruption of the relationship between the sacred and the secular. A few became spokesmen for the rejected side of human functioning. Mostly, these were men, for the women's movement had not yet found its voice and most of the concerned women were still quietly preparing themselves for later emergence into active roles in the struggle for a new world view and its implementation. Some of the most important contributions to this effort were made at the end of the fifties and the beginning of the sixties by four seminal figures. I could have included others equally representative, but I will focus on the work of C. G. Jung, Abraham Maslow, Alan Watts, and Huston Smith, because I have seen that each in his own way had broken through the boundaries of the Western intellectual tradition. These four had in common an interest in the Far East, and particularly in the philosophy of Taoism, which in a subtle way was beginning to filter into the counter-culture movement. These four had sufficient vision to be able to look beyond the value structure of the mainstream that was obviously not working for many of the best young minds of the country. Each of the four had a strong background in one of the traditional religions of the West. Jung was the son of a Protestant minister, and a scholar in the field of comparative religions; Maslow was reared in the Jewish faith and was well versed in the teachings of Judaism; Alan Watts was ordained to the priesthood of the Episcopal Church; and Huston Smith was the son of Christian missionaries to China. All four must have confronted the disparity between their inner images of a life where the human spirit finds support, and the disenchantment they saw around them. All four had the courage to mount their battles against the established orders in their own fields, and to set their own paths so that they might rediscover the treasures of the human soul. Jung left the psychoanalytic tradition at the very time it was becoming the "new wave" in psychology; Maslow took his leave from behaviorism when it dominated every major psychology department in the United States; Watts left the Episcopal Church to become a popularizer of Zen Buddhism and Taoism; and Smith brought the wisdom of the Far East to the halls of the Massachusetts Institute of Technology.

In the first half of the twentieth century, Jung had been almost alone among psychologists and psychiatrists to bring to the foreground of attention the numinous dimensions of psychic life. Only a relatively few people appreciated him during his lifetime. I had arrived to study at the C. G. Jung Institute in Zürich during his last days. The only time I saw him was in 1961 on the day before his funeral. He was laid out on his deathbed in a darkened room between the flickering light of two candles, wearing a white nightshirt, his face waxen pale against a white pillow. As I looked in silence upon that frail hull of a man, I felt that his radiance would emanate in ever-widening circles outward, far beyond the house by the Zürichsee in Küsnacht.

Jung's works did not begin to reach the English-speaking public in any sizable quantity until they began to be translated in the early sixties, and then they were mostly misunderstood. He was often called "vague," "obscure," or "mystical." A few years after his death, the children of a generation that had learned philosophy from Maslow and Watts, and had studied comparative religion with Huston Smith and Joseph Campbell and Mircea Eliade, were better able to receive and appreciate Jung's view of the sacred as an integral part of the individuation process, which is the process of growth toward wholeness.

Jung's approach contrasted sharply with the views of the prevailing Freudian psychology, especially with regard to its attitudes toward sexuality and the sacred. Freud had seen the human attachment to the Divine as a sublimation of the sexual impulse. This was, for him, a displacement that tended to manifest in psychopathology. Jung saw the human organism as a microcosm, participating in the Divine macrocosm and embodying its ordering principle in matter. To say that Jung stood in awe of the human impulse to religion, which Freud distrusted, would be an oversimplification. Freud's very denial had loosely cloaked his terror of the numinous, which he had once dismissed, according to Jung's report, as "the black tide of mud—of occultism."[1] Of deepest concern to Jung were the transpersonal realm of myth and mystery which, in his view, nourished and gave substance to the ego, and the ways in which the ego and the transpersonal realm related to each other. For Jung, the collective (or transpersonal) unconscious encompassed all the mysteries not yet known, the truth not yet manifest, the potentialities in nature and human consciousness not yet realized.

The drives and impulses of the Freudian id represented only a small part of the unconscious for Jung. The material that disappears from consciousness through repression, or forgetting, or which simply remains outside the scope of attention, belongs to the personal unconscious, which Jung saw as a thin film on the surface of the collective unconscious. Personal life stretched from birth, perhaps even from conception, to death; but the numinosum, the essence of the collective unconscious, was self-generating, self-sustaining, and ever-changing. To get some feeling for this, you would need to imagine that you could see into infinite distance over an eternity of time. You would see the stars appear and grow brighter, then fade away and disappear, while others emerged out of the deepest darkness. That is the ever-present mystery, the ever-present background, against which all *things* are in the process of changing.

Jung agreed that Freud was surely right to stress the sexual function of libido as that human energy which propels individuals outward into the world to form relationships, marry, and create new families. Jung saw that pathology could result, as Freud had indicated, from the damming up or the misdirection of the flow of this energy, or from defenses erected to prevent its release in healthy sexual expression. Jung never denied the importance of sexuality as a major force in human nature and human behavior. This assertion was, in fact, what originally drew him to Freud's early circle. Where he parted from Freud, apart from personal issues between the two men, was on the nature of this psychic energy, which Freud had called *libido*. Jung freed the concept of libido from its exclusive identification with sexuality. He saw libidinous energy as extending beyond the function of carrier of the life force from generation to generation through the medium of sexual reproduction. This psychic energy was, in Jung's view, the power that activated all aspects of human creativity, whether what was created was art, human relationships, or a personal relationship with the Divine. So psychic energy serves us as we extend ourselves outward in love to another human being; and it also serves as we expend this energy within ourselves as we enter into communion with our creative energies, those parts of ourselves which embody and give expression to the archetype of the Self. Inasmuch as we humans are an integral part of the universe, we come to know the universality of the Self in our own particularity as an inner experience, perceived by means of the psyche. So for Jung, the concept of sexuality has both an inner and an outer meaning. This is not to suggest a dualism; the two are sides of one coin.

That Jung understood sexuality as being a universal manifestation of Divine intent is suggested in his essay, "The Spiritual Problem of Modern Man": "Our studies of sexual life, originating in Vienna and England, are matched or surpassed by Hindu teachings on this subject. Oriental texts ten centuries old introduce us to philosophical relativism, while the idea of indeterminacy, newly broached in the West, is the very basis of Chinese science . . ."[2] "It seems to be quite true that the East is at the bottom of the spiritual change we are passing through today. Only, this East is not a Tibetan monastery full of Mahatmas, but lies essentially within us."[3] Jung was also aware that the demands of sexuality upon the individual that make themselves evident in late adolescence and early adulthood are as much universal and transpersonal as they are personal. "The extraordinary intensification of the sexual need that is so often felt at this time has the biological aim of forcibly eliminating the man's scruples, misgivings, doubts, and hesitations. This is very necessary, because the very idea of marriage, with all its doubtful possibilities, often makes a man panicky."[4]

Jung claimed to pass no sort of moral judgment on sexuality as a natural phenomenon, but preferred to make its moral evaluation dependent on the way it was expressed. He wrote: "Love is not cheap—let us therefore beware of cheapening it! All our bad qualities, our egotism, our cowardice, our worldly wisdom, our cupidity —all these would persuade us not to take love seriously. But love will reward us only when we do. I must even regard it as a misfortune that nowadays the sexual question is spoken of as something distinct from love. The two questions should not be separated, for where there is a sexual problem it can be solved only by love. Any other solution would be a harmful substitute. Sexuality dished out as sexuality is brutish; but sexuality as an expression of love is hallowed. Therefore, never ask what a man does, but how he does it. If he does it from love or in the spirit of love, then he serves a god; and whatever he may do is not ours to judge, for it is ennobled."[5]

Fundamental to Jung's conviction that sexuality is spiritual and transpersonal as well as biological and personal was the crystallization of his concept of the soul as contrasexual. He understood the soul, in part, as the compensatory factor in the unconscious—which balances the self-image that comes about in the process of gender identification. Jung observed that in most male children a conscious attitude of masculinity is cultivated, so that a boy grows up with the so-called "masculine" values which characterize the male role in a given society; while in most female children a conscious attitude is encouraged that will correspond with the culture's "feminine" values. Jung felt the "soul" too general a term for something he had found to be quite specific as he worked with the dreams and other unconscious material of his patients. The image of the feminine which men carried in themselves but often failed to recognize as aspects of their own hidden nature, Jung preferred to refer to as the "anima." The corresponding masculine image that existed as part of woman's unconscious, he called the "animus." Since both anima and animus belong to the category of archetypes, they cannot be observed directly. The contents of these archetypes produce distorted but highly visible images that women and men tend to project upon persons of the opposite sex. All too often the fantasy-images veil the humanity of the other person.

In the usual love relationship, Jung says, there are always four present: man and woman, anima and animus. A man relates to a woman on a conscious level while at the same time his own anima projections endow the image-of-woman he sees with attributes few others would recognize. The more one-sidedly masculine his image of himself is, the more his soul desires the unalloyed feminine in the other person. This meshes with the unconscious need of the dependent and submissive female for the man who embodies all the initiative and assertiveness that she does not find in herself.

Jung knew how difficult it is to distinguish between the image we hold of a person whom we want to love and the actual person. For one thing, the partner may collude with the tendency to project the shining image. Who wants to admit to being less than the partner imagines one is? And even if this is admitted and accepted, it is not so easy to construct a real relationship out of the shards of broken dreams. Finally, it is a matter of these projections being withdrawn and new ones springing up in the most improbable places, and blinding us again with their brightness. We seek new loves even while we are struggling with the newly seen realities in the relationships to which we have already committed ourselves. Often we shield ourselves with gentle lies, pretending that we are protecting the other. The lies suffocate our sexuality because they make us muscle-bound, tense and defensive. We need first of all to be honest with ourselves, and then with those nearest to us—otherwise we are merely living out our projections in our sexual relationships. And yet, no matter how hard we try to see around it, some part of the projective relationship is always present. For in some measure the depths of the soul are always unknown to us, and we only become aware that we are touched in those depths when another person recognizes in us that mysterious level of commonality. Then we are able to sense the Self in that other person, which may be a reflection of the Self within ourselves. A feeling of resonance comes about and we say, "This is right." We find ourselves in harmony with the other. Sexual love, Jung believed, is only one way through which that harmony may be expressed.

Jung refused to make sexuality the alpha and omega of his psychological concern. This was a major factor in his alienation from the Freudian doctrine. For Jung, psychic energy was the essential element, which might or might not be expressed through sexuality. He saw the process of individuation involving the movement of this psychic energy through successive phases in which opposing elements would be clarified and separated out, and then reunited in ways that were more refined, more conscious. In this process of individuation, psychic energy would gradually be transformed so that the potency of the individual would be released from the grip of unconscious conflicts. Empowering the individual to become what he or she is able to be is the goal of individuation. It involves all the channels into which psychic energy flows, including sexuality, personal growth, creativity, and the seeking after ultimate values. Sexuality itself was viewed by Jung as encompassing far more than matters of personal relationships. "The fundamental problem," he wrote, "is not sexuality *per se*, but the domestication of libido, which concerns sexuality only so far as it is one of the most important and most dangerous forms of libidinal expression."[6]

Jung saw in Taoism both the description of the fundamental problem and the possibility of its eventual resolution. The Chinese division of Tao into yin/yang reminded Jung of the familiar passage from Goethe's *Faust*:

> Two souls, alas, are housed within my breast,
> And each will wrestle for the mastery there.
> The one has passion's craving crude for love,
> And hugs a world where sweet the senses rage;
> The other longs for pastures fair above,
> Leaving the murk for lofty heritage.[7]

Here were two mutually contending impulses, both striving to drag people into extreme tendencies, whether on the spiritual or on the material side. What was needed was the harmony that is expressed by the "irrational third, *tao*." He recognized that Tao is not something that can be achieved deliberately, and a rational desire to bring it about does not lead to Tao. "The aim of Taoist ethics, then, is to find deliverance from the cosmic tension of the opposites by a return to *tao*."[8] "If . . . only the sexual problem is discerned, we get entangled in an insoluble contradiction, since the thing that harms is also the thing that heals. Such a paradox is true and permissible only when one sees the opposites as united on a higher plane, when one understands that it is not a question of sexuality, either in this form or in that, but purely a question of the attitude by which every activity, including the sexual, is regulated . . . What lies behind sexuality . . . is the *attitude* to sexuality . . . In so far as an attitude is not merely an intuitive (i.e., unconscious and spontaneous) phenomenon but also a conscious function, it is, in the main, a *view of life*."[9]

In an interview at Brandeis University, Abraham Maslow discussed his transformation. He related that in his doctoral studies many years ago he had discovered J. B. Watson and was sold on behaviorism. The birth of his first baby changed his perceptions as a psychologist. "It made the behaviorism I had been so enthusiastic about look so foolish I couldn't stomach it any more. It was impossible. I looked at this tiny, mysterious thing, and felt so stupid. I was stunned by the mystery and the sense of not really being in control . . . I'd say that anyone who had a baby couldn't be a behaviorist."[10] Abraham Maslow laid the basis for what came to be called Humanistic Psychology, a "third force" in psychology —a third, viable alternative to behavioral psychology and psychoanalysis. While his work did not totally reject the insights of the first two "forces," he was able to extract what was useful in them and place that within a large framework. His was an essentially optimistic view of humankind. Instead of attempting to study mental illness by working with abnormal cases such as the insane, the criminal, or the delinquent, he sought the basis of mental illness by examining the factors that characterize mental health. His interest led him to focus not so much on what made people "ill," but rather on what contributed to health.[11]

In Maslow's view, Freud had seen human personality as essentially mean, selfish, and aggressive, as he had pictured other animals. This followed naturally from the psychoanalytic doctrine that conscience, rationality, and ethics are no more than a veneer, completely different in character from what lies beneath. Maslow noted that behaviorists also studied animals which do not share our uniquely human characteristics, "martyrdom, self-sacrifice, shame, love, humor, art, beauty, conscience, guilt, patriotism, ideals, production of poetry or philosophy or music or science."[12] He engaged his students with questions like these: Why not study where humans are *different* from other animals, not only where they are similar? Why study humans as objects, in the same way that we observe rats? Why disregard the subjective information of human beings, like people's opinions about themselves, their feelings, desires, wants? Should we allow ourselves to become so preoccupied with unconscious functions, as Freud did, that we fail to take people's subjective feelings seriously enough?

Maslow observed that Freud had concentrated on intrinsic factors, processes within the psyche of the individual. Behaviorism concentrated on extrinsic factors, the effects of the environment upon the individual, and the person's ability to affect the environment. Maslow determined to combine these two positions, asserting that the objective study of human behavior was not sufficient in itself, but needed to be coupled with subjective feelings, hopes, and aspirations if human behavior were to be understood.

Clearly, all this could not be studied piecemeal, because the human brain and its functions were far too complicated. Maslow's approach had to be broader, more comprehensive and, finally, interdisciplinary. He criticized those behavioral scientists who used an atomistic approach, breaking things down into component parts and studying the components separately, saying that an individual must be studied as an entity, as a system. Each part is related to every other part, and unless you study them all as a whole, the answers are incomplete. The search for the whole led Maslow to study people who in their development had come to a high level of integration, sometimes called "wholeness." These people stood as symbols for the new human potential movement, in that they had actualized in their own lives a large measure of their potential as human beings.

As a result of his studies of "self-actualizing persons," Maslow was able to identify some of the characteristics associated with these healthy, vital individuals. In doing so, he provided new models for psychological development. Inherent in his models were hints as to the direction in which human sexuality could evolve. Self-actualization means "experiencing fully, vividly, selflessly, with full concentration and total absorption . . . The key word for this is 'selflessly,' and our youngsters suffer from too little selflessness and too much self-consciousness, self-awareness."[13] How important a concept this is for the education of our children as sexual beings! Maslow had recognized an equally pressing need in early childhood education to come to terms with the desacralization of human relationships. Young people, growing up in a permissive, affluent, pragmatic environment, were using desacralizing as a defense mechanism. This is, of course, one defense mechanism that psychoanalysts fail to mention. Maslow said that parents who are themselves confused about values, and who quite frequently are terrified of their children and never punish them for doing wrong, end up with children who mistrust anything that smacks of values and virtues. Such children may despise their elders, and often for that reason, and they then learn to make a big generalization: they won't listen to anyone over thirty, especially if the grown-up uses words resembling those of the hypocritical parents.

In their own homes they have seen that sexuality is commonplace, and that it is often used to manipulate the partner. Or they may learn from observing their parents that sex is not important; it is a natural thing, it happens, but it doesn't make a great deal of difference in the quality of human relationship. In Maslow's words, "they have made it so natural that it has lost its poetic qualities in many instances, which means that it has lost practically everything. Self-actualization means giving up this defense mechanism and learning or being taught to resacralize."[14]

In his essay "Various Meanings of Transcendence," Maslow's commitment to the principles of Taoism is clear. Less obvious are the implications for sexuality, but they can be discerned. He writes of the transcendence of ego that can occur ". . . when we respond to the demand-character of external tasks, causes, responsibilities to others and to the world of reality. When one is doing one's duty, this also can be seen to be under the aspect of eternity and can represent a transcendence of the ego . . . It is ultimately a form of meta motivation, and identification with what 'calls for' doing. This is a sensitivity to extrapsychic requiredness. This in turn means a kind of Taoistic attitude. The phrase 'being in harmony with nature' implies this ability to yield, to be receptive to, or respond to, to live with extrapsychic reality as if one belonged with it, or were in harmony with it."[15]

I am reminded of Maslow's Taoistic attitude toward sexuality at times when I work as a psychotherapist with newly married couples who are having difficulties establishing sexual relations that are harmonious and mutually satisfying while they are also trying to maintain their individual and personal autonomy. I have observed that couples who lived together and enjoyed sexual relations before they were married sometimes find that as soon as they are married the pleasure is diminished, and anything from irritation to indifference to rage enters in to destroy the very sexual acts that not too long ago brought them so much joy. Upon exploration it so often boils down to this: "Before we were married, I knew I could walk out any time, and so I was with my partner because it was where I most wanted to be. Also, s/he treated me with respect and consideration, showing that s/he valued the relationship. We didn't make demands upon another, but enjoyed what we had together; and in the meantime each of us went about his/her own business. Now that we are a 'corporation,' s/he is telling me how to spend my money, my time, where to go and what to do, and I can never please him/her. It seems as if each of us wants to be in charge and nobody can just let things be the way they are. We had looked forward to getting married, but now we want things to be better than they are."

Maslow suggested that what is needed here is "the transcendence of effort and of striving, of wishing and hoping, of any vectorial or intentional characteristics. In the simplest sense this is, of course, the sheer enjoyment of the state of gratification, of hope fulfilled and attained, of being there rather than of striving to get there, of having arrived rather than traveling toward . . . It is the Taoistic feeling of letting things happen rather than of making them happen, and of being perfectly happy and accepting of this state of nonstriving, nonwishing, noninterfering, noncontrolling, nonwilling. This is the transcendence of ambition, of efficiencies. This is the state of having rather than of not having. Then of course one lacks nothing. This means it is possible to go over to the state of happiness, of contentment, of being satisfied with what is."[16] Few newly married young people are prepared for this, but it may be an ideal to be stated, as one seeds the unconscious, hoping that something will take root and flower in its own time. It is only fair to remind the reader that Maslow wrote this near the end of his life.

To Alan Watts, known variously as philosopher, educator, lecturer, author, dancer, calligrapher, scholar, and devil-incarnate, at the end of one of his particularly brilliant seminars, a woman participant directed the question: "Dr. Watts, just how do you identify yourself?" "No doubt about it, I'm an entertainer, of course," he replied. I have felt that "celebrant," in two senses of the word, would have described him more accurately. As I saw him, first, he made of life a sacrament and, second, he took excessive joy in it. If you were to ask him whether excessive joy were possible, he would respond that everything he did was excessive, involving his whole being. He did not know the meaning of moderation. It would seem that he lived by Blake's precept "The road of excess leads to the palace of wisdom."[17] He managed to sustain the paradox of holding no thing sacred in a world which he saw in its totality as a manifestation of the sacred.

Impatient with traditional schooling, Watts managed to achieve a magnificent education through his self-directed reading and his association with an international crowd of intellectual luminaries which he termed "my own university." A relatively short period of formal study at a theological seminary led to his ordination as an Episcopal priest, a profession for which, by his own admission, he was quite unsuited due to his penchant for thinking outrageous thoughts and expressing them whenever the spirit moved him. He served as chaplain to delighted students at Northwestern University, Evanston, Illinois, until he could no longer escape the fact that the limitations of the institutional role were incompatible with his understanding of the meaning of spiritual freedom and his commitment to principles which resembled Buddhism more closely than Christianity.

He soon found himself more at home on the West Coast, and accepted the position of Dean of the American College of Asian Studies, in San Francisco. He read, meditated, conversed with many outrageous people, and became one of the leading forces in the making of the counter-culture. He traveled to the Far East and involved himself in the practice of Zen. Finally he settled on Mount Tamalpais, in a round house made out of a huge redwood wine-barrel. Its single window overlooked Mill Valley and San Francisco Bay. There he walked the hillsides and wrote prolifically, and from there he went out to give seminars all over the United States and Europe. He became a leading popularizer of Zen, Taoism, and his particularly personal philosophy.

A daring experimenter, Watts joined those intellectuals who for a time used psychedelic drugs to open pathways of knowledge that were not accessible through ordinary modes of consciousness. While his book *The Joyous Cosmology* probably led innumerable young people to rush into waters far beyond their depths, he was one of the first to recognize that any productive insights that might have come about after the use of mind-expanding substances needed to be quietly integrated, and that it was not necessary continually to repeat the experiments. He was fond of saying, "When you get the message, hang up the phone."

Alan Watts distilled his own experiences in the process of lecturing and teaching. I remember the first seminar of his that I attended. He began by taking a large white sheet of paper and, with a brush full of black ink, drew a large circle on it. Holding it up he asked, "What is this?" Most people gave the obvious reply. "No, it isn't," said Watts, "it's a hole in a wall"; and thus he would begin to upset the obvious mode of perceiving and set the stage for more subtle observations. His brilliant wit and affirming manner had the capacity to release people from their preconceptions and teach their minds to fly. He had little patience with those who held on to ideas or institutions just because they had invested themselves in them, and he took every opportunity to point out what traditional ways had become nonsensical.

One such occasion occurred in 1959, when Watts was asked to speak before a meeting of the American Psychiatric Association in Los Angeles. Learned papers had dragged long past the allotted time, and his turn came when it was already late for lunch. He abandoned his text and spoke spontaneously as follows (the address is reproduced here in its entirety):

"Gentlemen, this is not going to be a scientific paper because I am a simple philosopher, not a psychiatrist, and you are hungry for lunch. We philosophers are very grateful to you for showing us the unconscious emotional bases of some of our ideas, but the time is coming for us to show you the unconscious intellectual assumptions behind some of yours. Psychiatric literature is full of unexamined metaphysics. Even Jung, who is so readily repudiated for his 'mysticism,' bends over backward to avoid metaphysical considerations on the pretext that he is strictly a physician and a scientist. This is impossible. Every human being is a metaphysician just as every philosopher has appetites and emotions—and by this I mean that we all have certain basic assumptions about the good life and the nature of reality. Even the typical businessman who asserts that he is a practical fellow unconcerned with higher things declares thereby that he is a pragmatist or a positivist, and not a very thoughtful one at that.

"I wonder, then, how much consideration you give to the fact that most of your own assumptions about the good life and reality come directly from the scientific naturalism of the nineteenth century, from the strictly metaphysical hypothesis that the universe is a mechanism obeying Newtonian laws, and that there is no other god beside it. Psychoanalysis, which is actually psychohydraulics following Newton's mechanics, begins from the mystical assertion that the psychosexual energy of the unconscious is a blind and stupid outrush of pure lust, following Haeckel's notion that the universe at large is a manifestation of primordially oafish and undiscriminating energy. It should be obvious to you that this is an opinion for which there has never been the least evidence, and which, furthermore, ignores the evidence that we ourselves, supposedly making intelligent remarks, are manifestations of that same energy.

"On the basis of this unexamined, derogatory, and shaky opinion as to the nature of biological and physical energy, some of your psychoanalytic members have this morning dubbed all the so-called mystical states of consciousness as 'regressive,' as leading one back to a dissolution of the individual intelligence in an acid bath of amniotic fluid, reducing it to featureless identity with this —your First Cause—mess of blindly libidinous energy. Now, until you have found some substantial evidence for your metaphysics you will have to admit that you have no way of knowing which end of your universe is up, so that in the meantime you should abstain from easy conclusions as to which directions are progressive and which regressive. (*Laughter*)"[18]

In his book *Nature, Man and Woman*, Watts offered an approach to sexual experience based on a Taoistic conception of the universe entirely different from the Newtonian one. He analyzed the conflict inherent in the Western Judeo-Christian view of sexuality as it is bound up with the ego. He saw the ego, as the seat of the conscious will, charged with responsibility to restrain and control the impulses that arise spontaneously within the human organism. To gain this "control" the ego aligns itself with spirit, in opposition to nature and to sexuality. Attention to sexuality in our culture is the task of an ego that views itself as separate from other people and needs to find a way of relating to them while maintaining its own individuality. Since sexuality is one of the most powerful manifestations of biological spontaneity, it is especially difficult for the will to control. The willed control, says Watts, brings about a sense of duality within the organism, of consciousness in conflict with appetite. The more consciousness is increased by the sense of the individual will, the more threatening everything outside the individual becomes. With every success in control, the pressures coming from the biological necessities of nature gain in strength. Consequently, dualism arises between ego and spirit on the one hand, and nature and body on the other. Sexuality is set apart as a specially good or specially evil compartment of life, unrelated to other aspects of life, an abstract force divorced from the universal and concrete reality of nature.

Alan Watts insisted that "sexual problems" could not be resolved simply at the sexual level. We have set sexuality in a context of fruitlessly alternating dualism, now it is good, now bad, now lustful, now prudish. As long as sexuality continues to be the isolated area in which people are able to transcend themselves and experience spontaneity, sexuality will continue to be a problem. Sexuality must be one expression of a general permission that people give themselves to be spontaneous in their entire experience of inner feeling and in their sensory responses to the everyday world. This means being openly accepting of and sensitive toward the other, without grasping—and being aware of the other, without straining.

What was necessary, then, as Watts saw it, was to free sexuality from its subordinate role in the nature of things and to recognize it as essential to the total organizing pattern of person-environment. This cannot be done by setting sexuality about with rules and restrictions, for then there is no place for natural spontaneity. Such rules and restrictions are, in any case, limiting. "In the life of spontaneity human consciousness shifts from the attitude of strained, willful attention to *kuan*, the attitude of open attention or contemplation."[19] With this sort of attention, a Taoistic view of sexuality as experienced in love replaces the atomistic view. Watts described this view: "Love brings the real, and not just the ideal, vision of what others are because it is a glimpse of what we are bodily. For what is ordinarily called the body is an abstraction. It is the conventional fiction of an object seen apart from its relation to the universe, without which it has no reality whatsoever. But the mysterious and unsought uprising of love is the experience of complete relationship with another, transforming our vision not only of the beloved but of the whole world. And so it remains until the relationship is itself abstracted by the anxiety of the grasping mind to be guarded from the rest of life as a possession."[20]

Watts criticized the excessive interest shown by men and women in sexual techniques for the enhancement of sexual pleasure. He wrote of the possibility of something quite different, contemplative love which, like contemplative meditation, is only quite secondarily a matter of technique. "For it has no specific aim; there is nothing particular that has to be made to happen. It is simply that a man and a woman are together exploring their spontaneous feeling—without any preconceived idea of what it ought to be, since the sphere of contemplation is not what should be, but what *is*."[21]

His most powerful directive to young people who were seeking a new context in which to experience their sexuality was centered on the importance of returning the sacred dimension to sexuality: "For pleasure is a grace and is not obedient to the commands of the will. In other words, it is brought about by the relationship between man and his world. Like mystical insight itself, it must always come unsought, which is to say that relationship can be experienced fully only by mind and senses which are open and not attempting to be clutching muscles. There is obviously nothing degrading in sensuous pleasure which comes 'of itself,' without craving. But in fact there is no other kind of pleasure, and the error of the sensualist is not so much that he is doing something evil as that he is attempting the impossible . . . pleasure cannot be given unless the senses are in a state of accepting rather than taking, and for this reason they must not be, as it were, paralyzed and rigidified by the anxiety to get something out of the object.

"All this is peculiarly true of love and of the sexual communion between man and woman. This is why it has such a strongly spiritual and mystical character when spontaneous, and why it is so degrading and frustrating when forced. It is for this reason that sexual love is so problematic in cultures where the human being is strongly identified with the abstract separate entity. The experience neither lives up to expectations nor fulfills the relationship between man and woman. At the same time it is, fragmentarily, gratifying enough to be pursued ever more relentlessly for the release which it seems to promise. Sex is therefore the virtual religion of many people, the end to which they accord more devotion than any other. To the conventionally religious mind this worship of sex is a dangerous and positively sinful substitution for the worship of God. But this is because sex, or any other pleasure, as ordinarily pursued is never a true fulfillment. For this very reason it is *not* God, but not at all because it is 'merely physical.' The rift between God and nature would vanish if we knew how to experience nature, because what keeps them apart is not a difference of substance but a split in the mind."[22]

Alan Watts applied to the solution of the sexual dilemma a Taoist principle which supports, first of all, a world view in which the interrelationship of all physical processes, including sex, is seen as a dynamic principle underlying everything that we do. Watts explained the principles which led him to give permission for a natural, spontaneous expression of sexuality, but many of those who listened to him heard only the permission and did not understand enough about the principle of interrelationship. They failed to see that this principle requires a consciousness of the surrounding scene and all who exist within it—which is affected by whatever we do, and that we have an obligation not to exploit it or the persons in it in the service of our own freedom. Many people mistook his statements as suggesting an easy, almost casual relationship to sexuality. But Watts, while outspoken against anything the least bit coercive in the realm of sex, believed firmly that the expression of sexuality could be a form of art, to be cultivated with care and sensitivity, then offered up as a gift without any expectations or demands from the other. He put forth an ideal which few were capable of realizing in its totality, and which belonged to a view of the world that had not yet come into focus. Yet he lived his own sexual life according to his beliefs, and he became a master teacher to a privileged few in that most exquisite of all the arts, the art of love.

Perhaps the perspective of Alan Watts will be better understood in the future, when the consciousness of the East and the consciousness of the West have interpenetrated each other more deeply. In the last years of his life he made provision for that to happen. Quietly and unobtrusively, he approached some of his wealthy friends and admirers for funds to bring to the United States Tibetan holy men who had fled their icy vastnesses before the invading Chinese communists. This is the last great, scarcely known culture of the world, he told his friends, and it will not survive in its pure form on the continent of Asia. We must bring its representatives here and provide places for them to live according to their ways, and to teach those who wish to learn from them. Watts often said that his own knowledge of Eastern wisdom was relatively superficial, but he knew where the ancient and genuine tradition was to be found. At the time of his death his greatest wish and effort was being directed toward keeping it alive and sustaining it. Today in the United States several institutes devoted to the study of Tibetan Buddhism testify to that vision.

These three men, Jung, Maslow, and Watts, were all born and reared in the Western tradition. Only later in their lives did they discover the limitations of a monotheistic system in which one God set himself above "all other gods" and commanded his people to abjure all the others. All three eventually turned toward the East, and especially toward Taoism, for a view of the universe which was all-inclusive, with neither god nor human nor the smallest creature excluded from the natural rhythms of a pervasive order. Each of these men recognized that we do live in the world of the personal, first and foremost, and our senses guide us through that familiar world. They came to recognize that the personal was not independent, but rather embedded in the transpersonal, the ineffable presence which is in all and also transcends all.

The fourth man, although an American, had his roots in China, where he was born and spent his early years. For him, the spiritual practice of the East meant living daily in harmony with natural forces and energies, and not separating oneself from the rest of the universe to which one belonged. A scholar in the field of comparative religion, Huston Smith had written *The Religions of Man* in 1958 after his return to the United States. This book presented each of the world's major religious traditions in their individuality and variety. Smith became Professor of Philosophy at Massachusetts Institute of Technology at the very time when quite a few students in the hard sciences were beginning to suspect that something important was being left out of their highly technical education. He heard and responded to the requests of students for a different kind of course, one in which some of the ideas and practices that had begun to filter in from Eastern Asia might be explored. His students had looked to him because he was so firmly grounded in the religions of both the East and the West, and because he had treated the Asian religions with the same respect and seriousness as the Judeo-Christian traditions—an approach which was not frequently pursued at that time.

Huston Smith, raised a Christian in a non-Christian country, recognized that if there were indeed something one could call *Ultimate Truth*, no one religion possessed it entire. Each religion represented an attempt by human beings within a particular cultural setting to approach this Truth in its own way, following after its own images. As much as Smith is aware of the existence of what has been called *Great Knowledge*, unlike many of his theological contemporaries he has never laid claim to possession of it. He alluded to it in his talks with students, and those who were ready to hear it did so. But, for the most part, he guided his students in their studies of *small knowledge* in its many and varied forms, fostering a way out of narrow parochialism without either disregarding or disavowing any of the worldwide historical traditions. He taught Buddhism in its several forms, Taoism, and the *I Ching*, varieties of meditation including both sitting and moving meditation, dietary rules based on spiritual principles, and whatever other expressions of ancient wisdom those enthusiastic young people were newly wanting to explore.

I met Huston Smith in 1973 when we were members of the faculty of a summer program in Switzerland on Jung and Hermann Hesse, both of whom drew inspiration from Eastern philosophy. Each of us was leading a seminar, he on Eastern religious practice, including the T'ai chi movements and the use of the *I Ching*, and I was dealing with the psychology of the feminine as related to Jung's work. We met often over dinner or a glass of wine, and I learned that this man of profound intellect was also grounded in the body and in feeling. His example of how one can conduct every aspect of his life in consonance with his view of how the world moves led many of those present to a greater awareness of the intrinsic harmony in which we may be able to live. But granted, the little town of Vezia near Lake Maggiore was a summer paradise where one could easily abandon, for a time at least, the tensions of living that tend to tear consciousness into small bits and prevent a person from seeing life whole. There, in that lovely setting, Smith presented his model of a three-dimensional cross, with arms extending in all six directions, north, south, east, west, up and down. Those arms symbolized poles of infinite length, infinite possibilities, representing time, space, and levels of reality. He showed how it is that the farther we move from the center along any of the arms the farther we get from a resolution of the opposites. As we pursue our individual games and causes, we move away from center and endure the tension that is caused thereby. But Huston Smith saw that we nevertheless remain connected to that center, which is our own personal center, the soul's center.

Shortly after that summer, Smith left MIT and went to Syracuse University, where he developed the ideas he had offered in their barely germinating form at Vezia. He published them in 1976 in a significant book, *Forgotten Truth: the Primordial Tradition*. In this book, he writes: "If it strikes the reader as presumptuous to equate his personal center with the center of the cosmos, he must be reminded that physics requires him to do just that; because space is relative and curved, the center of the physical universe is for each observer the point from which his observations

proceed. If, still incredulous, still resisting the notion that the center of his self is in some way identical with that of creation at
large—have we not learned the lesson of Copernicus?—the reader
tries to position himself marginally by arguing that a single center
cannot occupy 4 billion bodies simultaneously, he forgets that the
spatial dimensions he has introduced have no bearing on the
mathematical point which, as we have seen, produces space without being implicated in it. The Hermetic formulation is exact:
'God is a sphere whose center is everywhere and circumference
nowhere.' "[23]

Huston Smith seems to be able to transcend the duality of East
and West in a way that had not quite been achieved by those observers of our time that were Westerners born in the West, or
Easterners born in the East. In Smith, it appears, there is a functioning union of opposites, a sense of centrality, which is able to
view with nonattachment the aspects of life which others would
see as separate parts or categories. Coming from a position of
inner union himself, he is able to comment on what he sees as
major causes for concern in our times: the spiritual alienation of
people on the one hand, and the under-realization of human resources on the other.

I think I understand his concerns as evidence of the decay of
"individualism," that wonderfully pat goal of the permissively
reared postwar youngsters who never acquired the discipline to
achieve what their capabilities promised. Seeking and striving for
oneself alone, consumed endless amounts of energy. Not only was
there the task at hand, but all the minor supportive tasks and obligations of everyday living also took their toll on the supply of energy. In addition, there was the strain of the competition, of making sure you got there before someone else did. So there was not
much time or energy to devote to reflection on matters that transcend the mundane necessaries of life. Weary and dispirited,
young people on college campuses looked about for alternative
modes of human relationships. Huston Smith helped them to see
that relationships could be transformed from casual and meaningless couplings to deeply centered and respectful connections between people who truly cared for one another. There were alternatives to the ways in which personal relationships were being

conducted, and Smith pointed them out. He recognized that many of the young people who studied with him were at a fork in a road, trying to peer into the future to see which way to go. He offered them a model which provided a choice.

First they had to ask themselves what it was they were seeking. One road led to *control*, the other to *participation*. Those who sought to control would be guided by empiricism, by mechanism. They would have to know just how everything worked, and how things and people could be used to further one's own goal-centered efforts. Those who desired participation would be led by their feelings and their perceptions of the feelings of others. Their way would value the "subjective" view, while the controllers would be more interested in "objective" reality. Those who would be controllers would see their environment only in terms of what their senses would report, or what information could be gathered from "responsible sources." Fearful of receiving unreliable information or of being deceived by the senses, they must be always wary, always suspicious. Finally, they find themselves victims of anxiety, which almost certainly leads to alienation. The alternative road, that of participation, is dependent upon trust rather than power over others. Those who would take that road might risk seeing *through* the eyes, not *with* them, to transcend sensory reality and to begin to penetrate the ground behind the illusions to which most people are accustomed. If this path is diligently pursued, the ambition to try to manage the universe is given up. In its place may arise the possibility of tuning in to the universe's rhythms, and harmonizing with them. At the end of that road, there may possibly be enlightenment.

6

Experimenting with New Forms

The mood of bewilderment that prevailed in the last stages of modernity, when the new leaders arose, was well characterized by Allen Wheelis, writing in 1958: "Now there is no great plan or pattern. The blueprint has been lost. Nothing is static. Everything evolves. We speak less of progress than of survival; and survival may be had only by adapting human nature and institutions to existing conditions of human life. The existing conditions undergo change at an accelerated rate, and seldom can a present problem be solved by a formula from the past."[1]

People on the threshold of manhood and womanhood were now beginning to resist actively the old hierarchical structures which they saw as blocking their development as individuals. Inspired by those few members of the older generation who had the vision to see what they were about, these young people proceeded to experiment mostly on their own initiative. Though the shape of the new remained indistinct and foggy, a path had to be cleared. The futility of the Vietnam War brought resistance to the draft. This provided a focus for the explosive energy that was being released in these young people. As they began openly to defy the "military industrial complex," individuals and groups directed their attacks against speed, dynamism, power, technology, complicated organizations, and the constant evaluations of people that were being demanded by schools, employers, the military, the government. They saw "big business" as the domination of the masses by the few, and they had little stomach for it just when they were beginning to get a sense of their own autonomy. Nor did they hold the traditional religious institutions in particularly high regard, but objected to the tendency of these institutions to define a public morality which supported the excesses of an atrocious and unjustifiable war. They resented the moral stance of people who would decry the abortion of a fetus conceived accidentally, when the parents neither wanted a child nor were capable of caring or providing for it, but who never cried out against the extermination of whole villages of men, women, and children, with napalm, and laying waste rice fields and forests.

As the young rebels met and worked together, sat-in and sang together, and lived together, at last they began to fashion their dreams together. When their vision opened up to new ways of looking at their surroundings, some of them began to imagine a possible society that would look very different from the one they were born into. Personal will and determination would count for more. Working people would not have to be swallowed up in huge, impersonal power structures. They would have more to say about the kind of work they would do and the manner in which they would live. Nor would their own personal lives continue to be determined by moral systems derived from the rubrics of the old hierarchical systems and their psychological counterparts.

The deterministic view of the psyche as exemplified in the psychoanalytic model of behavior came under close scrutiny. The young idealists chafed against the reductionistic view that the course of a person's psychological development was written inexorably during the years of early childhood or, as some of the experts insisted, even during the first few months of life; that only minor modifications of fate could subsequently be made, and those would have to do with adapting the individual to the existing social order. They saw the political implications of this system: power lay in the hands of the sexist forces of rationality and order; those forces were responsible for taming the archaic unconscious with all its spontaneity and impulsivity, and placing it under the control of the ego. They saw, also, how rationality, the *logos* principle, had become identified with the so-called "masculine" qualities—strength and domination—while the qualities of the nonrational—the emotive, the intuitive, and the mysterious— had been relegated to the domain of the "feminine." *Eros* had become associated with the feminine principle, despite the irony that Eros in the Greek myths is pictured as either double-sexed or male. But what a male! He is a weakling dominated by his mother Aphrodite, and he shoots his arrows on her command. The sensual Aphrodite is the same goddess who subdues Ares, the god of war, and brings him to her bed. There, she and Ares become enmeshed in a silken net dropped down upon them by Hephaestus, the antihero, exposing them to the ridicule of the Olympians. Eros-consciousness never becomes the model for male development, but Freud has used that of Oedipus, in whom the masculine principle is ordained to triumph over the feminine and dominate her. The repression of the feminine in the psychoanalytic doctrine had a double meaning—it not only reflected the need to depreciate the eros principle in men, but also lent support for the depreciation of women, since they are natural carriers of the eros principle as their leading function.[2]

The dream of a new society called for a "return of the repressed," in a far wider sense than that in which Freud had used the expression. Not only the psychological feminine within the individual male had to be redeemed, but her counterpart in the world, Woman, needed to be taken account of in a new way. There were profound political implications here, which became apparent later, with the rise of feminine consciousness in the Women's Movement. But even before that issue could properly be addressed, it would be necessary to deal with the issue of hierarchies which depended upon domination-submission relationships. A very different point of view from that of Western philosophy would need to find its way into the lexicon of images of reality. It would have to offer a perspective outside of and transcendent to political and psychological world views.

Now the young seekers had eyes for what had been hinted at by the avant-couriers of the new age, the Spirit of the Valley, the Tao. It found its own pathway, a watercourse way, blending with nature, overcoming through yielding to obstacles, and moving on. Although "the Way" is the closest approximation to the meaning of Tao, the opening of the central Taoist text makes it clear that one does not attempt to gain access to the Tao through understanding it. "The way that can be told is not the true Way." Although Tao belongs to the realm of Great Knowledge, it is not far from us; it permeates all of nature, and our own being in and of nature.

One characteristic of Taoism that these people found so attractive was that it was not a hierarchical system. Born of nature, the Taoist seeks to live in a dynamic relationship with all of nature, sensitive to her moods, seeking to be allied with her perfect ecological system. Such a person wishes to accept and cooperate with nature rather than to subdue her. As to nature's vagaries, they are regarded as neither good nor bad. They are and they change, even as we ourselves exist in a process of ongoing change. The Taoist finds all the lessons that are needed to be known within the natural world, ready to be observed and assimilated.

Leibniz, one of the first Western philosophers to be inspired by Taoism, stated it clearly in two of his famous *Twenty-four Statements:*

"And it follows, in general, that the world is a *cosmos,* fully adorned, that is, so made as to give the most satisfaction to the perceiver.

"For the *pleasure* of the perceiver is nothing but the perception of beauty, order, perfection. And every pain contains something of disorder, but only with respect to the perceiver, since absolutely all things are ordered."[3]

It was possible to accept the principle that the task of each person was to find his or her own place within this order, recognizing the harmony in feeling that accompanies the perception, even in the smallest part, of that overriding order. The so-called "opposites" are necessary to one another and to the dynamism of the whole: attraction/repulsion, creative/receptive, male/female. One does not exist without its counterpart, nor is one either superior or inferior to the other. In Tao the opposites are inseparable, although differentiation is possible. The Tao, the Way that cannot be told, is best expressed in the circular symbol of the Primal Beginning (*t'ai chi t'u*) ☯ in which the opposites are united like twins in their mother's womb. The dark twin, yin, is seeded with a point of light, and the bright twin, yang, bears the seed of darkness—and the matrix with its contents is always in motion. Where darkness was, shall be light, and where light, darkness, even as day and night, joy and pain, alternate with one another. There is not yin and yang, only yin/yang. Constant fluctuation is the dynamism of the cosmos.

It is no accident that an ancient Chinese book of wisdom appealed to people who were in search of new images to replace the figure of Oedipus, which would better express the shift in the collective consciousness that was taking place. Having lost faith in the constructed patterns of contemporary society, with its mechanistic forms and linear-sequential arrangements of parts put together, they sought a view of existence that was more organic and natural. They had begun to become aware of the intrinsic unity of nature, with all its elements interacting symbiotically to nourish, to grow, to dissolve, to decay, and thereby to provide the ground for something new to grow. This seemed to them to belong to a more authentic view of reality. They found profound meaning in the words of Lao-tzu:

> Those who would take over the world and manage it
> I see that they cannot grasp it;
> for the world is a spiritual (shen) vessel
> and cannot be forced
> Whoever forces it spoils it.
> Whoever grasps it loses it.[4]

Today, as ever in the past, the laws of nature must be taken into account; but they cannot, by themselves, provide the governance we need in human affairs. Yet human affairs inevitably go awry when the laws of nature are disregarded. Confucius knew this when, from time to time, he consulted the wisdom of Lao-tzu concerning the proper way to manage human relationships in various situations. Both men relied on the *I Ching* or *Book of Changes* in which the images of heaven, earth, and man were brought together in a model for human behavior. The *Book* was so significant that it has survived for thousands of years. By design, the *I Ching* is an esoteric doctrine. Jung wrote in his Foreword to the English translation that its message is not for everyone: "The *I Ching* does not offer itself with proofs and results; it does not vaunt itself, nor is it easy to approach. Like a part of nature, it waits until it is discovered. It offers neither facts nor power, but for lovers of self-knowledge, of wisdom—if there be such—it seems to be the right book. To one person its spirit appears as clear as day; to another, shadowy as twilight; to a third, dark as night. He who is not pleased by it does not have to use it, and he who is against it is not obliged to find it true . . ."5

I was very much aware of the interplay of opposing forces during a week's retreat at Puerto Vallarta, where I renewed my friendship with T'ai chi master Al Chung-liang Huang. On the beach we moved through the forms of the dancing energies, bringing heaven and earth, activity and receptivity into harmony within our own bodies. Gradually and with much practice, our movement became effortless, awakening the body to unsuspected vitality. During a long pause, I sat on the seawall and watched the waves as the tide was coming in. They would consume nearly all of the beach and then pull back, releasing a strip of wet sand and depositing crooked patches of lacy foam upon it. The foam quickly disappeared. The waves would return again and again, racing madly forward and flowing back reluctantly when they had reached their limit. Over and over, the tremendous force of the water hits the land. Ocean is the womb of earth. On every strand she yields up the earth and gives it birth. We who inhabit the earth build bulwarks against the sea, not so much to hold her back as to take notice of our own limitations. The relationship between ocean/land is not unlike that of woman/man, for in each case the primal power is unmistakably loosed where one engages the other; and the barriers we erect serve our immediate needs, but they do not contain the power.

It was in this setting that I told Chung-liang that I believed the *I Ching* could serve better as a more meaningful root metaphor for sexuality in our time than the Oedipus myth. Oedipus had been preordained to live out what had been determined for him by an arbitrary fate. No matter what tricks or wiles might be practiced to prevent the prophecy from being realized, fate would play itself out. The sense of the myth is that individuals have little to say about what will happen to them ultimately. They bear the burdens placed on them at birth or soon after, to carry out the sexual role for which they were destined as male or as female.

When they seek pleasure in ways that do not meet with parental approval (approval which is later internalized), they are beset by nameless guilts. Because of their inabilities to meet the demands they feel that society has made, they are also beset by shame. Only through extraordinary heroism is it possible to improve one's lot and thereby to feel that one is really worthy to exist. Using this oedipal model, fate is seen as an immovable obstacle that one tries in vain to overcome. This was a heavy load to carry—and the young rebels were ready to put it down.

Chung-liang agreed that the *I Ching* offers a very different image, one in which individuals are in a process of ongoing change within a world that continually changes. It is said that the holy sages in ancient times made this *Book* for the purpose of allowing human beings to understand and follow the order of nature. This order was not seen as capricious, but rather as a succession of events proceeding from oppositional processes within a network of relationships. Heaven (the spirit), earth (the world of practical reality, including the body) and man, all were taken into account. "[The holy sages] determined the tao of heaven and called it the dark and the light. They determined the tao of the earth and called it the yielding and the firm. They determined the tao of man and called it love [in the sense of humane feeling] and rectitude. They combined these three fundamental powers and doubled them; therefore in the Book of Changes a sign is always formed by six lines."[6]

We see various aspects of ourselves in these hexagrams and their images; we see ourselves as whole persons interacting with other persons, and we see ourselves as members in and of a universe that extends far beyond our capacity to imagine. We hear the eternal rhythms because they are part of us, too. As we become aware that we are being moved by them, we can listen to the pulse and the voice of the universe. Chung-liang had demonstrated for our class the various levels of *seeing* how we are in the world. First, we stretched out our arms and looked at our fingertips—a small world indeed. Then we extended our gaze to the beach and saw a wider world; and then beyond that to the sea itself; and then to the broad horizon, and beyond even that. We were able to extend the range of vision, and thereby to receive the universal energy which became manifest before our eyes. We do not need to assume an adversary relationship with the world when we are governed by a model of such limitless abundance and open receptivity.

In human relationships, love and rectitude are an ancient complementarity. But somehow, in Western thought, the corresponding principles, *eros* and *logos* had become separated. Eros, the function of humane feeling, intuition, and imagination, is empowered by love. Logos, associated with rectitude, is the rational function, master in the world of analytic thought, in objective reasoning, in a scientific method that establishes facts and avoids making value judgments. The danger of placing these opposites in contention with one another, or regarding one as superior to the other, was seen by Jung as far back as 1927, when he wrote, "It is the function of Eros to unite what Logos has sundered."[7]

Any attempt to comprehend this in its full depth requires a particular kind of vision. David Michael Levin speaks of this in his essay "The Opening of Vision: Seeing Through the Veil of Tears."[8] Levin sees the eyes as having two functions: *seeing* and *crying*. Seeing calls forth the usual associations: clarity, definition, discrimination, understanding—functions that have been highly valued in the past in our Western society. It is only recently that people other than poets and songwriters have had a good word to say for *crying*—yet crying belongs to the emotional side of people and, as such, is a reservoir of unimaginable power. If seeing separates and discriminates, crying relates and unites, hence crying can have highly sexual connotations, as Levin suggests:

". . . crying is the disclosure of the compassionate truth, or trust, which is immanent in seeing. *For it avows, between the being who cries and the being who is beheld, a primordial and indestructible kinship of flesh and blood* . . . Crying can teach us that seeing is much more than be-holding; it is always also to be be-held and be-holden, since every sentient being we be-hold can give itself to us only by virtue of its own enthralling hold, its own primordial existential *claim*, on our eyes. *What the eyes cry out for, then, is a new way to see with compassion: a way to see with our eyes, as we never have before, the kindred beauty and mystery of all sentient beings; a way to see these beings openly and accept-*

ingly, without dualities (including sexual polarizations) *which are painful and not fulfilling.*"[9] (Italics Levin's)

It was to this kind of sensibility that Maslow had given permission in the early days of Humanistic Psychology. The "third force" was a misnomer because the movement was less of a force than an absence of force. It encouraged the letting-go of constraints, in an effort to facilitate the natural growth potential of the human being. Humanistic psychologists saw their task as nurturing people so that they could develop in consonance with their inner design. Instead of laws and conventions, helpful and caring relationships were to provide the support systems for this process.

Humanistic psychology did not press its way into academic circles to protest "scientific" psychology. Nor did it take a stand against laboratory experiments on human subjects, or against the "neutral and objective" stance of psychoanalytically oriented therapists and analysts. Instead of occupying itself with what was "wrong" with the traditional practice of psychology, the Humanistic group put its energies into the creation of its own vision. What it did, symbolically, was to make space for the *crying of the eyes*, for the dimension of feeling to be *openly* expressed. It encouraged a freeing up of the feelings so that they could be allowed to flow. This often took place outside the cocoon of the consulting room. Settings were provided where people could share the intensity of their experiences with others. While this sharing may have been relatively easy for some people, others had been accustomed to placing a high value on privacy when it came to their own emotions. They felt that there was great virtue in being able to handle their own hopes and fears, pain, insecurity, even love, alone—or perhaps with one thoroughly trustworthy person. For this reason it was difficult to break through the armor and the masks people had created for public viewing.

Group therapists or workshop leaders provided elaborate rituals. These were not unlike tribal or family rituals, in which the power was centered in the group more than in the individual. Group games or exercises were devised for people who had always managed alone, or thought they did, so that they could experience what it would be like to rely completely upon others who were, in fact, strangers. Persons who had always made a great point of their "independence" were treated to exercises in which they were utterly dependent upon someone else; and later there were experiments in interdependence, where neither one could succeed at a task unless they cooperated and both succeeded. The attempt was to create a win/win climate, in which people could let go of some of their defensiveness and feel freer to grow in new ways.

Places were needed for psychological "proving grounds" where new ways of being could be tried out without the shadow of constant judgment hanging over them. Esalen Institute was such a place. It was the first and most seminal of centers from which many other growth centers would take inspiration and guidance for their independent development. Founded as an institute "to explore those trends in education, religion, philosophy, and the behavioral sciences which emphasize the potentialities and values of human existence," its activities consist of seminars and workshops, residential programs, community planning and community living, consulting, and research.[10] It was well known that the effectiveness and meaning of many seminars and workshops at Esalen derived from group activities with intense emotional content. Individuals were confronted by the group or in a group setting, and habitual ways of being were likely to be challenged at every turn.

My own initial experience at Esalen took me a long step on the road from humanistic psychology toward transpersonal awareness. It helped me to realize certain connections of mind/body/place/spirit in an immediate way, not an abstract context. Although I had known about Esalen for at least half a dozen years, I had resisted going there. I responded to what I had heard by becoming especially guarded about my private inner life. Beginning with my personal analysis and then in my training analysis, I had learned to cultivate the life of the soul in quiet inward ways, both in myself and later with those who were in analysis with me. This tender and delicate work needed to be protected through the exercise of skill, confidentiality, and trust. The work was often lonely, for it is essentially a process of self-reflection and self-examination. The analyst may serve as catalyst or guide, but the person with whom she works does the most important work alone. The idea of sharing what is inner and private with a group of strangers seemed to me potentially destructive of the precious and unique aspects of the individual, namely, myself. I therefore resisted subjecting myself to what I anticipated as the intrusiveness of the Esalen experience. All the same, I would not be honest if I did not admit that the idea of going to Esalen exerted a strong attraction upon me.

I had been living through a difficult time in which I had overcommitted myself both in my professional and in my personal life. I disregarded my growing exhaustion, and continued to drive myself into accomplishing everything I had set out to do. Only vaguely aware of bodily tensions, I refused to give in to lower back pain and sudden sharp twinges, until it had become agony to get up from a chair. I knew that I would soon have to do something—either go into a hospital or take off a month to attend a program on forms of alternative healing.

Driving down the coast road from Monterey to Big Sur and watching the waves smashing against the rocks and high cliffs so enchanted me that I nearly missed the sign marking the entrance to the Esalen Institute. I pulled off the highway, turned down the dusty road, and swung around hard to find myself facing into the orange glow of sunset. Great pine trees were black against a sky vibrating with all the intensity of glowing embers. A small stream tumbled out of the valley on my left and fell over rock ledges into the sea, reminding me that I was to take the watercourse way. I stayed the month at Esalen, obeying the order like a novice in a secular monastery, walking up hill and down, eating vegetables fresh from the garden, soaking in the water of hot mineral springs. After two weeks my pain was gone, and then I could begin to learn, as Jesus had known so well, that there is nothing like a miracle to attract people and ensure their attention for the real message.

It is different for everyone. Each person sees it through his or her own eyes, or tears. In coming to Esalen, people could leave their social personas behind. Here they would be free of the oughts and shoulds of the worlds from which they had come. They could participate in many different and creative experiences. As is to be expected with innovative projects, sometimes they are met with success and sometimes with less than the desired results. As people become loosened from their usual states of equilibrium, new ways of being are tentatively explored. These explorations would make important and, in most cases, positive impact on the participants. Naturally, much of what was happening was misunderstood, especially by the media, which operated largely from hearsay and made it all seem so threatening that many people who might have benefited were afraid to come. Some of those who did come were mature enough or sufficiently centered in themselves to stand the discomfort of exposing psychic contents from their own depths, and to come out renewed and rebalanced. Others found themselves toppling over. Even these were hardly ever alone in their predicament. The atmosphere was eminently supportive with someone invariably being available to listen to or act as guide to another who needed such help. The Institute made it clear to people that they came on their own responsibility. Esalen was not a hospital or a treatment center. If healing happened, as it so often did, it reflected the "making whole" quality of the human and the physical environment on the soul of the person who absorbed it.

What spread out from Esalen extended the human potential movement to Britain, Europe, Latin America, and even Australia. The movement filtered into the popular culture, casting a long shadow over the earlier psychological movements of psychoanalysis, behaviorism, and their heirs. The older psychologies remained important within their own strongholds, psychoanalysis within the frankly intellectual community and behaviorism in the academic community. But in the large segment of the population that was committed to neither of these alternatives, a rich source of stimulation for both mind and feeling was offered under the heading of "personal growth," in a proliferation of workshops and seminars. The human potential movement clearly did not use a "pathology" model.

What was the immense attraction of this movement, and why did it have such profound effect upon the lives of so many people? It seems to me that the movement provided opportunities for people to bypass the intellectual verbal skills and games which they had learned so laboriously, the "surface structure" of behavior, and to come into direct contact with the preverbal and nonverbal essence of being, which is not taught, but is an integral part of the organism, the "deep structure." Deep structures take shape and form, beginning with the development of the human embryo, and after birth they become the basic ground, the recipient of contouring influences that occur when the infant is most malleable and is still incapable of understanding through words or ideas or anything that we would call rational. In the human potential movement something happened in subtle ways, ways that you might not notice because you were busy receiving the input on an "adult" level and reflecting upon it as adults are supposed to do. Something else was occurring at the same time, profoundly altering the quality of consciousness, and this was what exerted its tremendous magnetic power. A few examples:

    Touching. Touching was allowed. It seems simple and natural enough, but remember, in all the recognized forms of psychotherapy until then, touching between therapist and client had been expressly forbidden. Of course Humanistic Psychology made it clear that whatever it was doing was not "therapy," and so the "rules" were not violated. Touching proved to be extremely therapeutic nonetheless. People began to rediscover what they had forgotten by the time they had learned to verbalize. They had forgotten how as infants they first came to know the world through the sense of touch, through the exploration of their own bodies, and how they discovered that all the world is not "my body"—though a good part of it is. So they remembered the twin discoveries they had made as young children, that pleasure and pain may come from oneself, or it may come from someone else, because there are others in the world. And by touching another, one can affect that other; by reaching out one can make connections, and one can feel the quality of the connection, the warmth or the chill, acceptance or rejection, nurturance or denial—but not in words—in touch.

    Touching was encouraged in nonthreatening or minimally threatening situations which were explicitly not sexual. Yet sexuality might be implicitly present in any encounter just because we are sexual human beings. Awareness of this, of course, brought to every interpersonal experience a certain excitement, a measure of fear and hesitation as well. Consequently, safe "games" were devised. These exercises helped people to cross over barriers to basically nonsexual physical contact, by permitting touching in a socially acceptable setting. So many people had come from nontouching homes, where as babies they were kept in cribs with stuffed animals around them as if to compensate for lack of cuddling from the parents. So many had learned when very small that touching is somehow connected with sexuality, and sexuality is only permitted under certain very restricted conditions. It is either for very small children, or for adults who belong to the acceptable category of spouse or family member.

Massage. This further extension of touching was quite different from the no-nonsense massage of the athletic club; nor did it resemble the frankly sexual manipulations of the massage parlor. The kind of massage that came to be practiced depended upon a recognition of the sensitivity of the body and respect for personhood. Though not explicitly sexual, it was thoroughly sensual in the truest sense of the word. It was smooth, gentle, and unhurried. It was loving without being exploitative. It was sensation for the mutual pleasure of the giver and the receiver, freely given and freely exchanged. It had the effect of helping people to become aware of the particular patterns of tensions to which their bodies had become accustomed, and thus to begin to release them.

I met a woman who works very hard in a helping profession. She is extremely conscientious in her efforts at healing and counseling. Often at the end of the day, having struggled with difficult patients and a demanding staff, she would return home feeling weary and dispirited. On one such occasion, she related, she asked her husband to massage her back and shoulders. As he was doing this for her, she began to wonder if it would work better if *he* were more developed psychologically. She asked him, "Would this be better if you were more individuated?" He responded, "This will make you well, because I love you so much."

Noise was something else for which permission was given. How used we are to inhibiting the sounds we utter! How carefully we shape them and with what precision we form them! Now comes the freedom to grunt and sob, to yell and pound, to let loose what we have been hanging on to so fearfully. The thunders roll. Then comes the freshness of the desert after rain.

Silence, too. Perhaps silence is one of the last taboos. Wherever people come together it seems to be necessary to engage in conversation or to listen to discourse. Could there be silence? Could a pause be attenuated without embarrassment? Meditation became a possibility. While some people today still regard meditation as "looking senselessly at a wall," more and more are learning to quiet their minds and enter into the spaces of silence where knowledge can make itself heard without words. They have learned to release themselves from incessant meaningless chatter about *things,* and return to essences.

Movement of the body came to be experienced in some different ways. Physical fitness was no longer just for athletes or health nuts. In the newfound silence, vast numbers of people began paying attention to their nonverbal bodies, listening to their bodies' messages, observing the language of the body, allowing oneself to "speak" through the body. At Esalen we discovered that the lips might lie, but the body itself does not lie. We became aware of ourselves and of others as wholes; we saw the total gestalt. What we saw and felt did not obey laws of logic, nor did it necessarily "make sense." We danced, as music evoked the harmony in the body. It was no longer necessary to be locked into the old patterns of male leading, female following. We could dance alone, with a partner, with many, or only in our imagination, but we were free to dance as the spirit moved.

Body therapies came back into popular usage, but these too were different from what they had been in the past. No longer were they essentially "physical," which is to say that they were intended to restore lost functioning or to correct structural problems. Now the body began to be regarded as a vessel of consciousness. The quality of consciousness could be seen as it was expressed through its direct effect on the body. Therefore, by regarding the body with great care, one might find a way into processes of consciousness that are not accessible through strictly verbal channels. And deeper yet, the quality of unconsciousness would also manifest in the body, so that the manipulation of the body itself could release unconscious pain and encapsulated memories into the stream of consciousness. It became clearer than ever that body and psyche are not two different things interacting with one another. Students of human behavior have begun to doubt that how we behave is *nothing but* the product of individual body chemistry. Nor is it *nothing but* the result of environmental influences. Nor is it an effect of that mysterious entity called "mind." We have read with interest statements like that of Carl Sagan in *The Dragons of Eden* in which he suggests that the brain's workings—what we sometimes call mind—are a consequence of its anatomy and physiology, and nothing more. This "scientific" viewpoint leaves me with a cold and unutterable sadness. I ask myself what there is in me that is unsatisfied by this terse explanation of one of life's greatest mysteries. Is it an archaic/infantile wish to be more than I am, or do I sense an intimation of a Divine principle innervating humankind? My answer does not come in words, but in an image from the ceiling of the Sistine Chapel. One looks up—as throngs have been doing ever since Michelangelo painted it—and finds oneself magically drawn to that small portion of infinity which vibrates between the right hand of God and the left hand of Adam. Are we *only* dust?

I am heartened by Buckminster Fuller's statement, which could well be a response to this question: "Now, in June, 1980, at 85 years of age, I have consumed over 1000 tons of food, water and air, which progressively, atom by atom, has been chemically and electromagnetically converted into all the physical components of my organism and gradually displaced by other atoms and molecules . . .

"Each one of us is a unique behavioral pattern integrity. The metaphysical you and I are not the coarsely identified 'cornflakes' and 'prunes' that we ate in the days before yesterdays . . .

"The metaphysical you and I qualify for continuance in the Universe as local/cosmic problem-solvers, and as we design our critical path delivering all humanity from fearfully ignorant self destruction, we have the obligation to assume as closely as possible the viewpoint, the patience, and the competence of God."[11]

Fuller's words are those of a visionary. The ideal state of consciousness that he describes has not yet been achieved by many people, although there are some who today are beginning to move in the direction toward which he pointed. But most of us have turned our attention toward attempting to become more fully human, both as males and as females, and to work within the framework of the society we know, or create better ones, before we move too far afield. In other words, the local pole of the local/cosmic axis has been in the foreground during the decade of the seventies, while the cosmic pole has been mostly in the background of consciousness. But, as we shall see later, this has begun to shift.

Beginning in the mid-sixties and continuing through the seventies, a significant segment of the population underwent permutations in their perceptions of themselves as sexual human beings. Contrary to the warnings that had been given them in their growing-up years, they had now learned to be more open about their sexual feelings (and other feelings as well), and consequently more vulnerable to others. They risked to give more of themselves and to act with more spontaneity in human relationships. They began to take an increasingly optimistic view of human nature; perhaps you *could* trust people; perhaps you *could* give yourself freely in love; decent people would not take advantage of you. Anyhow, you, yourself, were responsible for what happened to you. You could carry that responsibility.

One of the factors that contributed to this greater ease in sexual matters was, of course, the availability of oral contraceptives and devices that could put the control of woman's reproductive capacity in her own hands so that she had, in a very practical sense the freedom of choice as to whether she would have children and when, if she decided to have them. For better or for worse, depending on your point of view, it became possible to separate sexual intercourse from long-term commitment. It is impossible to overestimate the importance of this one matter on psychosexual behavior patterns of human beings. The whole system of man-woman relationships that had in the past been based on the biological differences between the sexes would have to be revised in the light of the new freedom provided by technology.

Sociobiologist Edward O. Wilson has framed the case for rigidly defined sex roles in his controversial book *On Human Nature*. He begins by calling attention to the anatomical difference between the two kinds of sex cell, the human egg being eighty-five thousand times larger than the human sperm. However, the woman can expect to produce only about four hundred eggs in her lifetime, while the man releases one hundred million sperm with each ejaculation. A man can, theoretically, inseminate thousands of women during his lifetime. Woman naturally places a greater investment in each of her sex cells, since a maximum of about twenty can become healthy infants, and the cost of bringing an infant to term and caring for it afterward is enormous. The purely physical commitment of the male ends with insemination. His investment will be far less than the woman's, unless she can induce him to contribute to the care of the offspring. This brings about a conflict of interest between the sexes. This is true not only in humans but also in many animal species.

Says Wilson: "Males are characteristically aggressive, especially toward one another and most intensely during the breeding season. In most species, assertiveness is the most profitable male strategy. During the full period of time it takes to bring a fetus to birth, from the fertilization of the egg to the birth of the infant, one male can fertilize many females but a female can be fertilized by only one male. Thus if males are able to court one female after another, some will be big winners and others will be absolute losers, while virtually all healthy females will succeed in being fertilized. *It pays males to be aggressive, hasty, fickle, and undiscriminating. In theory it is more profitable for females to be coy, to hold back until they can identify males with the best genes. In species that rear young, it is also important for the females to select males who are more likely to stay with them after insemination.*"[12] (Italics mine)

Clearly, as long as this scenario persists in the human race, women are at a distinct disadvantage in that they need men, or rather a specific man, more than men need any specific woman. Thus sexual economics have tended to favor the male sex. But if a shift takes place in which it falls within the power of the woman to decide when and whether she will have a child, then childbearing takes on a different connotation to a man. This is not something that *he* imposes upon a woman, but rather something that *she* confers upon him. No longer is the conception of a child assumed as the likely outcome of sexual intercourse. Now conception has become a matter of conscious decision mutually arrived

at, and furthermore it is a decision over which the woman ultimately carries the veto power. Naturally this demands a level of
consciousness that is not always present when the sexual juices are
flowing, but in theory, and often in practice, this kind of consciousness is present. Surely, in a fundamental way, the results of
sexuality in the bedroom exert a powerful influence on the domi-
nance/submission patterns of an entire culture. Is it any wonder
that abortion and contraception have become such important political issues, reaching far beyond any concern with the right to
life of the fetus? It is quite true that the developments we have
noted threaten to undermine the structure of the family as we
have known it until recently and, indeed, the stable marriage-
until-death nuclear family of our parents and ancestors is becoming increasingly rare. As woman's freedoms begin to approach
those of a man, the societal structure trembles. The important
questions that must occupy us now are concerned with what kinds
of alternatives may be found where the traditional family structure
no longer meets people's needs. How can the increasing participation of women be seen as a potential enrichment of the social
order, and not so much as a threat? How can we replace the
familial patterns we have left behind with something that reflects
the evolution of consciousness and carriers it forward?

Science and technics will continue to advance and our lives will
continue to be transformed by them, whether we approve of the
advances or not. It is a moot point as to whether the changing attitudes toward sexuality were brought about by the new secular
humanism or by technology or by other developments. Many factors have contributed to bringing about the sexual revolution.
While it is helpful to understand what some of them are, little is
gained by assigning more responsibility here and less responsibility
there. It seems necessary to accept the fact that a series of developments converged to free sexuality from the constraints of earlier
times. Many people have already accepted the new freedoms and
incorporated them into their lives in varying degrees, while others
resist them mightily. No matter what an individual's own stance
was, one could not help but be deeply affected by the changes taking place. The chasm widened between those who wanted to ex-

plore new approaches to sex, family, and morality and those who felt strongly impelled to support and strengthen the more traditional ways.

What was important was that large numbers of people felt free to experiment; what was new was that they could read about it, write about it, and speak openly about their own sexual lives. The people who were experimenting with new forms tried out open marriages, group marriages, and other arrangements with varying degrees of sexual commitments. Cohabitation between unmarried couples gradually began to be tolerated and then accepted by their parents or another generation. The term "living in sin" gave way to "living together." "Unwed mothers" became "single parents."

Tentative experiments entered into with so much caution and trepidation inevitably became prime-time material for the media. Television, in its hunger for novelty and the outrageous, skimmed off the most sensational expressions of the new sexual freedoms, making the experiments seem superficial and tawdry, or else so inviting that those most ill prepared were inspired to jump into the newest "in" thing. What was missing was the depth and beauty to be found in new forms of relationship, for these qualities are not readily translatable into television images. Television is not an instrument for lingering, for savoring, or reflecting on sensitive emotions, but rather for displaying a swift succession of passing images. What was most valuable about the sexual revolution failed to be communicated, while what was most widely shown often deserved the condemnation it received from those concerned with the public morals. There were, of course, exceptions. Some few public television programs dealt seriously with issues of common concern to young people, their parents and society. Some excellent documentaries on such themes as teenage sex, drugs, pornography, and venereal disease were shown. But for every one of these, many more programs displayed a callousness about sexual matters, a disregard of the implications of "private" acts upon other people, and the exploitation of sex for commercial purposes. Sex magazines, the public press, paperback books advertised "explicit sex" in boldface type. There was more open sex-mongering than ever before; there was more seeking, more craving, and more effort being expended to get what there was to be had. In an atmosphere of continuing titillation, the search for sexual satisfaction became a primary motivating force for individuals and a source of huge profits for the industries that exploited it.

7

Of Narcissism, Self-love, and Liberation

The affluent society of the seventies was able and willing to consume increasing amounts of time, energy, and money in the pursuit of the latest images of sexual desirability. Intense preoccupation with appearances; with discharging anger at parents, children, spouses, and lovers; with fulfilling one's own potential; with "feeling good"; with taking care of oneself in a hundred different ways hoping to attract other people to oneself; all this led to an epidemic of major proportions. This epidemic of egocentricity became known popularly as "the new narcissism." The subject filled journals of psychiatry and psychology, books of social criticism, and it filtered down into the popular magazines.

As usual, the elders supplied the backlash. The generation of parents who had raised their postwar babies so permissively now began to voice their concern about their children's becoming sexually active at an increasingly early age. A general outcry was raised against people who were "sexually liberated," and whom they considered to be, *ipso facto*, self-centered, manipulative, and self-serving. This evoked a revitalization of psychoanalysis or, to be more precise, it activated that radical element on the periphery of orthodox psychoanalysis that occupied itself with the syndrome of narcissism. In clinical practice, "narcissistic personality disorders" had replaced in importance the classical hysterical and compulsive disorders that had occupied Freud for so long and with such intensity, and several neo-Freudian psychoanalysts attacked the problem of narcissism with a will. We were reminded that Freud had identified narcissism as a factor in human personality which moves at cross-purposes with the sexually energized libido. Ideally, Freud had said, libido is directed outward and seeks relatedness with others. This is the impetus behind the development of normal sexual behavior. But narcissism, as Freud had described it, was a regression or inward turning of the libido. The narcissist pulls back the psychic energy that has been invested in persons out in the world and turns it inward so that it may fill certain egoistic needs—often at the expense of other persons or else in utter disregard of them. This narcissistic attitude is said to resemble that of sleep or organic illness or that state Freud called "being in love," all conditions in which the individual ego is deeply immersed in its own feelings and unrelated to the world of objects and persons. Here is where "being in love" differs from "loving"—for the former consists mostly in inner feelings derived from devoted contemplation of the love-object, whose image in the eye of the beholder may bear little resemblance to what another person might see. Then the image of the beloved merges with the ego ideal of the person "in love." A person then experiences that in the company of the beloved one feels greater and more fully oneself, as one really is meant to be or would like to be. One feels "truly wonderful." Loving, in contrast to this, requires a deep positive regard for the other's unadorned essence, including the weaknesses and imperfections as well as the beauty and strengths of the other.[1]

The original Freudian theory of sexual libido as an outpouring of psychic energy directed toward another person is only a partial theory. It needs the complementary theory of narcissism to explain the ingathering of this same energy and the holding it in reserve for the purpose of preserving and protecting the ego personality, or the person one knows himself or herself to be. If libido theory is essentially a description of the dynamics of the extraverted energies, then the theory of narcissism describes the introverted influx of energies. Clearly, no personality can develop without the interplay of these energic tendencies: like yin/yang, they are inseparable. When the relatedness of one tendency to the other becomes unbalanced or distorted, the personality may fall into disorder. If we make a pathological interpretation of these disorders, we then see illnesses that have to do with an overvaluation of the object, as in obsessive-compulsive disorders or hysterical disorders; likewise, the overvaluation of the subject leads to what we diagnose as narcissistic personality disorders. So then we treat this or that side of the individual and concentrate on the issues raised by the imbalance—why the imbalance has occurred, where it stemmed from, and what kinds of disabilities it has brought in its wake. We say it is the illness of the person; it is the illness of the times.

In a society where so much energy is expended in extraverted directions it should be no surprise that in our private worlds narcissism should play an important part. It remained for Heinz Kohut to clarify some problems growing out of narcissism which Freud had not sufficiently explicated.[2] When Freud had raised the issue of narcissism and suggested that narcissism and the capacity to love another person were inversely related, he laid the ground for a belief that all narcissism must be pathological. Kohut did not take such a stern view but placed the idea of narcissism in a developmental context. He delineated a psychology of the "self" (with a lowercase "s"). Kohut's use of the term "self" is not the same as Jung's usage of the Self as archetype but, rather, refers to an aspect of ego. The Kohutian self is defined as "the locus of valuing and esteem-formation—of esteem for the self and esteem given over to others."[3] Kohut sees psychological development occurring in three stages: the first, in which the infant-self has not differentiated clearly between self and other and thus derives pleasure from autoerotic experience; the second, in which a cohesive sense of the self as being something different from external objects begins to form; and the third, or oedipal stage, in which both the ego and the love object have become realities. Kohut saw narcissism as an independent line of development, proceeding along lines that are parallel to the development of interpersonal relations. Narcissistic developments are said to continue into adult life. At best, they can provide a person with the energy of ambition, the desire for self-fulfillment, and an ability to accept the inspiration and support of other persons whom the individual admires and respects. When this development runs a satisfactory course, the energies of sexual libido and the energies of narcissistic development function harmoniously in a dynamic balance. The

lines between inner and outer, between self and other, need not
be so sharply drawn.

Unfortunately the path to this happy state is not so easily tra-
versed, since there are many obstacles along the way. As Christopher Lasch pointed out in his book, *The Culture of Narcissism*,
the energy of ambition can become a compulsive driving force, an-
nihilating any relationship that threatens the goal of the person
bent upon his own aims. The desire for self-fulfillment can lead to
obsession with material goods and comforts, with political power,
recognition, and praise. One may be racked with pain between the
dependence on a vicarious warmth provided by others, and the
fear of that very dependence. Drawing back from relations with
others, one may have to confront an inner emptiness. At such a
time, insight does not solve the problem but only shows it up in
its true horror.

It is only when the suffering and passion lead the person to the
experience of transformation that the agony of failed introversion
can be healed. Jungian analyst Donald Kalsched in his exploration, "Narcissism and the Search for Interiority," points out that
the hero's isolation can only be overcome when he has survived
that "disillusioning 'moment' when the paradox of his own sub-
jectivity breaks through to him [and] he loses his 'image' and
gains a soul." The "moment" to which he refers is the simulta-
neous birth of otherness and interiority, paradoxically paired.[4]

The psychology of Jung provided a basis for reaffirming interiority without sacrificing the capacity to live in relationship
with others, even intimate relationship. The opposite poles of the
individual psyche will coexist whether we attend to them or not.
At one time the energy gradient may lie in one direction, at another time in another, and we do not live fully unless we give to
each the energy that is due to it. As Jung envisioned the individuation process, the guiding function of the soul would keep
the individual continuously mindful of the needs of self and other
as they impinge upon one another. Individuation involves two
movements, inward to discover who one is, and outward to learn
about one's place and function in the world beyond the personal
ego concerns. One of the outcomes of self-exploration was the de-

termination on the part of women to become at last what they were capable of being.

Women's Liberation was one of the great experiments of the dying paradigm of modernity. It started out as a movement of radical feminists who had found their voice and were raising it in angry tones against the injustice, restriction, and denial to women of political and civil rights. The perpetrators of these wrongs were seen as being either men in general, or the whole "system." Possibly historians of the future will regard the rise of the radical feminists as one of the major factors contributing to the decline of the power structures that emerged out of the industrial revolution. Women's Liberation began as a brave and vigorous movement, encompassing much wisdom and much foolishness, much pain and much derision. It was born out of agonizing labor and celebrated with joy. Although not many people have noticed it yet, the Women's Movement as a radical, feminist, separatist force has been in decline for some time now. Perhaps it is in its death throes, but I have heard no threnodies.

I first became aware of the Movement in the early sixties, before Kate Millett had written her book, *Sexual Politics*, that shocked so many, and before anyone ever heard of the Equal Rights Amendment. Living then in Switzerland where women had not yet obtained the vote, and where I was introduced to oral contraceptives, which were not yet available in the United States, I could visualize the changes that would take place when women began making use of their newfound freedom. I did not, however, fully anticipate the resistance that this would cause, both on the part of men who were relatively satisfied with the status quo and on the part of women who had not been reared to take the kinds of responsibility in the world outside the home that the new freedoms would offer them.

I belonged to a between-generation of more-or-less liberated women. My mother had been a career journalist, a rare job for a woman in the 1930s, but she was very good at it. She took pride in her writing and her professionalism. I doubt that it occurred to her that she was a second-class citizen, although she did not have an office at the paper but wrote her column at home, and her income did not give her financial independence by any means. The

title of her column was "You Can Be Glamorous." She specialized in informing women how best to spin their webs to attract
and capture men. She also interviewed the great and famous of
both sexes, and used her typewriter to reflect their glory as the
moon does the sun. She encouraged me to go to college, but
guided me into fields that were appropriate for females, which is
to say that accomplishment there would be nonthreatening to a
potential husband.

In the fifties, when I wanted to return to school for graduate
work, my application was initially rejected. For one thing, I was
already in my mid-thirties, and it seemed clear to the admissions
committee that no one could be expected to keep pace with college students at such an advanced age. Furthermore, my husband
was a professional man, so I was asked why should I want or need
a graduate degree? With some concerted energy I managed to
overcome the objections. I was informed not to expect any financial aid, and I did not seek it. The whole thing seems ludicrous to
me now, in view of efforts being expended to attract senior citizens back to schools and colleges; but that was then. In the mid-
sixties my own daughter was offered a graduate fellowship and
encouraged actively to pursue her studies. Her stipend was the
same as what a man in similar circumstances would receive.

In my mother's generation, I was led to believe, nice girls
steadfastly refused to engage in sexual intercourse, even if they
were engaged to be married. Virginity was highly prized, and a
woman's chances of finding a good husband were lessened if she
were sexually experienced. People actually got married in order to
be able to go to bed with the person to whom they were physically attracted, when there was little else to suggest that they were
suitable for one another as life partners. In my own generation,
when people engaged in sexual relations before marriage it was
generally done very discreetly, at least in the circles in which I
grew up. It was something you worried about, enjoyed, felt guilty
about, and imagined what would happen in the event that you
got pregnant. Suicide or double suicide were among the more
likely options. In my daughter's generation premarital sex was
taken for granted and parents were expected to accept it, if not to
approve it. Women were no longer willing to play the role of the

Sleeping Beauty until Prince Charming appeared to awaken them.

The Women's Movement was radical, it was necessary, and it was important for the evolution of consciousness. The burning of the bras was important. The same way that it was important that, on the day that Martin Luther King was killed, the houses and stores in the black ghetto of Chicago had to be burned down and looted. The same way that it was important that middle-class white women left their husbands and children in the suburbs and took buses to Selma, Alabama, to march for civil rights. Anger and righteous indignation are necessary. Not that they break the chains of slavery, because they don't. But they call attention to injustice. They prick the conscience of morally lethargic people, which includes most of us most of the time.

The consciousness-raising groups that enabled women to express their frustration and pent-up rage were needed. Even though they gave women an opportunity to consider collectively life changes they would not have dared to face alone, the Women's Movement really didn't solve most of the problems it set out to deal with. Women who went back to school, women who reentered the working world outside of the home, women who left unhappy marriages, did these things independently and alone after consulting with their own consciences. In the beginning there was much cheering from the sidelines from the Movement, but not very much substantive help was available for the individual woman. Most of those who secured jobs did so because they had prepared themselves, because they were qualified, and because they were able and willing to do what was required. The Movement helped many women get started in new directions, but each woman still had to deal with her issues in a most personal way, as an individual who happened to be female.

Working as a therapist in the early days of the Movement, I heard many women refer to themselves as "victims" of an oppressive society, meaning, of course, that they saw society characterized as men systematically oppressing women. Yet I observed that women themselves presented the image of victim to the public. As a case in point, I recall being present at the annual conference of the American Psychiatric Association in 1974. I had been invited to speak on ethics in psychiatry, as one of five persons in a colloquium, the other four being men. I felt that this was appropriate inasmuch as the membership ratio of women to men in that organization was then one to five. I was not a token woman. Between sessions, I walked around in the display area where various organizations of booksellers, pharmaceutical companies, and others show their wares. The salespeople were appropriately dressed for a professional meeting. Then I came to a booth manned—I use the word advisedly—by a group of females in jeans, hair disheveled, looking as if they had just come off a softball diamond. They were distributing poorly duplicated leaflets complaining of injustices visited upon women by men, and on their table was a goldfish bowl with a note attached asking for contributions. I felt sorry that women who wanted to be treated as equals had found it necessary to present themselves in such an unequal manner. Where was their pride in personhood? Perhaps they were trying to dramatize their wretched condition. If one behaves like a victim, I have come to believe, that is the way she will be regarded.

I may have been particularly sensitive to this because I have lived through years in which I, myself, had felt victimized. I firmly believed that I had been exploited, and I felt helpless to do very much about it. It took a long period of introspection, one might say of creative narcissism, for me to realize that the oppressors upon whom I fixed my rapt attention were, to some extent, at least, reflections of my own image of myself. Of course, I had not known this. But one day the terrible truth dawned upon me: the image I beheld was my own. The insight that followed this was that the woman who is oppressed is the one who allows herself to be oppressed. And it was much later when I could refine even this insight to: the *person* who is oppressed is the one who allows herself or himself to be oppressed. The number of the oppressed is great, but oppression is not limited to race or creed or color or religion or age or, for that matter, to sex.

If the Women's Movement was needed to break the stranglehold of the hierarchical male-dominated culture of modernity, then it has served its purpose. We will never go back to what we had. Nevertheless, while we move forward, it is necessary to view the deep inner context from which we have been emerging—

otherwise it is like quicksand which begins to pull us back down and in, the moment we slide too near the area of danger.

The major differences between man's and woman's consciousness that Jung described are certainly not as readily accepted today as they were when Jung first voiced them. And yet, they represent the matrix from which we have entered into another level of consciousness. The view of the consciousness of the sexes we were asked to accept, and for the most part did accept, sprang from a male perspective. Ego consciousness was seen as "solar" in nature, which is to say that it was light and clear and capable of generating its own power. It was the kind of focused consciousness that operated out in the world, its goals being the attainment of power, control, and domination. Jung identified this ego consciousness with masculine consciousness, and with that part of woman's consciousness which was not natural to her but which she had to struggle to attain. Woman's natural consciousness was more of a lunar consciousness, being diffuse in nature and identified with the soul instead of the ego. From a man's viewpoint the lunar consciousness was something to retain and enjoy for the hours outside of the workday, for the quiet introspective times, or the times of being in intimate relationship with a woman. Then her lunar consciousness could nurture his soul, without interfering in his day-to-day productivity. It might even enhance his effectiveness by providing him respite from ongoing pressures so that he would be better able to face the exigencies of the day ahead.

This might have worked, even in our contemporary society, if men had granted the soul equal weight with the ego, which is to say, if men were as attentive to the inward and sensitive sides of their natures as they have been to the development of their ego personalities. The separation of ego from soul that took place during the age of modernity, with the denigration of the soul and the elevation of the ego, contributed to the materialistic aspect of the age. Man neglected his soul and all those anima qualities in himself that are the expressions of the soul. Consequently woman, in her role of carrier of the soul, held diminished importance for him.

While women would not have described their own experience

in the male-dominated ego world in these terms, they nevertheless felt that their womanliness had been devalued in and of itself, but that it was highly desirable to men when it was employed to support their endeavors. Thus the woman with her "diffuse" consciousness was quite useful as a secretary who could carefully sort out her boss's various responsibilities and order his priorities; she was sufficiently focused to type his letters or his legal briefs. Women, who supposedly had less physical stamina than men, could work night shifts in hospitals and factories, then return to care for their children during the day. Women could be highly focused when they were needed to function in ways that demanded that. So the woman who was attracted to the Women's Movement was one who saw that she had capacities which went unrecognized, and that she needed support for realizing these. The support would not come from men, who were feeling their power structures threatened by aggressive and demanding women. The support would have to come from the ranks of the women themselves. And it did. Women gave permission to each other to express the rage that they had felt over the years at having to submit to a system in which they were second-class citizens, and from which there were not many ways out. Although they now had greater biological freedom than ever before, they were still a long way from freedom of opportunity. Their anger, fed by the realization that there were many other women who had suffered equally under a system biased in favor of the male, finally exploded. It took the form of women lashing out against the male establishment, of women forcing their way into areas that had been the private precincts of men, of projecting an overwhelmingly negative image onto men, of withdrawing into feminist enclaves, of refusing to trust men in general, and of finding the ultimate refuge in lesbian sexual relationships. There was a revolution going on, and men were regarded as the enemy. Men were, to say the least, dismayed.

If I were to try to couch these happenings in terms of the inner experiences of men and women, it would seem that both sexes have had sufficient reason to suffer from their alienation from the contrasexual aspect of themselves. While men were denying the feminine parts of themselves, women were giving vent to the long-repressed qualities that are commonly associated with the masculine. It has become apparent, however, that women do not make very good men, and they are not particularly at their best when they try to behave as if they were men. After all, if women objected to the masculine way of being in the world, what would be the purpose of reinforcing that way themselves by imitating it? The first generation of liberated women has had to learn the futility of this procedure. When men have bent over backward to adapt and adjust themselves to the demands of their female partners, the results have been devastating.

Gerd H. Fenchel, a psychoanalytic psychotherapist, has been observing and studying the effects on men of the changing roles of women and has summed up the major elements in the affectionate ties between the sexes. I cite them here because they come out of feelings that men shared with a psychotherapist of their own sex, which eliminates the middlewoman.

"Men, rather than a stereotyped powerhouse, have evolved into fragile creatures. They need companionship and caring concern from women in order to keep their psychological lives intact, to maintain drive energies and to feel needed and accepted. Feeling disparaged, fought against and boxed in by militant women, they have taken refuge behind various bulwarks. They have extinguished Eros and decided to fight women with their own methods. They hide behind narcissistic pleasures and sensations, abort intimate relationships and do not engage in heterosexual intercourse unless they are fairly sure that they can achieve an erection. They shy away from long term involvements, fully aware of emotional and financial losses in the event of marriage and divorce. They cut their losses, do not marry, and abandon fatherhood—their 'family jewels' are safe. Finally, they become affectually blunted. Sensations substitute for affect, and if they are lacking, apathy and depression become dominant. Others are turned off to women altogether and prefer male bonding with fewer demands and expectations. Still others save their traditional roles by openly declaring themselves male chauvinists. But nobody sits easy."[5]

Now we are coming into the second generation of the Women's Movement. We are beginning to recognize that we must first learn to balance the masculine and feminine energies within ourselves, which is to say that we must allow ourselves to function in natural and spontaneous ways as our temperaments and the situations require. This will enable each sex to move in the direction of inner harmony. In the process there will be much trial and error, but at least things will not stand still. Women will continue to experiment with their aggressivity in the world, and men with their vulnerability, their intuition, and their sensitivity to the needs of others. Also, women will continue to support women in the working world, as men have always supported men. It is a way in which each person discovers his or her own weaknesses, as well as strengths. Unless we risk this, unless we find out where our wounds are, we cannot get to our full strength nor can we heal ourselves. And when we have done enough of standing up for ourselves, and stumbling about, and raging, and weeping, then we can look again upon members of the opposite sex with true compassion. Then there can be an end to Women's Liberation, and an end to the reactive Men's Liberation.

It appears that now it is time to involve ourselves in a new movement, a movement of men and women affirming the cause of Human Liberation. I believe that it is inevitable that we do so. We need to look out for oppression wherever it is found, and this of course extends far beyond questions of sex and sexuality. Sexuality, itself, needs to be re-visioned in a far wider context. It transcends the needs of the individual person; it affects the family, the community, and the whole of society. Sexuality is a system within systems within a whole, which is the universe. Thus our concerns about the sexual generative parts of human nature are part and parcel of our concerns about the sort of life that will be generated in a world that is just now beginning to be defined as postmodern.

8
Sexuality in the Emerging Paradigm

Three centuries have passed since the Cartesian splitting of consciousness occurred, when the sacred and the profane were separated and each given its sphere of influence. The sacred had been relegated mostly to churches and religious communities, to private homes and to devotions performed primarily by women. The profane and secular had become the domain of science. The paradigm of modernity emphasized the role of science as man's supreme intellectual achievement. It was exemplified in classical seventeenth-century Newtonian physics, which deals primarily with matter and energy and their interactions. In this perspective, matter is viewed as real and as distinct from energy. Matter can be broken down and separated into its elements. Separate objects in this world view have an existence that is independent of human consciousness. Models in this system are primarily mechanistic, which is to say that the universe is imaged as a giant machine. Like any machine, it is made up of a number of parts, assembled in a particular way according to plan. Mechanistic models are constructed, supplied with some sort of fuel (energy), and they function in accordance with the way they are designed. When parts wear out or break down, they can be replaced with identical parts. Eventually, like clockwork, they run down, become obsolete, and fall into decay. They may or may not be replaced or superseded by new models.

Classical physics has often been drawn upon by other disciplines to provide metaphors that might explain certain phenomena. This has been particularly true in the fields of psychology and

psychotherapy, since the subtle processes that go on in the therapeutic engagement are difficult to describe, except by analogy.
Freud had talked of the movements of libido, or psychic energy,
in terms of a hydraulic system. The libido of a patient might be
dammed up due to an interfering complex and would not, therefore, be available for spontaneous functioning. It would be necessary to remove the obstruction in order to permit a free flow of
energies once again. Defense systems acted like brakes to impede
the forward movement of the psyche. Inertia and entropy also
worked against the capacity of the psychic mechanisms to achieve
their highest level of operational functioning. The ego held the
controls in hand, and so the goals of psychotherapy in this model
centered around developing the ego to the point where it would
be able to take charge and act in ways that would enable the "machine" to function as effectively as possible. This required first of
all that the ego be in charge of itself. The ego strove for autonomy and for authority as the leading element in the psyche. As
Allen Wheelis observed, the decline of the superego had occurred
by the middle of the twentieth century. The checks and balances
on ego functioning that had been provided by parental authority
and the demands of society had less and less influence among
many people who had experienced other places and other cultures
during the war and its aftermath. The paradox was that all the
time that people were fighting against the controls of their parents, and later against the controls of the established social order,
egos were becoming stronger and more stable. Many young people
achieved their maturity in the process of replacing the authority
of the older generation with their own hard-won freedoms. But
once the rebels had knocked out from under themselves the moral
support that tradition had offered them, once they realized that
they were not being resisted anymore, they hardly knew what to
do with their freedoms.

In preceding chapters we have seen how the "aspiring ego"
gained in strength, reigned briefly as a "mature ego," and then in
all too many cases gave way to the narcissistic "grandiose ego"
which operated from a center in the here and now and did not
have much interest in learning anything from the wisdom of the
past. At the very height of its powers, the dominant patriarchal

structure of society's institutions had begun to feel the rising influence of the archetype of the feminine. Women found themselves face to face with opportunities and challenges to modify the social order in ways that embodied their own values more than ever before. Sometimes women blundered by falling into the trap of the masculine, by trying to imitate masculine modes to gain a stronger position. But on the whole, the strengthening of feminine values offered the promise of bringing closer together the opposing attitudes that had so long been identified as "masculine" and "feminine." *Androgyny,* meaning the coexistence of masculine and feminine principles in *each* person, was a word that one began to hear. It was an idea that gave men permission to increase their consciousness of their heretofore repressed inner receptivity, and at the same time it gave women permission to allow their active, energetic, probing capacities to find expression out in the world. Each sex could begin to allow the secret, the sacred, soul quality of its nature to emerge into daylight and participate in those areas of life which before had been entirely practical, mundane, and profane. The ideal of "wholeness" began to be more than a psychological abstraction. It bccamc a goal toward which many people were impelled to strive. What this meant was that one did not have to be less a man or woman than before, but that one could maintain one's own sexual identity while cultivating the complementary aspect of oneself, the contrasexual, which makes for wholeness.

Wholeness has been symbolized by a sphere which encompasses everything known, or by a circle which has no end, or by a mandala which engages the eye and draws one to a center by way of labyrinthine paths. Wholeness implies an absence of limits and boundaries. We as human beings are whole, in a certain sense, for we are total organisms; and yet we are also part of a larger whole. On one level, we as human beings know that our bodies occupy a certain space, our lifetimes have their beginnings and ends, and we as individual selves cannot fully grasp the totality. We do well enough to acknowledge that there *is* this oneness.

The newer paradigm that is now emerging begins with awareness of a total unified scheme of reality. It entails a sense of participating in an overarching oneness, not as a separate being, but as a particular manifestation of the whole. The salient characteristic of the newer paradigm is the converging of the sacred and the profane aspects of life. If this sounds like a theological concept, it is, in the broadest sense; because the whole of which we speak is Source, Creator, and Essence of all that is and all that will be. But in another, more psychological sense, it is a world view which is reflected in every discipline, both scientific and religious; and so it cannot be said to relate only to things religious. When boundaries are erased between the pairs of opposites that we employ to define a world as dualistic, we approach a holistic consciousness in which there is no longer any duality. More and more members of the scientific community begin to see that disciplines which they thought were dealing with completely separate phenomena are really exploring aspects of the totality from different points of view.

The increasing confluence between Eastern wisdom and Western scientific progress has contributed to the beginnings of a reawakening to the essential unity between matter and consciousness. We saw how some of the leading postmodern psychologists found in the philosophy of the East a more open and flowing sense of reality, and taught this view to their students. The wisdom that is based upon Eastern sacred traditions reminds us that it may be necessary to free ourselves at times from the limitations that logic imposes on thought. At the same time, logical methods impose their limitations by demanding that for statements to be meaningful they must be verifiable analytically or, at least, confirmable by observation or experiment. Thought seems to require an aggressive attitude, one that seeks to penetrate the unknown and bring its contents into consciousness—like a fisherman sitting in his boat and hauling a few fish from the sea. Eastern wisdom offers another, alternative mode of coming to awareness. This is through meditation. Meditation differs from thought in that meditation is essentially receptive. The thinker goes after how things work. The meditator seeks that purity of perception through which may be revealed the essential reality behind the appearances of things. He is like the diver who knows what it is to swim about in the ocean.

Fritjof Capra, a physicist who operates in both the thoughtful and the meditative mode, pointed out in *The Tao of Physics* that

Taoist philosophers and atomic physicists not only hold a similar world view, but even the language they use to describe it is sometimes remarkably similar. In essence, the shared view sees "the universe not as a collection of physical objects, but rather as a complicated web of relations between the various parts of a unified whole." Capra cites two examples of statements made by Eastern mystics about the way they experience the world:

"The material object becomes . . . something different from what we now see, not a separate object on the background or in the environment of the rest of nature but an indivisible part and even in a subtle way an expression of the unity of all that we see." (S. Aurobindo)

"Things derive their being and nature by mutual dependence and are nothing in themselves." (Nagarjuna)

Next, Capra cites statements of how nature appears to certain atomic physicists, and we can see how they resemble descriptions of the mystical experience of nature:

"An elementary particle is not an independently existing unanalyzable entity. It is, in essence, a set of relationships that reach outward to other things." (H. P. Stapp)

"The world thus appears as a complicated tissue of events, in which connections of different kinds alternate or overlap or combine and thereby determine the texture of the whole." (Werner Heisenberg)[1]

The emergent paradigm takes its direction more from post-Einsteinian physics than from the earlier classical physics. It views matter as a form of energy rather than as something distinct from energy, and states that matter and energy can be transformed into each other. This new paradigm regards the world not as a machine driven by energy but, rather, as a living, generating organism, in that it is continuously undergoing development and change. While parts of it may wear out and decay, other parts are being renewed. Unlike machines, which function according to linear chains of cause and effect, organisms function according to cyclic patterns and respond to multiple sources of information. A plant, for example, responds to its inner structure; to light, air, water, soil, wind; and to the manner in which it is cultivated. Where branches are pruned, it will grow more profusely to restore the cut-off parts. Periodically it will produce seeds that germinate and ensure the continuation of the strain. Organisms fluctuate with a degree of flexibility that enables them to adapt to changing environmental conditions. We can regard this organism we call our world from the perspectives of physics, biology, psychology, sociology, or culture, but however we look at it we will see that all of its aspects are interrelated and interdependent. The sharing by many disciplines of this concept of the unity of nature and the interconnectedness and interdependence of all its parts is the essence of the paradigm that is emerging in our time.

Since human consciousness is a work of nature, we need to recognize that consciousness is rooted in a mystery which transcends it. Beyond all of our individual and collective potential for acquiring knowledge and wisdom lies the inescapable message that Absolute Truth cannot be encompassed by limited human consciousness. Absolute Truth is another expression of what the ancient Chinese referred to as Great Knowledge, the mystery that always exists behind whatever we may have come to know. This mystery is and always has been fundamental to the world's great religions. The important development of our own times is that science, so long alienated from religious precepts, now begins to acknowledge its limitations in the face of Great Knowledge. Yet, even as scientists discover the limitations of their individual disciplines, they are finding more and more that other branches of science offer complementary knowledge that crosses over what had formerly been perceived as boundaries, and enlarges the scope of the participating disciplines. Over the past fifty or so years new fields have been created, such as molecular genetics, biochemistry, and astrophysics, by effecting syntheses between formerly independent specialties. In the rapidly developing area of the neurosciences alone many disciplines, including neurochemistry, behavioral science, experimental psychology, physiological psychology, neuropharmacology, electrophysiology, and neuroanatomy, are explicitly concerned with the brain.[2]

As the boundaries between disciplines become ever more permeable, the cross-fertilization increases. New questions are being asked by some people in the forefront of the physical and social sciences today. The scientists are concerned with the implications of the discoveries they are making as they penetrate more deeply into that which yesterday was the realm of the unknown. Instead of demanding answers, these questions carry forward the spirit of search and discovery. Small knowledge becomes enlarged, even though we cannot expect that by linear progression it will become Great Knowledge. It is possible to intuit, however, by means of an unfocused holistic vision, something about the nature of Great Knowledge, or the transpersonal unconscious, or that vast realm beyond our ken which is known by many names, yet scarcely known at all.

Theoretical physicist David Bohm has formulated such a vision in the broadest terms. He has also been able to present for the consideration of the scientist supporting data for his understanding of the new world view that has arisen through a synthetic view of quantum physics, neuroanatomy, and the boundaryless spiritual systems of the East. It is no mere coincidence that two important sources of inspiration for Bohm have been Karl Pribram's holographic theory of brain functioning and Krishnamurti's philosophy of consciousness. Bohm is one of the intellectual giants of the new paradigm. With an almost mystical vision he has brought together apparently disparate views so that they can be contemplated within a unity that incorporates their particularities.

It is possible to draw an analogy between Chuang Tzu's Great Knowledge/small knowledge and David Bohm's implicate order/explicate order. Bohm re-visions as implicate order all that part, or aspect, of the universe which lies beyond ordinary knowledge. We can know nothing directly about the implicate order, since it is enfolded upon itself. Bohm tells us that the roots of man's problems lie in the nonmanifest, and that the "one mind of mankind" will be changed when we realize this. In a conversation with Renée Weber,[3] he illustrates his point using as an example the live oak tree that grows in California and never loses its foliage. "The leaves are continually forming and dropping off at the same time, so that it looks as if it's a constant tree. But it's from the nonmanifest that the tree is continually forming, and into the nonmanifest that it is dying. And therefore you don't understand the tree by considering it to be static or more or less a static object which is just manifest at this moment to our concepts."

Weber responds: "You mean, you would say that to understand the tree you have to understand that as much or more a part of what you see is something you don't see, that gives rise to it."

Bohm: ". . . a tree which is living, that comes out of the soil and the air, whose matrix is the water, the sunlight . . . there's a nonmanifest energy out of which it's coming."

But Bohm sees that this is not ultimate truth of which he speaks. He says that "physical matter has its roots in the nonmanifest. And also thought has its roots in some nonmanifest consciousness. But all of that is limited."

This world reveals itself to us measure by measure, through the process of unfolding, which is to say, through the ways in which it manifests or incarnates itself. Manifestation means becoming accessible to consciousness. The world of the collective or transpersonal unconscious, in Jung's terminology, is essentially the same as Bohm's implicate order. It is the archetypal world, which is nonmanifest by its very nature. In the process of *unfolding,* archetypes become conscious as archetypal images, then as ideas and, finally, in matter itself.

As we reflect on all this, many questions spring to mind: Is what Bohm offers for our consideration a philosophical view of creation out of the increate, or is it a scientific hypothesis? Is Jung's suggestion, that the ego as the center of consciousness emerges out of the matrix of the unconscious, similar to Bohm's description of the process of unfolding? And are the processes of forgetting, repressing, denying, or ignoring all part of the enfolding process by which that which was once conscious, or could have been conscious, is reabsorbed into the mysterious unknown? Is being born, in a spiritual sense, unfolding, since it is an emergence from the matrix-womb of unconsciousness? And is dying, being once more enfolded in the matrix-now-tomb, of unconsciousness? Is this transiting, this flowing, between the implicate and the explicate orders of reality, so powerful a truth that it helps us to understand the profundity of religious experiences, as, for example, that of one who has "found Christ"? It is as though the implicate universe now is understood as the infinite mystery we call God; it unfolds, yielding up a part that incarnates as God-on-earth, God-as-man, the Christ figure. Seeded by the omni-present Godhead, this Christ can only manifest through the womb of Woman; and, finally, when his task on earth is finished, he is reabsorbed into the Godhead through the gateway of the tomb. He returns, to be once more enfolded in the universal God.

If the nature of Ultimate Truth lies beyond the grasp of ordi-nary human consciousness, at least we can recognize that we live in a universe that is continuously revealing itself. As we learned more about the nature of nature, and the nature of human con-sciousness, we have seen that the old paradigm functions within the limitations of the everyday world that is accessible through the senses, but that there is far more that we can bring to our awareness. The emerging paradigm is not a single, monolithic world view, but rather a synthesis of many perspectives drawn from many disciplines. Synthesis is the key word here. It means that the disciplines all function under the aspect of eternity. Ev-erything that happens, happens not only in one place in time, but also in a larger sense in all places and for all time. The thought is not new, for Jesus had said, "Truly, I say to you, as you did it to one of the least of these my brethren, you did it to me" (Matthew 25:40). What is new is that these ideas are beginning to surface in the minds of those who had not considered themselves especially religious.

When we begin to re-vision sexuality in terms of the emerging paradigm, we rediscover the fact that sexuality is not altogether a private or personal matter. Sexual relationships have implications which extend far beyond the boundaries of the personal experi-ence. Based upon our consciousness of the transpersonal dimen-sions of our lives, we know that we do not function as fully au-tonomous individuals. All are part of the interconnected web of relationships. How we behave and how we feel about our behavior colors the environment in which we live. If our loving helps us to feel happy and contented, we vibrate with a warmth and openness that is felt by others. If we bring to another a sense of worth and value, that person also is able to place his or her weight on the positive side of Being, for we are a part of all that is. We know that our desire and our will is responsive to a total situation, rather than independent of nature or of our surroundings.

Nowhere do the patterns of nature reveal themselves so clearly as in the realm of sexuality. Nature's concern is with the continuation of Life, and she is profligate. Individual lives come and go. But we are human beings, not animals of the field. We cannot altogether give ourselves over to the demands of nature. For us, life must have meaning. Whether it is to have meaning for ourselves alone, or whether the meaning goes beyond our personal needs and enters the realm of the transpersonal is an important question. The answer we give will go a long way toward determining the kind of world we and our children will live in.

As we view human relationships in this wider context, we realize that the people whom we know intimately are and always will be in our lives, because they belong to the interconnected web in which we too are enmeshed. Each person bears some responsibility for relationships with others whom we may meet and from whom we may separate. They are, in an important way, always there. At times, someone may be in the foreground of our lives; at other times, in the background. It is necessary to be aware that every sexual relationship leaves its mark on those who join themselves together in this way. It changes them and, in doing so, it changes the context in which they exist. Joy or sorrow, trust or deceit, bitterness or ecstasy, all affect the soul which, in turn, touches the soul of the world and leaves its imprint. We keep no secrets from the unconscious, even if we try to keep certain matters from our partners or even from ourselves. Whatever we live out in the manifest world, affects that world in more profound ways than we could ever imagine. When all is over and done, the residue of our own lives is swept up and enfolded into that other world of which we have received only hints—and there it remains, to be born again in another generation.

In the earlier paradigm, experiences of the senses provided the data from which scientists tried to discern the patterns inherent in nature. More and more instruments were devised to augment the direct sense perceptions of human beings. We came to a pass where everything from the most sensitive microscope and the most comprehensive computerized systems provided so much information that the mind could literally choke on it, were it not for the machine's capacity for sorting it all out and arranging it in usable categories and making disposition of what had been gathered. But, finally, all that can be gotten out of the machine is what we, ourselves, have perceived and put into it.

From the viewpoint of the emerging paradigm, information received through the senses is to be regarded with some reservation. Things are not necessarily what they seem. In fact, "things" are not things at all. They are events, happenings, that have their meaning in how they are related to other events. In a world view which sees that all is in flux, there is room for simply allowing oneself to go with the process that is unfolding. There is increasing room for imagination and wonder. The person is encouraged to see figure and ground as interchangeable. Subject and object dissolve into relationship, and relationship exists within a larger context. Since human relationships are determined by more variables than can possibly be counted, it makes sense to encounter persons in their totality and in their natural settings rather than trying to "engineer" relationships.

When we re-vision sexuality in this light, we welcome the delights of the senses. These become more than an end in themselves. Personal pleasure becomes a gateway to something beyond oneself.

Sexual feeling expressed through the language of the body, through sensitivity to the partner's every response, through exquisite receptivity to the varieties of touch and to the warmth of closeness, gain in intensity when experienced as a part of something beyond senses, beyond words. As a drop of fine perfume contains the fragrance of the ten thousand petals, so this other human being in these moments embodies the concentrated essence of the whole world. Through this person's humanness, you participate in the dynamism of life, you merge with life itself, your individual boundaries are pushed to their limits. At the same time, it is all so very personal. The center of your being is touched. It is infused with life-energy until it can no longer contain it. Then orgasm explodes the shell of the personal and you experience another dimension of consciousness. Your vibrating center becomes the center of all there is.

The earlier paradigm had it that observations and measurements were demonstrably "objective." Every possible effort was to be made to remove any subjective factors that might creep in unawares. Observations were to be made with as neutral and impartial an eye as possible. In contrast to this, the emerging paradigm reflects the recognition accepted by most scientists, that the observer is always part of the observation and the experimenter is a factor in the experiment. The nature of the questions asked determines to some degree the nature of the answers that will be obtained. Complete objectivity is an impossibility, because for every step by which we attempt to remove ourselves from subjective involvement there is someone, self or other, who is making the subjective judgment that we are being truly "objective." This parade of watching who observes the observer could continue through a series of infinite regressions, and arrive nowhere.

Transcending the subject-object dichotomy is essential to the re-visioning of sexuality. A transpersonal view of sexuality will assert that we are not separate, autonomous beings, nor is one person to be dependent upon another for support. One does not exist for another's pleasure. Or pain. We are interdependent. What happens to one or to the other concerns us less than what happens between people, because we are not alone. In our relationships we are equal as individuals in our intrinsic value, although we may differ greatly as to our natures. This makes it possible, ideally, for us to respond fully and mutually to one another. According to our capacities we are able to give to one another and according to our needs we may receive. This is a true communion of the spirit. Whatever each of us does affects the others, and in turn reflects back to us, so that it is impossible to separate "mine" and "thine." Knowing this, experiencing it in wordless wonder, in the wisdom of the heart, enables us to break through the wall of isolation that was a consequence of our futile search for autonomy, independence, and self-fulfillment. We are not alone. We cannot be alone for long. We cannot survive alone. One of the gifts that sexuality can confer is nurturance offered freely. A sexual relationship that is truly dynamic both fluctuates and endures. It is tough and flexible, strong and yet sweet.

We saw that the older world view tends to explain events by reducing them to prior causation. Early in our lives we learned that if we do *that*, this will happen. In a pragmatic sense this often proved to be true, and on a certain level there will always be some truth in it. But the causal sequence had long ago acquired a moral tone, and the relationship between human beings and the God-head became, among other things, a matter of certain behaviors evoking either reward or punishment from Him. It was all relatively simple for many people who remained within the comfort of these explanations and directions for living. In a time of rapid changes in the way we understand the physical world and the human capacities for expanding consciousness, these people have remained steadfast in their commitment to a tradition which was somewhat predictable and apparently manageable.

In contrast, the emerging paradigm disturbs established patterns. It relies upon holistic rather than reductionistic explanations for events. The world is imagined as an infinitely complicated organic system, and events are seen as moments in an ongoing process that is consonant with the patterning of that system. When with limited intellects we attempt to understand that which appears to us as unlimited, there is not much about which we can be absolutely certain. High-energy physicists tell us that specific events are not predictable in the world of the infinitely small. They can only talk about statistical probabilities. They speak of subatomic events having a "tendency to exist." This casts doubt as to whether anything is finally and perfectly predictable. One might say that patterns of functioning are inherent in the nature of nature, becoming manifest as they unfold. Process continues, with neither beginning nor end, or so it appears from our human perspective. Life, in the transpersonal sense, goes on and on in a living and continuing universe, although individual lives cease to exist as entities and new lives come to birth. As the Taoist saying goes, "The sticks of wood are consumed, but the fire continues to burn." So also do we participate in the continuity that transcends our existence as individuals. But unlike the wood in the fire, we can reflect upon what is happening to us and all about us, and wonder at it. The system is teleological; it moves forward as an expression of an unfolding evolutionary design. Only the past is determined. The present and future are free.

In a reductionist vision of sexuality, people engage in sexual relations for mutual pleasure or procreation or both. These relations are seldom viewed outside the personal context, except when restrictions are imposed by some external authority of church or state or social custom. Then, the laws of cause and effect are invoked, with concomitant reactions of self-satisfaction, ambivalence, or guilt, depending upon the degree to which one adheres to collective standards.

The emerging paradigm suggests the holistic image of persons actively participating in the creation of a new generation by lending their own total beings to the procreative act. Yet there is the recognition that consciousness has evolved to the evolutionary state where it is possible to have a free choice as to the outcome of our sexual relations. By loving consciously, we further the evolution of consciousness. We can choose to guide our sexual impulses toward procreation and the life of the family; or toward intimacy that can be expressed through the body, the emotions, the spirit; or any combination of these. From time immemorial, the privilege of living and loving and enjoying offspring has been the reward received for carrying out nature's purpose. In premodern societies, it made sense to conceive and bear children without placing any kind of limitation on the size of the family. Children were an economic asset; they helped with the work and took care of you in your old age. But we do not live in such a society, nor have we for a long time. The scientific developments during the age of modernity made it possible to reduce infant mortality rates throughout the world. In developed countries particularly, premature infants are being saved who previously would have had no chance of survival. Populations are no longer subject to devastation by famine and disease. The changing demands of human ecology require that human consciousness be applied to the problem of population control. This means that we need to be concerned on the transpersonal level, where we are dealing with national and world issues in this area; but also we need to be concerned in the most intimate areas of our own personal lives, since we are also, individually, manifestations of the larger issues.

The older paradigm rewarded aggressivity and competitiveness not only in economics, but also in sexuality. In the economic sphere, the vast majority of people were interested in their own security and comfort, while a relative few were fighting their way up the mobility ladder to higher status and greater tangible reward. Yet these few were the trend-setters, the media idols, the fantasy figures that enabled the many to enjoy vicariously the dramatic risk-taking existence of the few. The scenario of the "beautiful people" went something like this: The prospective mate was someone to be seduced, to be captured, to be conquered, to be won over against odds. Every possible means to gain advantage in the manipulation of the relationship would be employed.

Gradually, something of this frenzy trickled down to the wider public. The longing for power and beauty in sexuality lent itself to a high degree of commercialism. Some of the most profitable corporations in the United States were in the business of making products that enabled people to feel more attractive sexually. The national obsession with superficial beauty often obscured other values that were grounded in the spiritual and emotional lives of human beings. A mate was more like a possession, in the sense that there were certain legal and moral rights that you had over your partner. This had little to do with feelings, because when feelings of affection found expression outside of a formal and committed relationship, the party who remained steadfast and loyal to the original commitment felt cheated, wronged, and diminished—even though he or she was being loved in much the same way as before.

The new economics of transpersonal sexuality do not allow a person to regard a sexual partner as an object to be acquired. What is to be sought is a human being who is able and willing to share in that most precious, abundant, and ever-renewable resource of the human spirit which we call love. Because such love is unlimited in supply, relationships in which it is present will be able to survive many transformations. Individuals, being less threatened personally in relationships, will be able to become more conscious of the needs of those they care for. If less energy is invested and less attention paid to competing for, or with, a partner, then more can be directed toward the quality of the relationship.

In the older paradigm, power politics have been hierarchical and authoritarian. The impetus has been toward increasing productivity and material growth. This is predicated to a large degree on the premise that we will continue to have access to an abundant supply of raw materials and energy. As human institutions have grown in size and complexity, individuals have become less and less able to comprehend them. So the institutions of government, of industry, and of education have become increasingly compartmentalized. Each person acquires familiarity with a limited area of specialization and focuses on that, with little time or energy or concern for the total picture—whether that be a sense of international politics, world economics, or the breadth of educational opportunities available to oneself and one's children. The effect of this is that most people feel that they have little chance of influencing their government substantially, that their voice is ineffective in making changes happen. Consequently, a feeling of despair is abroad. This often manifests itself in a pseudo-joy, which is a frenzied search for immediate pleasure before everything collapses.

At the same time, new ways are emerging. Decentralization (in contrast to compartmentalization) is a word that is being heard more and more by those who are moving into the new paradigm. Decentralization is an attempt to break down society into smaller units which are, nevertheless, wholes in themselves. This leads to the political organization of communities that limit their size to something that can be understood and managed by the people who participate in them. Leadership is less authoritarian than participatory, and the governing and the governed work together, often exchanging these roles, as they determine the standards, practices, and modes of cooperation by which they will live. People in these communities can know each other personally and feel responsible toward one another. At the same time, each community contains the essence of the larger political structure to which it belongs, like a hologram, or like a drop of seawater that contains the essence of the ocean. Networks join these communities together so that they can share their knowledge and experiences. On another level, these communities see themselves as seeding elements in the systems in which they are embedded: the cities, the states, the nations, and the entire planet.

Political concerns are reflected in some of the currently held attitudes toward sexuality. It is not only the supporters of the newer paradigm who have seen the need in our times to re-vision sexuality. The more conservative element within our society has also taken a firm position on sexual practices. Not government, but a group of citizens, self-appointed as guardians of the nation's morals, are assuming the hierarchical and authoritarian role and determining how others shall behave. Quite correctly, they have observed over the years a dissolution of restraints on sexuality. The kind of selfishness that demands instant sexual gratification seems to be increasing at an alarming rate. They point to the breakdown of the nuclear family, forgetting that this family grouping is a fairly recent and not too successful experiment that never fully supplanted the extended family, which had a more secure support system. They point to the increase in illegitimate births, to teenage sex, the proliferation of pornography, promiscuity, and prostitution. They see wide-open sex shops, they note a widespread preoccupation with casual sex and so-called "deviant" sex—on film, on stage, and on the television set in everybody's living room. They see that in sexuality exists the ultimate in profanity and, by God, they want it stopped!

Many of the issues that have been raised by the conservatives must be addressed. Some of the means proposed to address them are open to question. To attempt to cure the moral problems of a nation by force and by fiat will only drive the symptoms into hiding. It is no longer possible to return to the morality of the past. Pandora's box has been opened and her secrets are out. Once woman's only "natural" career was marriage and bearing as many children as possible. Today, woman has proved herself capable of managing home and family as well as of working in the world, especially if she has her partner's loving support. She need not feel forced to go out to work, or forced to remain at home giving her complete attention to her family. Today she has many choices. Yet, there are groups who seek to place constraints upon her, to keep her "in her place." For example, this would be effected through the prohibition of sex education in the public schools under the pretext that sexual activity increases when young people are informed about their sexual and reproductive functions and guided into taking personal responsibility for their behavior in intimate relationships. Or, it is suggested that children should learn about sex from their parents. Well enough, if parents are equipped with adequate knowledge and the capacity to transmit it. But why should not sex, like any other important aspect of living, be a part of the curriculum and taught to young people by teachers trained to do so?

Sexuality occurs in an environment, and the consequences of our sexual behavior affects that environment. Does society have the right to require sexually active women to bear children whether they wish to do so or not? This is a much-debated subject, to which there are no easy answers. It appears that those who believe most firmly that society has the right to impose childbearing upon women, are often the ones least willing that society should bear a substantial part of the burden for their care. A prominent spokesperson for the defeat of equal rights legislation said: "The role of motherhood is the most socially useful role in our society . . . we are asking Congress to evaluate all proposed and recent legislation on this standard: Is it an incentive or a disincentive to the role of motherhood? If it contains any disincentive to mothers caring for their own children, we simply must use our ingenuity to search for other ways to solve the problem." This was translated to mean support of federal legislation to prohibit abortions, to refuse information to minors on contraception unless their parents have been informed and agree, and to deny federal support to day-care centers which might have enabled mothers to work outside the home and support their children.

Is morality to be controlled by ignorance and fear? Or is morality more likely to develop naturally out of the realization that private acts have public consequences? Legislation imposed through hierarchical structures cannot make people more responsible, more caring. Care is bred into them from birth onward, and more by example than by precept. Transpersonal sexuality under the emerging paradigm needs to be cultivated over a lifetime. Concerns about our sexuality are best seen in the total life-context.

The foregoing observations may be sufficient to suggest that in a major paradigm shift, such as we are experiencing, scientific and social changes are not merely superficial; they are deep and pervasive. Hardly an aspect of life escapes being affected, although the effects of change may be perceived only slowly and in fragments at first.

As we begin to consider what kinds of changes we will make in our own lives in the process of re-visioning sexuality in a transpersonal context, a warning is indicated. As evolution proceeded through the centuries, it brought some hard-won achievements to consciousness. The older world view contains the core values of all time. It is not that we wish to cast them away, but only that we are moving on, and that we have broken through some of the constraints that were needed in an earlier day. Much of what was valued in the past must be maintained in the changing world. We would do well to heed the words of Alfred North Whitehead:

"There are two principles inherent in the very nature of things, recurring in some particular embodiments whatever the field we explore—the spirit of change, and the spirit of conservation. There can be nothing real without both. Mere change without conservation is a passage from nothing to nothing. Its final integration yields a transient non-entity. Mere conservation without change cannot conserve. For after all, there is a flux of circumstance, and the freshness of being evaporates under mere repetition. The character of existent reality is composed of organisms enduring through the flux of things."[4]

9

The Jerusalem Metaphor

I give you the end of a golden string,
   Only wind it into a ball:
It will lead you in at Heavens gate,
   Built in Jerusalems wall.[1]

      *   *   *

Now I a fourfold vision see
And a fourfold vision is given to me
   . . . May God us keep
From Single vision & Newtons sleep[2]

Always, underneath the rational peregrinations of the mind, lies
the moist ground of the soul. Even while we consider, evaluate,
and judge, a process goes on below that gives substance to the
thought, the idea, the problem or the solution. It is the intangible
essence of human experience that we know as consciousness, although it extends beyond the boundaries of what we know. Jerusalem, for me, belongs to that essence.

    Jerusalem serves as metaphor par excellence. It is the City of
the Center, the manifestation on earth, according to tradition, of
the archetypal City of God, the archetypal City of Peace, over
which peoples have shed their blood since David the King wrested
it from the Jebusites a thousand years before Jesus was born outside the City gates. All this I knew intellectually long ago. That it
now carries such symbolic weight for me will not be clear unless I
provide some personal background. Unlike so many people who
make their pilgrimage to Jerusalem guided by a strong spiritual de-

sire to absorb the historical and religious atmosphere of the place, I made my first visit to that city prompted by purely rational considerations—or so I thought. I needed some local color for a novel I was writing, part of which was set in the ancient city of Jerusalem. *I*, which in this case meant *ego*, decided to go there. I had never been an enthusiastic supporter of the Jewish State in the past; on the contrary, I regarded its development with some impatience, having long believed that the creation of a bi-national state, with Arab-Jewish cooperation, would have been preferable. What I now sought was firsthand knowledge of the topography of the area; that was all.

My journey had taken me through Egypt, Lebanon, and Syria first. In those countries I had felt foreign, everywhere eyed with suspicion. Our party arrived by bus from Jordan via the Allenby Bridge. We alighted on the barren sandy stony ground of Israel and immediately stepped into a barbed-wire enclosure presided over by the Immigration Service. Our group was led into a small squarish building where we stood in line a long time waiting for our baggage to be inspected. I looked up and saw before me a large poster on the wall, a panoramic photograph of the Old City as it looks today in the warm glow of sunset. The Dome of the Rock, shining like molten gold high atop the Temple Mount, dominated the City. Suddenly, and to my great surprise, my eyes overflowed with tears. This "crying of the eyes" gave onto a new vision. I felt a deep surge in the inmost part of my being. This was something so atavistic, so profound, that even now I cannot put words to it. I knew only that I had arrived, and the *I* was not my ego, but my soul.

As I walked about that Golden City, I walked in history and out of time, as I know time every day. Layer upon layer of the residue of the structures are here. Each is built upon the rubble of the previous one, each supported by the fallen stones and the fallen heroes of the past. I knew that in a certain sense we all walk in this way, supported by what has gone before, until we ourselves crumble into dust. We are our own history, our own developmental history as individuals. We are also more than this: we are the latest of the generations. And yet more than this, also. I climbed the Temple Mount to the very top, where the Dome now stands. On the way, I passed the Jews praying at the Wailing Wall—praying for the lost Temple of Herod's time, and the Temple of Solomon before it, and how many temples in Germany and Poland and Vienna and Prague, and in the heart! Praying and wailing for time past but not lost to memory. And placing little slips of paper between the stones in the wall—messages to be carried from time into eternity, for all I know.

"Put off your shoes from your feet, for the place on which you are standing is holy ground!" Barefooted, I entered the Dome of the Rock. This mosque has been built over the Rock, the rugged gray summit of the Mount which has been understood variously as the headstone of the tomb of Adam, the place where Abraham raised his knife to slay his son, the altar on which the ram was sacrificed in Isaac's stead, the spot from which Muhammad ascended to heaven. This Rock is the symbolic center of the earth; it is both womb and tomb for humankind. It is here, all together, past, present, and future: the Uncarved Block.

"Now I a fourfold vision see . . ."

This is the vision against which the development of humans as sexual beings will emerge. The vision is built up of many layers of experience, with the dust and the stones of each layer finding the way to the surface in the course of time.

Most developmental theories associated with the older paradigm are linear-sequential. They begin, as a rule, with birth and proceed through the stages from childhood and youth to maturity. Theories of personal development regard the zenith of human achievement to be the attainment of life's basic goals and a healthy adaptation to the world as it is, which includes an ability to function constructively within its social and political structures. This is a single vision, centered on personal ego.

A transpersonal developmental theory cannot be linear-sequential. It springs from a world view that is not based on straight-line relationships of antecedent causes and subsequent effects. A cyclical movement would better describe a transpersonal view of developmental process, because this allows us to see stages repeated over and over again, as we experience birth and rebirth more than once and we die many deaths before we die at last. In the repetitions of these psychological realities, however, a different level of consciousness is reached every time. Each cycle incorporates the insights derived from previous experience, so we come to the same vista, but we regard it from another level. The helix, then, would be a better symbol for the unfolding stages of human development in a transpersonal context. The cycle of eternal return is experienced over and over, and on many levels, ascending and descending like the angels in Jacob's dream, going between heaven and earth.

I conceive of the process of human development as moving through four stages: the pre-personal, the personal, the transpersonal, and the nonpersonal. The first three stages belong to human experience and are known primarily through a person's conscious experience.

The pre-personal stage begins at birth and concerns itself with the formation of the personality out of the blending of the raw potential with which the newborn infant is endowed and the experiences to which the child is subjected during the early years.

The personal stage which follows is under the domination of the ego, the functioning personality. By the beginning of puberty, the ego has become the center of a personality that has form and structure, that has arrived at an age of sexual potency and receptivity. The ego will be engaged in making its way in the world in some vocation, with finding a mate, with founding a family and rearing children.

The transpersonal stage begins usually at midlife or beyond, when the ego ambitions have mostly been fulfilled or modified or given up. Then attention is turned to the gathering-in of the fruits of the earlier life and to other goals, other meanings, that extend beyond ego concerns.

About *the fourth stage, the nonpersonal stage,* we can only speculate. There are no words for this stage, since it is precreation and preverbal, so we conceive it in symbols: the Rock, the Temple in Jerusalem, the dark side of the hero's journey, Jonah in the belly of the whale. Here knowledge has not penetrated and only intuition can guide. Nevertheless, much has been written about this place by poets and wise men, children and fools. According to the Judeo-Christian tradition this realm existed when there was nothing but primordial chaos, *tohu v'bohu,* when all was formless and void. This realm has no attributes, yet everything that shall ever be exists within it *in potentia*. It is the mystery of Tao, in which all things have their beginning and end. In our own time, David Bohm has called this realm the implicate order.

Not by studying physics, but through a direct exploration of human consciousness, Jung came to a similar point of view when he wrote of the collective or transpersonal unconscious as the fundamental basis of consciousness. He understood this realm as being a teeming void without explicit content, but with formative elements within it which he called archetypes. The archetypes were active tendencies in the unconscious. They manifested as patterns of human behavior in people's lives when they were in a condition of readiness to experience them. These tendencies to behave in certain ways are experienced as archetypal dynamics, according to Jung, and they give rise to inner models of behavior or archetypal images of how things are. The images usually take their specific content from the particular culture in which the person lives. Consequently, the guiding mythologies of any people contain both universal and local characteristics.

Jung's theory of archetypes and the collective unconscious recently has been given added substance by the work of Rupert Sheldrake, a plant physiologist who has proposed that all life systems are regulated by not only known energy and material factors but also *invisible organizing fields*. These fields have no energy in and of themselves but are causative in that they serve as "blueprints" for form and behavior. Sheldrake calls these invisible matrices "morphogenetic fields," from *morphe*, form, and *genesis*, coming into being. As in Jung's concept of the collective unconscious, Sheldrake's "M-fields" not only act in the formation of behavior, but also are affected by the behavior as practiced over time. Whenever one member of a species learns a new behavior, the causative field for that behavior is changed, however slightly. If the behavior is repeated often enough, it creates a "morphic resonance" which affects the entire species. Then animals in different parts of the world begin simultaneously to behave in new ways, and human beings invent the same new instrument on opposite sides of the globe at about the same time.

What Jung, Bohm, Sheldrake, and others have suggested is another dimension of existence which contributes to human experience, a dimension which is neither heredity, as passed on through the genetic code, nor environment, but a level of reality that stands outside of consciousness and which gives form and direction to the evolution of consciousness. Sheldrake has described the nature of this realm in a way that is comprehensible to the contemporary mind:

"These ideas are extremely unfamiliar and are perhaps easier to grasp with the help of an analogy. Imagine an intelligent and curious person who knows nothing about electricity or electromagnetic radiation. He is shown a television set for the first time.

"He might at first suppose that the set actually contained little people, whose images he saw on the screen. But when he looked inside and found only wires, condensers, transistors, etc., he might adopt the more sophisticated hypothesis that the images somehow arose from complicated interactions among the components of the set. This hypothesis would seem particularly plausible when he found that the images became distorted or disappeared when the components were removed . . .

"If the suggestion were put to him that the images in fact depended upon invisible influences entering the set from far away, he might reject it on the grounds that it was unnecessary and obscurantist. His opinion that nothing came into the set from the outside would be reinforced by the discovery that the set weighed the same switched on or switched off . . .

"This point of view may resemble the conventional approach to biology. By contrast, in terms of analogy the hypothesis of causative formation does not involve a denial of the importance of the wires, transistors, etc. (corresponding to DNA, protein molecules, etc.), but it recognizes in addition the role of influences transmitted from outside the system, the 'transmitters' being past organisms of the same species.

"Genetic changes can affect the inheritance of form or instinct by altering the 'tuning' or by introducing distortions into the 'reception.' But genetic factors cannot by themselves fully account for the inheritance of form and instinct any more than the particular pictures on the screen of a TV set can be explained in terms of its wiring diagram alone."[3]

Sheldrake's work, like Jung's, suggests that only a part of what we know derives from personal experience and personal memory. Both hypothesize a nonpersonal unconscious realm that has the capacity for formation. For Sheldrake, the formative factors are *morphogenetic fields*; for Jung, they are *archetypes*. For Plato they were *ideal forms*. Over the ages, proponents of the perennial philosophy have always pointed to a hidden reality that cannot be grasped through the senses and that lies behind the reality we see and touch and believe in.

The stage of development that centers in the *nonpersonal* realm begins with death and ends with birth. It is the fourth stage, but it may also be understood as the first stage, since it is symbolized by not only the tomb but also the dark womb from which the infant emerges into the world of light. So let us leave it where it stands, as beginning and end.

The Judeo-Christian religious tradition tells us that the dawn of human consciousness came about when the first couple was roughly ejected from the Garden of Eden. We all reenact this painful propulsion from the uterine paradise when we are born. Our psychosexual development begins with the event of conception, when we begin our transit from the darkness of the *nonpersonal* toward the dawning of the *pre-personal* stage. It was the sexual act in which the parents engaged that set in motion the process that will be marked by the gradual unfolding of the child's consciousness. The pre-personal stage may be said to begin at conception (although most psychologists would place this at birth or even later), when the new entity begins its life in secrecy and darkness, establishes itself and grows according to the order which is of its nature, until at last a child is ready to be born.

I see birth not only as a beginning, but also as an ending. It marks the separation from the womb environment, the mythic banishment from Eden, and the passing through the gate guarded by "the cherub with his flaming sword," who prevents the one being ejected from ever returning by that same way. The original wholeness, that sense of being totally enclosed as a part within a whole, must give way to the gradually dawning sense of being apart from the whole. The mother matrix formed the entire universe for the child about to be born. The infant was immersed in nature, which was synonymous with Mother. The physical attachment of the child to its mother is supplanted after birth by psychological attachment and identification with her. Then a kind of psychic fusion with her, or with parental figures, takes place, and an individual psychology is only potentially present.

Psychoanalysis views the early and archaic struggle of the infant toward consciousness as an attempt at conquest of the primitive instinctual id. The process of acculturation requires the recognition of and the taming of the natural instincts, a process which enables an individual to participate in its cultural environment and eventually make an adaptation to it. Perhaps the most profound of the instincts *is* that of sexuality, as Freud thought. He saw it as an urge to life, a response to nature's demands upon the organism to perpetuate itself. For human beings to live together requires the exercise of eros, the capacity for relationship: therefore the element of sexuality is seen to be essential to the quality of relationship. Blind, instinctive behavior in humans defeats the very purpose of social interaction, which is for human beings to come together in productive and fruitful ways. The major early developmental task, then, is to deal with the conflict between the primitive id and the developing ego.

In such a conflict there are, necessarily, many woundings. The immature ego finds protection through exercising an instinct of self-preservation, which seeks to form a cohesive sense of self as differentiated from other, and to discover ways of maintaining integrity while relating to others. The psychoanalyst would hope to facilitate the patient's relinquishing of the archaic past and to increase the ego's capacity to adapt to the rigorous demands life makes upon a person who wants to exist and succeed in the world as it is. Ego psychologists move from a preoccupation with the conflicts between the ego and the id to the development of the ego itself. They see the interplay of instinct and experience during the complex series of maturing processes as enabling the young ego to gain a sense of coherence and personal power. Behaviorists deal with particular behaviors that interfere with a successful mature adaptation, and concentrate on modifying or controlling those behaviors. The work of cognitive-developmental psychologists enables people to form expectations of how and when the tasks of the pre-personal stage will be negotiated, and the processes through which the individual will pass on the way to coming to a level of ego development associated with maturity.

These traditional psychological approaches deal with the movement of individuals from the pre-personal stage—which is basically pre-egoic, prelogical, natural and instinctive, to the personal, or ego, stage—which is rational, acculturated, and adaptive. In the course of this development, science is to be regarded as holding the potential solutions to all problems, and any attachments to mystery and magic are discouraged. Religion could survive if it preached a social gospel and functioned to aid adaptation and to further human relationships. But when religion was perceived as a nonrational system that could support human weakness, or that had no discernible practical purpose, its value was depreciated.

As a counterpoint to these psychologies, we saw how, in the sixties and early seventies, so many young people who were approaching the time when they should have achieved a well-adapted ego, turned or re-turned to the nonrational dimension of life. Instead of going back to their traditional religions, they embraced all kinds of new religions that were springing up, many with a distinctly cultist flavor, in which blind adoration of a "spiritual teacher" and blind obedience were expected. Others found something psychology had not provided, by rediscovering ancient traditional religions of the East. Still others sought a personal experience of transformation through the use of mind-altering drugs, or through other means of moving from one to another level of perception. On all these pathways walked the seekers, and each was attracted by the hope for something that the mainstream culture did not provide on the way from the pre-egoic stage of childhood (or a level of consciousness resembling that of childhood) to the mature stage of ego dominance. They were dimly aware at first, and more clearly aware later on, of the possibility of transcending the ego stage, to find another level of consciousness. This would lead them toward new perceptions and finally toward a new world view. Although this view often was not consonant with what was being discovered in the burgeoning fields of science, it nevertheless made its contribution. The counterpoint, or countercultural position, supported people in breaking through boundaries of their own thoughts, to use imagination in ways that they had not been free to attempt before.

I do not mean to imply that creative people have not always broken through the limits of reason and allowed their fantasies to carry them into the vast unknown, for this has been the experience of some individuals. The new scrambling-up of consciousness was unique in that it involved so large a portion of the population of young people moving toward the height of their intellectual and energetic capacities, and sent them off in directions of which their parents had never even dreamed. Some returned with precious ores, to be refined in a more stable setting, some were burned out in the process, and some never returned at all.

Traditional psychologies, which were still firmly entrenched in the universities and in the American Psychological Association in the sixties and seventies, and the "counter-culture" movements, during the same years, are two positions that represent, in the extreme, two world views which are important for our consideration here. Ken Wilber, a leading theoretician in the field of transpersonal psychology, has delineated these world views and analyzed the nature of the relationship between them. They are particularly important in the consideration of the directions that sexuality has taken, because these are directly related to the world views out of which they have come. The position Wilber characterizes as world view one (WV-1) is the one from which the traditional psychologies come. The major focus of interest starts with the prepersonal archaic stage of infancy and proceeds toward the development of a well-established ego. World view two (WV-2) begins where the first world view left off, with the assumptions that the ego can and must be transcended, and that there are higher values than those of the ego, from which the ego has been alienated, and which must be reclaimed.

Wilber writes: "World view one (WV-1) sees development moving from a personal source in nature, through a series of intermediate advances, to a culmination in the 'high point' of evolution, that of human rationality. It recognizes no higher source or goal of development, and it vehemently denies the necessity of even mentioning such supposedly 'higher' levels. Man is a rational being, and rationality is all that is necessary to comprehend and order the cosmos. It looks very much like science.

"WV-2, on the other hand, sees development moving *from* a spiritual source ('in heaven') to a culmination in a 'low point' of alienation, that of a sinful humanity or of the individual and personal ego. History is thus the history of a falling down, not a moving up, and mankind (or personal ego) is at the *end* of the fall . . . It looks a lot like religion."[4]

Wilber describes WV-1 as a linear progression from the preegoic (pre-personal) phase to the ego (personal) stage, and WV-2 as a linear progression from the ego stage to the trans-egoic (transpersonal) stage. He sees the two lines of development as mutually exclusive, although they are often confused, as will be explained later. Wilber states that both of these world views are partially correct and partially in error. WV-1 is correct in maintaining that the pre-personal and irrational component of our lives did indeed precede the rational both in individual lives and in the course of human evolution, and that the general evolutionary trend is from the lower to the higher, from the simpler to the more complex. WV-1 is wrong, however, in its denial of the transpersonal dimension and its unwillingness to recognize that there can be and indeed has been a falling-away from a primal union with Spirit, the sacredness of life. WV-2 is correct in insisting on the transpersonal component of the cosmos and the sense that we are almost all in some sense alienated from an identity with Spirit, the sacral aspect of our lives. But WV-2 errs when it depreciates the value of the ego as an organ of perception and of consciousness, and when it blames the ego for having separated itself from its earlier identification with the undifferentiated wholeness of the womb-paradise-mother-matrix-mythic dimension of existence. WV-2 is wrong also, when it elevates that primordial Garden to a higher state than that of the condition of consciousness, in which we now live most of our waking lives, and to which we were brought by man's first disobedience.

Wilber calls attention to the "pre/trans fallacy" that exists in these views, because both world views are part true and part false. They are true when dealing with the portion of human development upon which they have concentrated their attention, and false in their devaluation of the importance of the opposite position. He makes a clear distinction between primitive collective material and transpersonal collective material. *Primitive collective material* comes from an earlier evolutionary stage and has much to do with myth, magic, superstition, and identification with and dependence upon power objects or persons representing them. *Transpersonal collective material* is based upon a wider understanding of the nature of universal processes, and an attempt to understand how we can live harmoniously with them (instead of being dominated by them). So evolutionary progression moves from the pre-personal to the personal to the transpersonal stage. He suggests that there may be a counter-movement, from the transpersonal toward the pre-personal, but he does not seem to see this involution as an integral and necessary aspect of evolution, in its widest sense. He rejects Hegel's idea that Nature (the pre-personal) is simply "slumbering Spirit" or "God in his otherness," and that our life-task is the return of Spirit to Spirit through the overcoming of self-alienation. Yet Hegel, in his recognition that Spirit is always present, and that, whether we recognize it or not, it operates in us and through us, suggests that the involutional phase is more important than Wilber is willing to admit. Wilber has limited his concept of the involutional stage to "simply the phenomenon of regression." Consequently, he finds himself in a view of evolution which is basically linear, the process moving forward from the pre-personal to the personal to the transpersonal, for the most part, with occasional regressions when the transpersonal dimension becomes confused with the pre-personal dimension.

Wilber takes Jung to task for sometimes failing to distinguish the archaic primitive stage from the ideal stage, where human beings find themselves in harmony with nature but more consciously so, than in the earlier oneness with nature. Perhaps one reason for Jung's reluctance to differentiate the end, or goal, of human development from its beginning, is that Jung does not view the process as linear but, rather, as circular or, better yet, helical, with alternation between progression and regression, between evolution and involution as an essential feature of the life-cycle. One always comes back to the same view, but with increasing consciousness and from a different level. Jung teaches that in the beginning of life the ego exists within the larger Self only *in potentia*. Gradually the ego begins to differentiate from the "other" and to become aware of its own identity; however, *at all times* there remain portions of the personality that are not conscious. In the growth process, the ego's potentialities are gradually being actualized but, at the same time, much is being rejected from consciousness. Residues of the rejection are carried along as archaic baggage into the more advanced stages of psychological development, as one moves toward awareness of what Jung called the undiscovered Self, and what Hegel called Spirit. Ever-present, even though not recognized, the psyche knows the Self on a deep level, even before one reaches the most primitive stage of awareness. This essential Self is the wholeness that exists before any differentiation occurs. It may be understood as the universal wholeness out of which all life evolved, or it may be understood in terms of individual awareness of an earlier stage of oceanic oneness which is not ordinarily accessible to memory. Jung had acknowledged this presence in the inscription he had carved over the doorway to his home in Küsnacht, *Vocatus atque non vocatus, Deus aderit*, Called or not called, God will be there.

Jung's position on the relationship of the ego to the transpersonal dimension of consciousness bears directly upon our attempt to re-vision sexuality. He saw sexuality as an essential part of the life-cycle of individuals, but also as an important aspect of human evolution. Of course, we can say that there is nothing new about this. People have always looked at sexuality as an important consideration for every individual, and people have talked about sexuality in the broad terms of biological, sociological, and ecological trends. What Jung's work suggested, which had not found its way into either scholarly or general interest commentaries, is that it is important to consider our personal sexual behavior in the context of the transpersonal implications that it will have. We begin our life without ego, and we surrender the ego at the end of our life. But during our conscious hours we concern ourselves mostly with matters relating to the development of the ego—how the ego fares and how it achieves its wants or needs. The pre-personal stage is addressed to the acquisition of a strong and effective ego. The personal stage is spent in the exercise of this ego so as to form and shape the environment, even while it is being formed and shaped by it. The ego stage is the one in which the most active sexuality is experienced. The ego or personal stage, as Jung would see it, is not stable within itself. It partakes of both the archaic past, which has predisposed it to behave in specific ways, and the vision of wholeness toward which it is purposively drawn. It wavers back and forth between these two, seeking a connection with the Self— which is the beginning and the end, the darkness from which the dawn emerges and the darkness into which the twilight fades.

The way in which Jung conceptualized the stages of life would take into account Wilber's "pre/trans fallacy" and would even expand the concepts of pre-personal and transpersonal. Jung's stages of childhood, youth, and maturity, and later maturity into old age may correspond in some degree to the pre-personal, personal, and transpersonal stages of Wilber. Jung believed that early childhood and extreme old age extend beyond these categories. Although utterly different, they have one thing in common, submersion in unconscious psychic happenings. The difference here between Wilber and Jung is that Jung recognizes the involutional character of extreme old age, which is the resolution of the transpersonal dimension. In youth we may have an inkling of it, in maturity and old age we enter into it, and in extreme old age we lose ourselves, which is to say we lose our egos, to it. This is the completion of the cycle and the beginning of a new cycle.

This is not to say that the transpersonal dimension is altogether inaccessible earlier in life. The child is capable of regarding the world with awe and wonder. The youth may experience limitless passion in devotion to a cause or to a lover. The young adult may follow a spiritual quest and encounter numinous visions along the way. But in the course of the development from the pre-personal to the personal stage the view is necessarily limited. It is like climbing a mountain. Before the summit has been reached, it is not possible to see over to the valley on the other side. So one looks back at the earth below, which symbolizes the nonpersonal past. It has a sacredness about it, for it is, in fact, the same earth that is on the other side; yet it is seen in its archaic aspect—as myth and legend and the religion of the fathers. When the personal stage is mastered, it is as though a crest had been reached, and now the person can look beyond into the not-yet-known. If the earlier stage entailed the tearing away from the womb (Egypt), the ego now looks forward to exploring new territory (the Promised Land).

This pilgrimage entails a return to the Rock, which is at once the undifferentiated source and the top of the Holy Mountain, the City *in potentia*. The building of the City is, in part, an ego task. It is built around the Self—symbolized by the Rock. The person's sense of cohesiveness grows more extensive and complex with time, as does a city. Many of the structures of an earlier time fall into ruins or are broken down in battle, but their substance is not lost. It forms the rubble upon which the new construction is built, as in the ancient city. At the end of the journey one stands inside the Dome of the Rock, in the center of Jerusalem. So the Rock and Jerusalem are the beginning and the end of the cycle. Under the great Rock, as legend tells us, the body of Adam lies buried. Seeds from the Tree of Life rest upon his eyelids, placed there by his son Seth, his first son born outside of the Garden. Adam's tarnished innocence is a mark on the Uncarved Block. From the Mount the pilgrims wander through the labyrinthine ways of the Holy City. Not far away, although it may take a lifetime to get there, is the Street of Sorrows. There stands the Church of the Holy Sepulchre, built upon the spot where Christ is believed to have died on the cross. Here the ego, achieved through so much difficulty, is at last surrendered. Where one man died alone, there now stands a church frequented by many peoples. Each of several denominations controls its designated part of the church. Pilgrims offer their prayers in a multitude of languages.

Both the Rock and the City represent unity. The first is an undifferentiated wholeness, while the second is a well-articulated and complex structure in which all the interrelated parts radiate out from the center and form a single mandala. Here disparate peoples live together, not always without conflict, but they survive; and the City survives, and its evolution continues.

It is with this sense of permanence and flux as the essence of being that I would turn to an examination of ourselves, as pilgrims on the evolutionary way. What is there in our natures that is as permanent and predictable as the Rock? What in us is constructed like the City, ever changing, ever growing, reflecting what has gone before and planning for the future?

10

Re-membering and For-getting

The metaphor of Jerusalem could be carried further. Let the Rock, which was there in the beginning, represent the archetypal characteristics that derive from our genetic heritage and the evolving morphogenetic fields. These comprise the basic patterns of our psychic structures. The City represents that which is built upon the Rock, the product of all we learn in our interactions in the world. The City stands as the acculturated part of ourselves. The Rock is the fundament, relatively fixed and stable; it is the essence of our being. The City is ever-changing, the expression of our becoming.

What if our explorations into the complex nature of cognition could be reduced to these two absurdly simple questions:

Is it possible that I came into the world knowing nothing?

Is it possible that I came into the world bringing with me the seeds of all knowledge?

The City perspective implies the first question—that at the start there was nothing of significance in consciousness; that we began life as a *tabula rasa* upon which events and experiences would inscribe their images and impose their expectations. The Rock perspective implies that people begin their lives as complex organisms, systems teeming with potentials to feel, to respond, and to behave in ways that to a considerable degree have been predetermined by the process of natural selection and the accumulated experience of the species during a long evolutionary period that still continues.

In recent years, the position that we are formed and shaped primarily by events and conditions that impact upon us in our life-time has been favored over the alternative view. This has been particularly true in the United States, which declared its indepen-dence in the same breath as it proclaimed its egalitarian ethic: "We hold these truths to be self-evident, that all men are created equal, that they are endowed by their Creator with certain una-lienable Rights, that among these are Life, Liberty and the Pur-suit of Happiness." The belief in the equality of all men has not only been consistently supported by the government of the United States, but the concept of "all men" has been enlarged since the initial Declaration to allow slaves to be freed and women to vote. If people differed among themselves in their abili-ties and achievements, much of the responsibility for this was placed at the doorstep of the environment. It was poverty, or lack of parental care, or poor education, or other insufficiencies in the environment that accounted for the failures of so many people to measure up to the norms of society. Ethics and morals, right be-havior and appropriate exercise of sexuality, could be achieved by attending to the processes of early rearing and education, and set-ting up social structures in which people could grow and flourish. For getting what you deserve in this world, it would be necessary to have a fair chance at a good education and a generally facilitat-ing environment.

There is no way in which I would minimize the importance of an enabling environment in shaping the character of developing human beings. We learn to come to terms with our natural en-dowments in socially and sexually acceptable ways and, if we are guided constructively, we are likely to flower. But, it seems to me, we can only determine how to carry out this guidance, how to ed-ucate and serve as models for the succeeding generation, if we have some idea of the natural psychophysiological structures that come under our influence. Biologists have long been studying, classifying, and describing the multitude of life-forms. Ethologists have been particularly interested in comparing the behaviors of different animal species, including the behavior of human beings. Sociologists concern themselves with the interactions of individ-uals in group situations, and with the impact of groups upon their members. Psychobiologists, in their attempts to understand the basis for human consciousness and human behavior, look to the neural structure and organization of the brain itself. Physicists and biologists agree that brain research is the ultimate intellectual challenge for the last two decades of the twentieth century. The brain/mind (and at this point it is not necessary to make a distinction between the two) possesses the uniquely human capacity for self-reflection and for self-regulation as the human organism adapts to an environment and/or alters that environment to meet its needs. The special qualities of human consciousness as compared with the consciousness of other species is that human beings are capable of shaping the world at the same time that they are being shaped by it, and that they are able to observe and re-member the process as well.

Sociobiology deals with human beings as the evolutionary outcome of natural selection, and with the social systems they construct as being directly related to their genetic endowments. Sociobiologists place particular emphasis on the red thread of instinctive behavior as a determinant of culture, a position which is obviously at odds with the psychologies that look to learning as the major determinant of behavior. We know that human development occurs in the process of the interaction of genetic and environmental factors. When we examine the factors that contribute to human development we are struck by their complexity and the real impossibility of sorting out what can be ascribed to nature and what to nurture. As a culture, we tend to preach the importance of the environment in providing favorable conditions for psychosexual development, even while as individuals we practice the exercise of the instinctive components of our nature, with little awareness of the implications of what we are doing. Furthermore, in recent years we have apparently been successful in outwitting the evolutionary plan of natural selection. We have decreased the rate of infant mortality; we have increased the average life-span. We have learned how to avoid the natural consequences of sexual intercourse. We have learned how to use artificial insemination to impregnate a woman whose natural mate is unable to do this, or who has no sexual partner, and we have managed to find surrogate wombs which can carry a pregnancy when a woman is unable to bear a child. Consequently we no longer need to rely on natural selection to solve the problems of a decaying species. Why, then, should we be dismayed to discover that we may have to use our brains to find ways to improve the human race other than the methods imposed by the ordering processes in this universe as described by Charles Darwin? We come face to face with the crucial questions: Can the brain understand itself, and can it understand the body of which it is, of course, an integral part? The answers are yet to be found, but the provisional conclusion must be that we can only continue to make the attempt. Sexuality is a good area with which to begin because, after all, the survival of the species depends upon this.

Sexuality comes into focus as one of the most important determinants of how human beings will fare in the eternal struggle between that intrinsic nature which is more or less genetically ordained, and the other impulses which lead us toward controlling and shaping our natural instincts in favor of the development of culture and society. Sociobiologist Edward O. Wilson begins a discussion of sex and society with the following quite surprising statement: "Sex is an antisocial force in evolution. Bonds are formed between individuals in spite of sex and not because of it. Perfect societies, if we can be so bold as to define them as societies that lack conflict and possess the highest degree of altruism and coordination, are most likely to evolve where all of the members are genetically identical. When sexual reproduction is introduced, members of the group become genetically dissimilar. Parents and offspring are separated by at least a one-half reduction of genes shared through common descent and mates by even more. The inevitable result is a conflict of interest."[1]

Wilson is observing and describing the wide range of living organisms, including those which reproduce themselves asexually, with each of the offspring being like the parent, as well as those which reproduce through the mating of the male and female of the species. The fact that there are two sexes allows for a diversity among offspring, a diversity which increases in geometric proportions as every generation adds its new combinations to the genetic pool. This wide variation within the species produces differences in ability to survive within the native environment. Those who are best fit to survive, that is, those whose genetic endowments are most effective in the struggle against external influence, are selected out to survive. As these then reproduce, they give birth to strains that are more fit, while those which are less fit are eliminated. Thus the entire character of the species undergoes evolutionary changes in the process of adaptation.

What, then, is fitness? Nature would determine this as consisting of the capacity to survive and the capacity to reproduce. These two objectives, however, are often at odds with each other. Sexual reproduction entails actively pursuing instinctive behavior, and this involves a kind of competitiveness for mates which can be extremely aggressive and self-serving. It may also be destructive to the weaker individual. On the other hand, survival often depends on cooperation and altruism. Bonding is more related to survival needs and hence is conserving, while sexuality serves the diversity that evolution requires to ensure development, dynamism, and change. Perhaps this helps to explain in part why sex and marriage are often incompatible!

According to sociobiologists, human courtship is based on the same or similar instincts as the courtship behavior of many other animals. This statement would have been self-evident some years ago, before the advent of sexual technology. But now that we have contraceptives, sexual behavior does not automatically put the woman at the risk of bearing a child; she can choose not to do so, if that is her wish. Disposable napkins and tampons mean that the woman does not have to set limitations on her regular activities and contacts during her menses, as in some earlier cultures. Now she can engage in almost all her usual behaviors, including sexual intercourse, at any time. The advent of nursing bottles means that infants are not necessarily dependent upon the presence of their mothers in order to ensure their nourishment and care—which frees mothers of babies for a wider choice of activities either at home or away from their homes. This calls into question whether the sociobiologists are correct in their assumption that men and women are likely to maintain the same courtship behaviors as they used before these technological advances, and whether humans retain their similarity to other animals in the manner of their selection of sexual partners.

I was pondering this question after having read Wilson, when I came upon a feature article in a Sunday newspaper. The subject was the current scene at the most popular of the dating bars in the city of Chicago. I found myself comparing Wilson's statements about the breeding habits of birds with the newspaper reporter's observations of how supposedly sophisticated and knowledgeable men and women behave in these social watering places.

According to Wilson: *"The displays of male birds are ordinarily directed at both males and females, and sexual selection is based as much on the territorial exclusion of rival males as on competition for the attention of potential mates . . . The males are highly variable in color and display frenetically on individual territories that are grouped tightly together in a communal area."*

The Chicago *Tribune*: The atmosphere is at its best when it is extremely crowded; usually you have to elbow your way in. The men in the better bars are impeccably dressed, with a certain amount of flamboyance, a jacket of excellent cut and fine material, a delicately colored shirt set off by a bright but tasteful silk tie, gold cufflinks, well-tailored slacks in the latest fashion, and so on. They walk about, surveying the entire room, sizing up their competition as well as the women.

"Females wander singly or in groups from territory to territory, expressing their willingness to mate by crouching."

Women walk up and often seat themselves at the bar and lean over it, while the men come up from behind to talk to them.

"The sex that courts, ordinarily the male, plans to invest less reproductive effort in the offspring. What it offers to the female is chiefly evidence that it is fully normal and physiologically fit. But this warranty consists of only a brief performance, so that strong selective pressures exist for less fit individuals to present a false image. The courted sex, usually the female, will therefore find it strongly advantageous to distinguish the really fit from the pretended fit. Consequently, there will be a strong tendency for the courted sex to develop coyness. That is, its responses will be hesitant and cautious in a way that evokes still more displays and makes correct discrimination easier."

The man who approaches a woman will utilize any one of a number of prepared lines, and he will persist in trying to flatter her in order to persuade her to go home with him. The woman tends to tease and extend the conversations as long as possible, so that she can get some idea of what the man may have to offer. She finds out what he does for a living, where he comes from, and as much as she can about his income and family background. She tries to see through his games to decide if she really wants him.

"Two distinct processes were judged to be of about equal importance in the competition [for sexual partners]. To use Darwin's own words, the distinction is between 'the power to charm the females' and 'the power to conquer other males in battle.'"

Women are interested in men who appear especially attractive, who approach them with a certain amount of gentleness, and who openly admire them. But the women also expect some toughness from the men. A man who wants to connect with a woman ought to be able to know whom he wants and to push aside other men if he has to, to get to her, and then to protect her from the advances of other men.

I could continue the comparison of the courting behavior of birds and other animals with the behavior of human beings in the meet markets of Chicago, but my point is clear: What we believe we do as autonomous and liberated individuals may to a very large degree be an expression of our evolutionary heritage, relatively uncontaminated by all that we have learned in the developmental process. Our tendencies to develop along certain lines, and our capacities for learning certain forms of behavior and not others, are both potentiated and limited by the "program" which is inherent in our nature, all the way back to the cellular level. This "program" does not determine actions *per se*, but it does determine the potential for becoming. It seems to me that the basic thrust of our lives is toward the actualizing of these potentials.

As we attempt to re-vision sexuality from a transpersonal perspective, it seems vital to emphasize the evolutionary character of human behavior and, most significantly, of sexual behavior. The relations between the two sexes are based upon instincts that are primarily absent from consciousness. These instincts do not belong exclusively to the realm of the personal unconscious but to the collective unconscious as well, stemming as they do from residues of archaic and even prehuman social interactions. While every society and every generation provides forms through which these instincts may find "appropriate" expression, the basic instincts remain essentially intact and effective as motivating forces in human behavior. As tendencies to behave, these instincts appear in consciousness in the form of "ideas," "wishes," "thoughts," or "concepts." All the same, they arise out of the collective or transpersonal unconscious, as Jung said, and they function as structural patterns which act to give form to the contents of consciousness.

The universal patterns that lie behind our perceptions are archetypal in nature. Yet only individual persons can perceive the larger context in which they are embedded. Our images are manifestations of archetypal material, which comes to us through the lens of our own consciousness and which we claim as objects of our awareness. Every image acquires a subjective cast. Whatever else it may be, what we perceive is, at least in part, the product of something that occurs within a single human brain. We do not see the thing itself; we do not see the light waves that reach the retina. We only see our subjective image of it. This brings us back to the earlier question: Can the brain understand itself? We have already come a long way in this direction, even by recognizing that the brain is an agent of transformation which actively transforms impulses it receives from outside itself into perceptions that it is able to experience and transmit to the rest of the body.

Here re-visioning becomes necessary in order to transcend the familiar subject/object dichotomy. This requires a leap of faith. It is not so easy to get beyond the distinction between what is in me (my subjective perception) and what is outside of me (the objective world), and to become aware that there is only one world with no dividing line between what is subjective and what is objective. I am in it, thus I am a part of it; it is in me, thus it is a part of me. But is there really a boundary between myself and it? I know what "I" am and where I leave off and the rest of the universe begins. At least I "know" it on one level. But if I allow my consciousness to transcend the immediate perceptions accorded me by my senses, and to flow through my own skin, I find it not impossible to re-vision myself in a new context.

The re-visioning begins with the knowledge that we are limited by our preconceptions only when we take our images as "real." We need to re-member that we are part and parcel of the totality that consists of ourselves enmeshed in the intricate webbing of the functionally related universe, as Blake reminded us:

> How do you know but ev'ry Bird that cuts the airy way,
> Is an immense world of delight, clos'd by your senses five?[2]

For-getting with child, we re-member the primary union of male and female. As woman and man become one in a moment of sexual meeting, so male and female cells join in conception and become one also. How much each cell remembers we do not know, but it is clear that, at the very least, the potential for consciousness is present in the moment of conception. When does consciousness begin? When does life begin? These questions acquire new meaning as we re-vision sexuality. The event of conception is transformative. It transforms a generalized life process into an incipient individual life-form. What could not occur naturally when human beings were separate, now becomes possible through sexual union. Out of this union something may be generated that will someday become a separate human being, if that is to be its destiny.

Conception, then, is as good a place as any to begin to re-vision sexuality as a developmental process—although arguments could be made for beginning at almost any other moment in the life-cycle: at birth, with the infantile sexual feelings, with a child's learning about sex and sexuality, with puberty's sexual changes, with sexual feelings that lead to courtship, with all that has been said and written about mature sexuality, or with any of the unlimited variations on sexual patterns that our society has come to regard as human. Beginning with the product of conception is consonant with seeing the person from a systems view.[3] The world of the cell is embedded in the world of its surroundings, the receiving and nurturing uterus, and that uterine system in the system of the mother's being, which itself is in a larger setting, and so on. Not even the smallest organism exists in and of itself; it is always a part of a larger world which exists within a still larger universe. Each organic unit is also a system with subsystems within it, and all are related through dynamic interactions.

Is it possible to re-member what we have forgotten about our uterine existences before we were born? I have cited some evidence that suggests that it is. These memories belong to a level of consciousness that is extraordinary. Because we do not easily accept that there may be a reality beyond the familiar one, we are apt to dismiss the possibility that there could be memories of a time before childhood, memories of birth and beyond birth, and even before conception.

The Australian aborigines, who are not so informed as we are in recognizing the limits of consciousness, tell stories of the time before time, the Dreaming, as they call it. They comprehend the life principle as *spirit*. Neither is it born nor does it die. Spirit is ever present to them, appearing when the time is right. A Worora elder of the Kimberley people talks of the birth of his little daughter and says:

> In its own Wunger* place
> A spirit waits for birth
> Today, I saw who the child really is—
> That is how a man
> Learns to know his child.
>
> Namaaraalee** made him,
> No one else,
> No one.
> But not all things are straight
> in this day.
>
> As I looked at the water
> of Bundaalunaa
> She appeared to me:
> I understood suddenly
> The life in our baby—
> Her name is Dragon Fly.[4]

> * *Wunger means Dreaming/spirit.*
> ** *Namaaraalee is a Wandjina spirit.*

Every Australian aboriginal child can tell of the Dreamtime

when the parents found or dreamed of the spirit totem that would be born in the child. The stories go like these:

In the Dreamtime the fish used to go round and round, but one fish broke out and as he was flapping along he broke up the bank. That is how the Sale River came to be. One day when Gertie Garndur's father and mother happened to be out fishing, a spirit child, who was Gertie, speared her father's eye. He cried out that a fish had speared his eye, and went to lie down in the camp. The spirit child came into his dreams and said, "Father, it was I who hit your eye and my name is *Jarnanya,* which means fish." *Jarnanya* (Gertie) was born in Bugudu . . .

Winani, May's spirit name, means the shadow of the cliff. May's father and mother were living at a place called Wundulle, which is the biggest spirit water. One day her father, while drinking, happened to see a shadow reflecting in the water. When he saw the reflection of the stone in the water, he could see a child. When he looked again she wasn't there anymore. He knew it was a spirit child. Whenever parents, either the mother or the father, see a spirit child, they don't tell anyone for a month, until the mother is pregnant. When they had gone home, Winani's father dreamed that the child had come back and said, "It's me, Daddy, the spirit child." So *Winani* was born near Pantijan . . .

This story is from a long time ago, back in our Ancestors' time at Kunmunya. The spirits had dug the roots of the grape, and where the vines were pulled out the seawater rushed in and started a waterfall. It is spirit water. Now it happened that when the aboriginals were living there, Jack Wherra's parents dug for grape roots and got plenty. They cooked them and peeled them and after they had eaten plenty of the roots they slept. His parents dreamed that a big peeled grape root was lying down and at the end of the grape root they heard the spirit child say, "It is I, Jack Wherra." They both kept it in mind until the mother became pregnant. *Wherra,* Jack's aboriginal name, means peel.[5]

With these as introduction, perhaps the tales re-membered by people today will not seem stranger than those recounted by the outspokenly primitive folk of the antipodes.

A young pregnant woman was telling me about a curious happening. Several months ago, she and her husband had been out house hunting, since they wanted to have a larger place when the baby would be born. They looked at many places, and at last there was one to which the wife was particularly drawn. Not that this house was more beautiful or better priced than the others, but it had a special charm, a great attraction for her. Because of this, the couple bought the house and moved in. Shortly thereafter the woman's parents came to visit from the distant city where they were now living. When the parents arrived they found, to their amazement, that this was the very house in which they had lived when they were first married, years before the daughter, who now lived there, had been conceived.

Coincidence? Yes, that is one way of explaining it. Or, perhaps, one way of explaining it away. But I cannot totally disregard the sense I had, while the woman was speaking, of a great deal of energy behind her words. I could not help but ask myself: How much do the cells remember?

"Re-member." Put the members, the parts, together again into their totality. Is consciousness something like a huge jigsaw puzzle we work on, gathering and arranging bits and pieces and putting them together into coherent sections that progressively approach a sense of the whole? If that were so, given enough time and patience, I could imagine that it might be possible to re-member, to put back together again the entire fabric of our lives, and even, eventually, the history of the lives of the cells that at any moment constitute our bodies. In my experience as an analyst, I have many times been present at re-memberings, when individuals have been able, in the process of highly focused attentiveness to inner process, to bring up details of the past which had been long forgotten, if, indeed, they had ever been in consciousness. Later some of these experiences were validated, as in the case of the young woman with her new house.

Sometimes we see a place in dreams that looks awesomely familiar. I had such an experience once, when I was living in Switzerland. I dreamed of driving through an Italian village. The hills and winding streets were vivid and every building stood out in its characteristic centuries-old architecture complete with narrow windows and turrets. I saw the local church with tiled roof and its campanile on one side of the town square. A few months later I made my first trip to Italy. We were driving in our Volkswagen, and all of a sudden I was there, in that very place. Every detail was as I had recalled from my dream.

Years later I told my mother about this. "It's very curious," she said, "and I don't believe there's a thing in it, but did you know that one of your ancestors on my father's side was Chief Rabbi of Abruzzi?" Remembering this incident just now, I got out my atlas and turned to a map of Italy. I found no city of Abruzzi listed, so I looked for the cities through which we were traveling at that time. They were clustered in an area due east of Rome and across the Apennines. The district, I discovered to my amazement, was called Abruzzi.

Dreams come in their own time, when they will, and often we have the sense that what we re-member of them are only fragments of longer and more elaborate narratives. Nevertheless, they offer glimpses into realms beyond consciousness, revealing the presence of a matrix from which consciousness flows. Jung's own dreams and those of his patients showed him the collective nature of the unconscious, the racial memory of a phylogenetic past. Bits and pieces float into consciousness, sometimes in the form of instinctual desires and sometimes in the experiences of ancient mythic forms. Jung found other sources of this archaic, nonpersonal material in the visions and hallucinations of his psychotic patients. These led him to investigate ancient and esoteric writings in order to uncover parallels in human experience. Jung perceived a tangled skein running through the psyche and attempted to untangle it. Yet he had to take it as it came, on its own terms. He understood this material as products of the mind, or soul, or spirit, and he dealt with it on those levels. "Just as the body bears the traces of its phylogenetic development, so also does the human mind," he wrote. "Hence there is nothing surprising about the possibility that the figurative language of dreams is a survival from an archaic mode of thought."[6] Jung's observations provided a conceptual framework for a psychology of the unconscious. But it was not until the discovery of new and more direct routes to the unconscious that other investigators could systematically explore certain awesome mysteries of our unre-membered lives.

11

Awareness Between Conception and Birth

The course of prenatal development is being monitored and studied in greater detail and with greater precision than ever before, due to new instrumentation and advanced methods of research. We now have objective measures which can inform us on such questions as whether birth defects or inherited diseases are present, what is the sex of the child, and how the course of development is proceeding. About the subjective experience of the fetus, what the fetus is feeling, we have much less information, since it has little opportunity to express itself. If, however, we can make the assumption that the successive transformations that the fetus undergoes make impressions and contribute to something we might call the *experiences* of prenatal life, then it is possible that through memory regression we might be able to trace the experiential path backward in time to the time before birth. Birth is, after all, not the beginning of life but rather a rite of passage in a life that has already begun.

That we can, and probably do, remember the experiences between conception and birth, given the necessary conditions, has been demonstrated by Stanislav Grof in comprehensive reports of his pioneering research studies over a period of more than twenty years. Dr. Grof's observations were based upon experiences triggered by the experimental use of LSD, which he describes as "an unspecific chemical amplifier."[1] The initial decade of research with LSD began in Prague, Czechoslovakia, where the drug was freely available to qualified professionals as an experimental and therapeutic agent. Specialized training and supervised experience was required for each therapist or research worker to be licensed to use the drug. The general public knew almost nothing about psychedelic drugs in the late fifties, since reports on the research were published almost exclusively in scientific journals. When Grof left Europe to pursue his research in the United States, Prague had no black market traffic in psychedelics and no non-medical use of them.

When he arrived in the United States in 1967, Grof suddenly found himself in the midst of the national hysteria that had been generated by widespread self-experimentation with illegal psyche-delic substances on university campuses and in the drug subcul-tures of hippie communities. Newspapers were filled with sensa-tionalist stories about psychotic breaks, suicides, murders, and changes in personality, which were attributed to the use of LSD. Less frequently reported was the influence of the psychedelic movement on the releasing of creativity and the freeing of creative people to develop new forms in the graphic arts, poetry, music, theater, television, and in designing more aesthetic life-patterns, and still less on its therapeutic value in certain illnesses. The pow-erful drug had created a new opening to the depths of what Jung had called "the collective or transpersonal unconscious." The sub-stance cleansed the doors of perception, and what emerged to view was awesome. Not everyone had the psychological consti-tution to contain the powerful stimuli that could assail the sen-sibilities after the drug was ingested. It was as though all we had read and heard and dreamed of about the brilliant worlds of the unconscious, with all their glowing light and color, fantastic shapes and terrifying monsters, we could now *experience* in their full intensity in every part of our being, and especially bodily. No longer a pure "psychic" experience, this world became a total ex-perience in which every fiber of every nerve and every capacity of awareness were engaged in a world beyond the world we know.

And people were playing with it! It was just as Albert Hofmann had predicted. Unprepared, uninitiated, unwilling to take the time and effort to reflect seriously upon what unfolded before their inner eyes, many people found themselves overwhelmed by the potency of the psychological material that issued forth. There is little wonder that legislation was demanded and passed to suppress the availability of the drug. But what unfortunately resulted was that the legislation proved quite ineffective for suppressing the drug's nonmedical use, while it succeeded in reducing legitimate LSD research to a bare minimum. Just at the time when new scientific information about the drug and its effects was most needed, it became nearly impossible to secure money for the study of psychedelic substances. There were no longer funds or facilities available to train the many psychiatrists and psychologists who were being called upon daily to deal with people who had fallen into dangerous states after using these drugs and who required emergency treatment.

Recognizing the need for placing information on LSD research before the professional people who were needed to deal with the drug-related problems, Grof decided to devote himself to presenting the findings based on the research he had already done. In a series of five volumes he would summarize the basic information about LSD, focus on the "cartography of inner space," and deal with various aspects of LSD research, psychotherapy, and the spiritual dimensions of the LSD experience.

The first of these books, *Realms of the Human Unconscious*, is particularly important in that it brings a new dimension to the study of sexuality. This new dimension is a *subjective view of our individual beginnings*. Were this to consist of a look into life in the womb through individual views of intrauterine existence, this would have been sufficient; but there was much more. Grof presented an amplification of the infant's early core experiences around the birth process, complete with the visual, affective, and bodily involvement that were, and often remain, locked into these experiences.

For the most part, Grof's work in Czechoslovakia had been *psycholytic* therapy. *Psycholytic* derives from *psyche* and *lysis*, and means the releasing and dissolution of tensions and conflicts that are psychological in nature. Psycholytic therapy relies on a low dosage of LSD, enabling the gradual release of material so that each level of awareness can be worked through and integrated into the totality of consciousness and thereby resolved to the degree that the new work can build on what has gone before. Were this not done slowly, there would be the danger of a hopeless jumble of incomprehensible material suffocating the consciousness of the person subjected to it. The higher dosage *psychedelic* therapy was utilized only in special situations where the subject was believed to be able to deal more immediately and intensively with internalized elements.

In psycholytic therapy, subjects under the influence of LSD regressed to early childhood and even to infancy. They were able to relive early psychosexual traumas—relive, not merely remember them—in all their complexity and with the accompanying sensations and emotions, some of which had occurred even before the onset of the ability to use language. Some subjects worked through what Freud had identified as basic psychoanalytic constructs: oedipal and electra complexes, castration anxiety, and penis envy, to name a few. This is the more significant because the psychoanalytic constructs could not have come from any indoctrination of cultural information—as would have been likely, had the research taken place in the United States. Freud had been blacklisted and psychoanalytic literature had not been available in Czechoslovakia since the Germans occupied that country in 1939. Psychological research had been oriented strictly toward psychopharmacology and behavioral studies. Therefore we can be quite sure that when subjects in Grof's Czechoslovakia research produced early developmental material, the source of this material was not external to the person who experienced it.

From his extensive observations Grof was able to recognize specific memory constellations, for which he used the name "COEX systems" (systems of condensed experience). He explains that a COEX system consists of "condensed experiences (and related fantasies) from different life periods of the individual. The memories belonging to a particular COEX system have a similar basic theme or contain similar elements and are associated with a strong emotional charge of the same quality. The deepest layers of this system are represented by vivid and colorful memories of experiences from infancy and early childhood."[2] These early memories were the core. In the course of the individual's lifetime the core had attracted to itself many layers of accretions. These accretions were composed of later experiences that had been based upon predispositions or situations resembling the core experience

—in a sense, they were variations on the original theme, now elaborated and charged with the original emotion that had become complicated and intertwined with new constellating events, and with the mechanisms the individual had unconsciously devised for dealing with them.

Jung had long ago embarked on the exploration of the many-layered collective psyche, as expressed in the complexes of the mature individual. In "A Review of the Complex Theory," Jung had predicted what the outcome would be when these core experiences of the human soul were revealed to conscious awareness: "Where the realm of complexes begins the freedom of the ego comes to an end, for complexes are psychic agencies whose deepest nature is still unfathomed. Every time the researcher succeeds in advancing a little further towards the psychic *tremendum*, then, as before, reactions are let loose in the public, just as with patients who, for therapeutic reasons, are urged to take up arms against the inviolability of their complexes."[3] "Complexes," he asserted, "are in truth the living units of the unconscious psyche, and it is only through them that we are able to deduce its existence and its constitution."[4] The complex, for Jung, is what is experienced with a high degree of feeling tone. "It is the *image* of a certain psychic situation which is strongly accentuated emotionally and is, moreover, incompatible with the habitual attitude of consciousness."[5] These complexes, which appear on the surface in the form of neurotic symptoms or other kinds of psychological conflicts, have been traced by Grof backward in time, through the successive layers of accretions that make up the COEX systems.

Grof was able, through his painstaking work in psycholytic therapy, to penetrate many layers beyond what Jung had imagined could be possible in a scientific experiment. Although Jung had pointed to a collective level of unconsciousness so archaic that it even preceded in time the conception of the individual and was grounded in the phylogenetic patterns, in practice Jung's explorations were limited by his methodology. If collective material emerged, he investigated it. But his views—that true individual consciousness arose in the child only with the psychological separation from the mother, the attainment of a degree of independence, and the emergence of moral conflicts—led him to conclude that one could not expect to make a systematic exploration of the unconscious contents that had originated in the individual much before the age of puberty. Grof established that the psyche of a much younger individual could indeed be systematically explored, and that a very real form of consciousness exists in the child's preverbal stage, and is present during the birth.

In the process of resolving and integrating the COEX systems, Grof observes that "sooner or later the elements of the individual unconscious tend to disappear . . . and each individual undergoing psycholytic therapy enters the realms of the perinatal and transpersonal phenomena."[6] What is particularly interesting is that in reexperiencing the birth process, the individual undergoes sensations not only of birth, but also of death. A new philosophical awareness may emerge from this experience, as the person realizes the frailty of the individual and the impermanence of the individual's life relative to the larger course of Life itself. The realization that one must leave the world exactly as one came into it, bereft of everything one has acquired during a lifetime, points up the similarity between birth and death: birth is not only a beginning of life in this world, it is also a death to the world from which the infant issues—the womb-world—which is nourished by the seed of the generations. It is at this point, then, that the prepersonal flows out of the transpersonal, and the beginning of birth heralds the ending of immersion in the oceanic oneness.

Taking his lead from Otto Rank's *The Trauma of Birth*, Grof describes four stages belonging to the birthing process. He calls these the "Basic Perinatal Matrices (BPM I–IV)." Under the influence of LSD, the barrier between consciousness and the sacral dimension of life disappears. Each BPM has two facets or components. One is biological and one is spiritual. As the person returns in awareness to the biological matrix, its spiritual dimension reveals itself; so the pre-personal and transpersonal experiences are blended.

In BPM-I, the biological stage of undisturbed uterine existence is experienced in its spiritual dimension as a sense of cosmic unity.

BPM-II, which corresponds with the onset of delivery, is accompanied by feelings of universal engulfment. The contractions of the closed uterine system give rise to the spiritual experience of "no exit," or hell. It is felt as antagonism with the mother.

The biological component of BPM-III is the propulsion of the child through the birth canal. This is experienced as a death-rebirth struggle. Now the infant experiences synergism with the mother as its movement and hers become as one.

The final stage, BPM-IV, is the termination of the birth process. It entails the physical separation from the mother, the cutting of the umbilical cord, and the formation of a new type of relationship with her. The spiritual experience that accompanies this is the death of the ego and a rebirth to a radically different orientation toward life. Here it is necessary to experience the total annihilation of everything that has gone on in the womb, to experience it on all levels, physical, emotional, intellectual, and transcendental, before the vision can be swept clean of the debris that surrounded the ego potential and inhibited its freedom and growth.

The sexuality of the womb is (or should be) the peace of containment and the first fully satisfying feeling in life. It is re-membered only dimly, if at all, unless subjected to psycholytic or otherwise induced recall; yet the proto-memory is present in the growing child and in the adult as a vague feeling of longing that draws to itself expressions leading to hope and to love. Dimly remembered, this is a period of contentment against which all other experiences will appear incomplete. It is toward the renewal of this contentment that sexual activity will be directed in the future. Nor has it been entirely peaceful within the womb, as the reactivated memories at times may make evident. Some people experience parts of this time of containment as suffocating, filled with noxious smells and evil tastes, with disturbing movements, and even with an awareness of being in some way wounded (as though an abortion had been attempted). Despite such negative feelings, there is usually an overall recollection of having all one's needs met, and of being totally protected. If, on one level, both males and females experience the yearning to return to the womb, then in the process of forming one's own gender identification the male's desire will be directed toward returning to the womb through his penis in sexual intercourse, while the female's desire will be to *be* the womb, the container which experiences a symbiotic relationship with the contained.

As we go on to consider how the development of sex differences occurs, we will realize that human beings are not "only masculine" or "only feminine," either from a physiological or a psychological perspective. Although we identify ourselves as belonging to one sex or the other, our sexuality and, indeed, much of our nonsexual functioning are determined by the interplay of both male and female hormones within the total structure of the organism. Always, we are both the container and contained. We alternate between these two ways of being, sometimes one predominating and sometimes the other. If the containing principle is essentially "feminine," man functions out of the containing feminine side of his nature when he exercises it. When a man wishes to be contained, either in the sexual act or in a more inclusive relationship with a woman, he is experiencing his masculinity. Even so, at the opposite side of this is his desire to be born into the world, and to be thus freed from his containment.[7]

The most traumatic aspects of the birth process are activated with the onset of delivery. Similarly, adults may feel psychological pressures which are akin to the early contractions of the uterus. The first mild contractions produce a discomfort, and this is like that experienced by a person who has been engulfed and now *feels* the engulfment as something different from what was before. The walls begin to close in, there is not enough space, one cannot breathe freely, one is in a place that is too small. How well most people know the ways in which adult life assails us with such feelings when we are growing psychologically and no longer are able to exist in the same limited environment which was tolerable before. There is an urge to move, to get out. This increases with the added pressure we feel. We know what despair is like: there is no way out, no solution, we are stuck, we are dammed, we cannot do anything.

And then there is an opening, a tiny one to be sure, but it *is* an opening. This is the moment of breaking through what seemed to be an impasse. In our later sexual lives, we will have many occasions where something is required of us, or we require something of ourselves, that is different from what we have known before. It may be the discovery of pleasure that comes to us as we explore our own bodies and begin to learn about body-mind responsiveness to touch and to imagination. It may be the new experience of sexual feelings for another person that turns our values around and charges our vitality. We only know that we have to move, that things must change, that we are being pushed or squeezed or shoved; and then, that we are on a roller coaster that we cannot control and that we simply have to go with it. This is akin to the experience we will know many times in coitus, being compressed within the narrow vaginal passage, or feeling the compression, feeling the slippery fluid about us that makes the resistance pleasurable and finally allows us to yield ourselves up to it, feeling the mounting excitement as we rush breathlessly toward climax. We are simply all there, all in this moment of centered awareness. Nothing else exists for us. Crazily oblivious to the whole world, we hit the cosmic center. It explodes in a vision of golden light. For an instant, life is suspended. Too soon, we notice that we can breathe again. Gradually we feel the release from pressure. We can expand again in space. We are free, we are home, we are liberated, we are redeemed! It is possible to feel love again, to offer forgiveness or compassion to the other with whom we have joined in our entirety. These feelings can be experienced fully only when we have truly surrendered ourselves, our self-seeking ego selves, and allowed Eros to come alive in the sexual act.

Grof has shown how pre-personal and transpersonal modes of consciousness are joined in the processes around birth, and also in the reliving of the perinatal matrices. Our own experience of sexual intercourse shows us how these two modes of consciousness may be joined in one of the core experiences of our ongoing lives. It is neither a matter of living altogether in the transpersonal setting, nor exclusively on the pre-personal or instinctive levels. The two modes are present in us at all times.

Grof returned again and again to the perinatal matrices in order to gain an understanding of the roots of psychosexual functioning in the later life of the individual. The sociobiologists explore the evolutionary development out of which individual development emerges. They look to the processes of natural selection for an explanation of how the instinctive behavior of humans has come to be what it is, and they compare this development with that of other species on this planet. Jung had traced the roots of psycho-sexual behavior to the beginnings of human history as handed down to us through the ancient creation myths and sacred stories of many peoples, describing the psychic life of archaic generations. When the contents of any of these pre-personal stages appear in dream material, they are usually overlaid with something sugges-tive of personal and subjective experience, however remote. The pre-personal is inevitably embodied in the personal, just as the dream filters through the veil of sleep and is remembered in the waking state. And so the suggestion that we can peer into the ex-perience of our own birth, as Grof has demonstrated so impres-sively, has the capacity of stretching our imagination sufficiently to enable us to move back earlier still. If the birthing process and the remembering of it provides an important key to an under-standing of how sexuality will develop later on, then what about conception and what follows immediately after conception?

The period between conception and birth is the time of the most rapid growth of the organism, a time in which each day witnesses changes so significant that at no time later on will so much happen to a human being within so short a space of time. If, as seems to be the case, the earlier an experience occurs in human life the more it may influence what will happen as the per-son develops, then the subjective experiences of the period imme-diately following conception should not be overlooked. A warning is necessary here. No matter how profound such an early experi-ence may be, there is always the likelihood that its effects can be moderated later on. The human organism has the magnificent ca-pacity to transform itself over and over again every day of its life, to adapt to changing conditions, to repair injury, to heal itself, to re-vision and to revise concepts, to learn and to incorporate learn-ing, and to make out of what to some would appear a catastrophe an opportunity for development. So, when we speak of early for-mative influences, it is necessary to bear in mind that re-forming is always possible. In fact, re-forming is always taking place, whether we plan it or not, so it seems essential that we apply as much con-sciousness to the transformative processes in which we are en-gaged as we are able to do.

Birth was a forgetting. As life in the world begins to unfold, the life in the womb is folded up again, folded away and forgotten. This was the "death" that accompanied the emergence of the infant from the darkness into the light.

In England, between 1953 and 1969, another psychiatrist was using LSD psycholytic therapy to probe the mysteries of the beginnings of individual lives. Frank Lake,[8] who identifies himself as a clinical theologian, discovered independently what Grof had found: an astonishing frequency of instances in which perinatal and prenatal experiences were spontaneously relived by subjects under the influence of LSD. Dr. Lake was one of about 160 British psychiatrists who were utilizing LSD in their research at the time, so he found himself in a climate that was receptive to his explorations. Again, invaluable work in the exploration of the deepest levels of psychological disturbance was possible, and was done quietly without raising the outcry that made such research nearly impossible in the United States.

Lake based his teachings in part on Grof's topographical analysis of the four Basic Perinatal Matrices. Working mostly with claustrophobic patients, he found that lasting remissions would occur in patients who were able to relive their traumatic birth experiences. He also came to realize—partially due to his theological background—that some people were unable to get all the way down to the crushing, suffocating terror of the anatomical-theological emergency of birth. Instead of reliving the birth process itself, they transformed it into symbolic experiences. They found themselves involved in communication of a mythic, visual, or orgiastic nature, or in apocalyptic experiences with every possible horror elaborated beyond imagination.

Lake turned to other methods to elicit intrauterine experiences after 1969. The technique of hyperventilation—under careful supervision—provided access to an altered state of consciousness without the use of any drugs. In this state, persons were assisted in regressing to the prenatal state, first through simulation, and then through a transformation of awareness which changed the character of the experience into something that involved the whole person on many different levels. Lake found that he subscribed to two fantasies, which were not untypical of psychiatrists working in this field: one, that life in the womb is utterly peaceful and tranquil; and two, that to enter into the prenatal would be to risk precipitating a psychosis. These fantasies were, of course, incompatible.

Speaking to members of the International Association of Transpersonal Psychology in Australia in November 1980, Dr. Lake confessed, "As a reasonable psychiatrist it didn't occur to me to ask any questions of the fetus." But about four years earlier he *had* begun to question the fetus. In the context of working with over a thousand persons, mostly health professionals, in three-to-five-day workshops, he had come to a dual hypothesis, namely, 1) that certain experiences that occurred very early in fetal life were projected into later life as psychological disorders and 2) that these same experiences were projected into later life as the way groups are experienced. It was Lake's belief, based upon his observations of material engendered in his workshops, that people can sometimes use groups to get in touch with so-called fetal states. Parenthetically, I should like to add that from my own experience in facilitating regression to birth and fetal life in psychotherapy I am in full agreement with Lake on this. Also, I have observed that responses to these early prenatal experiences are often projected into the interpersonal relationship of couples, and especially in sexual relations. For here, more than anywhere else, the connections are made between sexual intercourse and the potentiality for conception. Consciously or unconsciously, the couple moving together in the act of love—whether experiencing it as transcendent joy or whether it is touched by pain or conflict—connect this with the beginning of life. Entering the womb again and withdrawing from it, holding on and letting go are familiar feelings. They belong to the only lives the partners organically know—their own.

While Grof had elaborated the last trimester of fetal life and the birth process, Lake turned his particular attention to the first days following conception and the first trimester of fetal life. Lake came to this by starting, as Grof had done, with the recognition that various psychological disturbances of adult life appeared to be related to unconscious reenactments of earlier experiences. Both researchers found that the birth process is a substantial core of the multitude of enactments of it. Some afflictions of adult life could be understood as expressions in physical and symbolic form of earlier systems of condensed experience. As they traced back through the COEX systems, strongly negative experiences would be encountered. Birth itself was fraught with terror and danger, pain and the fear of total annihilation.

Lake went back further still. In his work with groups he was able to facilitate the experience of pushing awareness backward, through the distress encountered by the fetus as early as the first trimester; and then suddenly there would be a change. It was possible to identify a sense of sheer bliss, of free-floating wonder, free of attachment of any kind. Lake links this to the brief period between fertilization and implantation. The ripe egg has left the ovary and entered the Fallopian tube. If intercourse has taken place within hours or no more than a couple of days, the egg may accept the sperm, and conception occurs. The fertilized egg, the zygote, now begins the long journey to the uterus. It is only a matter of inches, but the zygote is so small it is barely visible to the eye, and the journey takes three or four days. Lake reports that at least one person in three in psycholytic therapy experiences "blastocystic bliss" as the fertilized egg travels freely down the Fallopian tube and comes to rest in the domed chamber of the womb. The blastocyst is self-subsistent, since it has no attachment. There is no time, no space, no light, no dark, no right, no left, no up, no down, no masculine, no feminine—only experiential wonderment in a completely monistic state. It is as though "I encompass the whole universe. It is I and I am it."

All this comes to an end about the tenth day, when the connection with the lining of the mother's womb is made. Now comes the union with the "other," a first inkling of dualism, which grows into an exchange of physical substance and human love ascending and descending through the umbilical cord. Viewed from the context in which this initial union is reexperienced later in the course of regressive therapy, and feeling into the sensibilities that it arouses, it may be possible to recognize whether the union was an event from which the individual is fleeing, or a state to which he or she aspires to return. If this moment can be brought back into our experience, we have a precious ore with which to work. The backward movement brings us to an earlier state that is pre-personal.

But the blastosphere itself moves forward in its development, into the complexities of interaction with the mother. The quality of this interaction depends to a great extent on the feelings in the mother during this time. The mother's general responses to her own life situation *before* she knew she was pregnant appear to be "discovered" as the subjects relive what comes through to them from their first contact with the womb. The image that the mother has of herself, her sensations, her movements, her anxiety level, can be recognized as having affected the fetus. During the primal integration (the reliving) the strong change in the mother on her discovery of pregnancy may take the form of fetal response to maternal delight or maternal distress. The fetus experiences the mother's affect as it is chemically transmitted through the umbilical cord. If this affect is positive, in the form of attention-giving emotional regard, the fetus develops a feeling of comfortable skin, which may be the basis of later self-esteem and feeling of personal value. But if the fetus receives negative affect, it cannot as easily thrive. It wishes to feel its presence recognized. When this is denied, the ground is set for the anticipation of being disregarded, hence of being of no interest or account in the world.

I had occasion to think of this recently when the mother of a sixteen-year-old girl consulted me. The mother had just learned that her daughter had undergone a third abortion, without having mentioned it to her parents. The mother expressed concern about the daughter's promiscuity, her use of alcohol and drugs, and her general alienation from the rest of the family. This mother wanted to know how to treat her daughter, how to get her daughter to care more about herself, to be more selective in her friends and more self-protective.

I asked the mother about her relationship with the daughter over the past few years. I was given a recital of incident after incident of the daughter's rebellious behavior, of her inordinate demands on the family, of her unwillingness to measure up to the standards the family had set for her. Looked at superficially, there seemed to be no good reason why this daughter had become such a problem. All the more so since her brother, two years younger, growing up in the same household, was a cheerful, well-behaved, and trouble-free youngster.

I shifted my questioning to the situation existing at the time the daughter had been conceived. The mother had not wanted this child; in fact, the pregnancy occurred when a contraceptive device failed. The mother was so upset when she discovered that she was pregnant that she seriously considered throwing herself down a flight of stairs. It took her several months to get used to the idea that she would have to postpone her career plans to have this child. At last she accepted it with good grace, or so she thought. When the child was born, the mother was disappointed to have a girl and not a boy. While she was nursing her daughter, her breasts became abscessed, a condition which she resented bitterly as an attack on her femininity. By the time of her second pregnancy, the woman had become reconciled to her maternal role, and this pregnancy was a totally positive experience.

If Lake's findings apply, the distress that must have been experienced by the first blastocyst at the influx of the initial maternal distress would have registered as an invasion of anxiety, fear, anger, distrust, bitterness, and pain. The subsequent improvement in the mother's attitude possibly saved her daughter from severe psychotic disturbances. The child's responses to the unmet uterine needs were long-lasting. Distress of the order that must have been experienced could not remain connected with the consciousness of the growing child, for it would be impossible emotionally to bear. Consequently, the affect was split off, and the hurtful environment of the beginning was not remembered. The catastrophic sensations were dissociated from the emotions that accompanied them. What was left was a feeling of being worthless, of living a meaningless life, of not deserving anything from the parents or from the world. This young woman could not expect people to treat her well but, on the contrary, she felt that she had to make every kind of concession in order to make herself acceptable to people. Furthermore, she would have to be satisfied with anyone who would associate with her—and so there was no discrimination in her choice of associates. Her sexuality was perverted into a means of compensating for her poor self-image. She betrayed her sexuality, and was in turn betrayed by it.

Clearly, problems like those of this girl and her mother are sexual problems, but they are far more than merely sexual; they find expression in sexuality as well as in other areas. Psychotherapists who try to deal with complex situations of this kind often approach them as purely personal issues, without recognizing their early pre-personal basis. There is reason to believe that many of today's sexual and other interpersonal difficulties could be understood in the context of the first interpersonal connection ever made, that between the newly fertilized ovum and the mother.

Important as this first connection may be, it is necessary to ask the question as to whether all subsequent difficulties are traceable to these beginnings. Just how far-reaching were the results of the inhospitable reception offered to a tiny bundle of cells as it arrived in the womb after its journey down the Fallopian tube? My tendency is to believe, with Jung and others, that experiences all through a person's life as he or she interacts with the environment affect the individual. Trauma can occur at any moment in a lifetime, and can have a profound effect on the future of the individual. But how the person responds to trauma, and how the person interacts with the environment, tends to be a variation on an earlier way of responding. We cannot know for certain in which life experiences a current problem may be embedded. But there are people whose history shows that they have "always" been somehow at odds with their world. These children were "always different"—even though the nature of their differences and difficulties may have been presented in a variety of seemingly unrelated ways. They are usually referred to in diagnostic manuals as psychopathic personalities or sociopaths, or cases of character disorder. These labels denote that the individuals' problems stem from unknown origins and are particularly resistant to treatment.

Every disturbance of attitude and behavior begins somewhere. Psychoanalysis has asserted that the crucial predisposing events occur in early childhood or even in infancy. Although psychoanalytic treatment may continue for many years, the patient who is enabled to regress to the first few years or months of postnatal life does not necessarily find the key to the resolution of the disturbance. One reason for this could be that the events of the person's life and that person's response to those events have built up such a mountain of accretions that it is impossible to dig through them. The original events that started the process could be buried in the complexities that surrounded them and the later experiences that related to them. Another reason could be that the investigations simply did not go back far enough.

Both of these explanations could be true. Recognizing the complexities that underlie human behavior, and the impossibility of ever sorting out all the contributing factors, must frustrate the searcher. It is not fruitful to look at events piecemeal, as though they were discrete. We have learned that nothing in this world happens independently of everything else, but we have not yet learned to apply this realization to dealing with the misadventures of the human personality. We need to begin thinking in terms of wholes, to observe the total responses of people in their extended environmental context.

The second explanation, that we may not have gone back far enough, applies to those persons for whom the traditional approaches to the psyche have been ineffective, or to those on whom such methods, if tried, would not work because they do not reach into the roots of the personality structure where the disorder had its inception. Furthermore, if we wish truly to envision our own development in the total ongoing life-context in which we participate, we cannot overlook the moment when we began to be, as individuals.

The sexual act which results in conception may be considered on many different levels. The most obvious one is the subjective level, the experience of the participants. It involves the intentionality with which they enter into sexual relations, and the feelings that they have about each other, about themselves, and about the place they are in their lives individually, together, and in the larger environment. Another level is the biological level. What exactly is happening in these people? What happens when making love becomes making life? And third, what are the unconscious dimensions of the act, and what are the unknown feelings that will rise to the surface when the fact of conception is known?

Reflecting on all of this, the inescapable conclusion is that most of the time we are not nearly conscious enough, in our exercise of sexuality, of the implications that transcend our personal concerns. We are insufficiently aware of exactly what our intentions are. One important aspect of this is that we are often not clear as to whether we are or are not willing that a child should result from this union. We do not pause to remember that in this act we are engaging the fundamental life-force. Unless a developed consciousness intervenes, we are borne along on the winds of our archetypal natures. We feel little conflict, because we *are* acting in accord with pure instinct. The joy of being at one with our true natures may lull us into a blissful state of dreamy consciousness at the border of unconsciousness long enough to conceive a child.

Even the most naïve, the most uninhibited, the most natural human beings are, after all, somewhat rational, which means that we bear the burden of judgment and responsibility. We see, perhaps a little late, but eventually, the consequences of our acts. It seems to be necessary to make an effort to consider in advance the implications of what we may do, rather than having so often to gain insight through hindsight. For this reason, it has been important to discuss the work of Grof and Lake, and others who deal with roots of sexuality in the beginning of life.

One should not feel, however, that the die is cast if there are difficulties between conception and birth. Human beings, especially at an early age, are amazingly resilient. Whatever difficulties they may have encountered, they are inevitably responsive to affection and warmth, to being given attention and to being touched in a loving way. The miracle of human life is its capacity for transformation, and this can happen at any stage of life, from conception to the moments before death. Errors can be made and errors can be corrected; and tenderness, care, and understanding can help to bring about new beginnings at any age.

12
Human Development
in a New Context

The psychological theories of child development in use today have grown out of the old paradigm. Their purpose and goal is development of an ego as a relatively autonomous center of consciousness. The psychological systems are designed largely to liberate the conscious ego from factors that inhibit the fulfillment of the individual's potential. These potentials may be described in terms of the exercise of creativity, as growth—in the sense of becoming what one is capable of being, as differentiation from the morass of social pressures, and as adapting to what are seen as desirable social norms. Ego development with regard to relationships in these psychological systems revolves around becoming loosened from the control of others, as well as deriving personal benefit from human relationships.

These psychological systems reflect the dualistic world view in which subject and object stand in opposition to one another and the role of psychology is to serve a mediating function at best, and a manipulating function most of the time. Manipulation is a reasonable enough concept in a world in which people, places, and things are seen as separate entities, and the capacity to move these separate entities around is seen as advantageous to the individual who masters the necessary skills to accomplish this. The areas of human experience in which these psychologies function most effectively are the areas of thought and feelings. Feelings, with their accompanying physiological effects, often are seen as factors that control individuals and limit their ability to be strong and independent. People who are powerful are those who are able to manipulate the feelings of others, while keeping their own under control. This means that they do not let their personal feelings interfere with the path which through logical reasoning processes they have chosen to take. They are able to make methodical plans and carry them out without undue influence from the affective side of their nature.

Psychotherapies based on this perspective, to which Ken Wilber refers as "world view one," are the traditional therapies which have been discussed earlier: behavioral therapies, psychodynamic therapies including psychoanalysis and its many derivatives, and cognitive developmental psychologies. In addition to these, the old paradigm spawned innumerable "self-help" therapeutic movements which have as their purpose becoming more effective in the world—where effectiveness means primarily getting what you want for yourself. There is nothing wrong with people helping themselves *per se*, but all too often helping oneself means doing so at the expense of someone else, or simply to improve one's self-image and bring it closer to an ego ideal. So the logical processes are, more often than not, imposed upon the feeling processes. People learn how to direct their actions toward fulfilling their desires. Furthermore, these psychological systems studiously avoid reference to any possible spiritual aspects of life. The field of psychology, dealing as it must with the imponderables of the human psyche or soul, has long sought to make its principles sound as scientific as possible. This involves applying the scientific method to evaluating the "results" of psychotherapies, to making diagnoses, and to predicting the "outcome of treatment" for the sicknesses of the soul—even to being able to inform the health insurance companies how long it is expected to take for a mentally ill person to recover from his illness—based upon actuarial records, of course. All of this is consonant with the paradigm of modernity: everything that counts can be measured.

World view two is still inchoate, as it must be in this time of rapid change and redefinition. Yet it has been clear enough that as the newer paradigm embraces the area of psychology and psychotherapy it must offer ways to approach the human organism that are consonant with the holistic and contextual perspective. Beginning with the humanistic psychology movement of the sixties, when individuals were freer from the hierarchical and authoritarian modes of psychotherapies than in the past, the person-in-society and the person-in-a-planetary-context have received a fair share of attention. At first this movement encouraged enlightened self-interest and self-love—and for this it came in for a good deal of criticism from the schools of psychology which required people in need of psychological help to make great personal sacrifices for the sake of personal development. But it soon became clear that unless a person had high self-regard, it was difficult, if not impossible, for that person to work generously and constructively with others. The humanistic mode required first the fulfillment of the ego, and only then would the ego be free enough from concern with its own needs to listen attentively and empathically to the needs of others. Humanistic psychology has two primary aims: the fulfillment of the individual's potentiality for growth, and the enhancement of interpersonal relations. These are no mean objectives, and yet somewhere in the mid-sixties some of the leading figures in the humanistic psychology movement found themselves not wholly satisfied with the very movement that they had been instrumental in founding and guiding.

The rumblings of the inner storms came out of the mystical and transcendent experiences that people were having in ever greater numbers. Increasing use of psychedelic substances enabled many people to break through their fixed notions of the limitations of mind and psyche. Of the many people who discovered through the use of mind-altering substances that levels of consciousness could be attained exceeding anything they had been able to imagine, a few were willing to explore in depth this meta-world and the varieties of meaning implicit in it. For these relatively few who were serious pioneers in the field, it was not a matter of enticement to take the "sacred medicine" over and over, but rather to assimilate slowly and with utmost care whatever could be derived from each experience.

The other influence that brought about the uneasiness with the humanistic movement and the desire for something more was the growing interest in Eastern philosophy and psychology. Here the Westerner began to enter in where Jung had feared to tread two or three decades earlier. It is as though the psyche, or our understanding of the psyche, had matured somewhat between the thirties and the sixties. In 1938, Jung had traveled in India and, during the years following, he wrote about his hopes and misgivings concerning the possibility of the ways of the East ever being assimilated into the Western psyche. In the sixties, the pilgrimage to India had become fairly commonplace among a certain group of students and other seekers, and by then many people were practicing yoga and meditation. They had changed their lives radically to take into account what they had learned during their journeys to the East and to their inner selves.

The "something more" that was sought in the field of psychology was the topic of discussion throughout the sixties and into the seventies by those philosophers, psychologists, and educators who had undertaken the serious study of the so-called altered states of consciousness. Leading among these were Abraham Maslow and Anthony Sutich. Sutich, writing about those early days (1966–70) in his doctoral dissertation, which he completed shortly before his death in 1974, referred to his personal contacts with Krishnamurti, Alan Watts, Swami Ashokananda of the San Francisco Vedanta Society, and others, and to his wide reading in a variety of Eastern and Western religious traditions. He said that one of the things that impressed him about Maslow was that he read rather extensively in Eastern literature and that he talked about the Eastern perspective, especially after Maslow met Alan Watts in 1959. By 1966, Maslow had clearly taken a position for a psychology that concerned itself not only with "self-actualization," but also with self-transcendence, unitive consciousness, peak experiences, ecstasy, mystical experience, ultimate meaning, transformation of the self, and species-wide transformation. These terms, and others, helped to formulate and define the purpose of the new field of psychology that was now considered the "fourth force," following the third force, humanistic psychology.

Transpersonal psychology was the name finally chosen for the fourth force, on the suggestion of Stanislav Grof, who had been familiar with Jung's use of the term *transpersonal* much earlier in relation to the transpersonal or collective unconscious. It was Grof's research with LSD that had given solid experimental validation to Jung's intuitively arrived at concept.

Transpersonal psychology was, indeed, the right name for a branch of psychology that transcended the personal or ego realm in psychology and addressed itself first and foremost to the wider context in which the concept of ego had so long been embedded. Transpersonal psychology does not negate ego; it recognizes ego as a concept, a necessary tool for understanding ourselves and our being in the world and in the cosmos. Ego is a point from which we view the totality, hence it is not a solid, irreducible entity but, rather, a description of where we happen to find ourselves at a given moment in our experience. Our attachment to ego is a function of our personality, our individuality—which is a necessary part of our experience. We need a sense of ego coherence, especially during the first half of our lives and possibly much longer. We need to experience ego as the place from which we move into the world and from which we gain our personal identity.

The importance of transpersonal psychology is that it admits of ego but is not limited by ego states. Ego is, after all, an intellectual concept that psychologically unsophisticated people manage to function well enough without. Ego also has emotional overtones and social implications. As we have suggested earlier, the experience of most human beings is that the intellectual, emotional, and social aspects of their beings are often in conflict with one another. This makes for discomfort, dis-ease, illness, and the many varieties of neuroses and asocial functioning. When we are shown ways to extend our consciousness beyond the limitations and constraints of ego, we have opportunities to experience new forms of relatedness based on a redistribution of energies. As we begin to know ourselves as participants in an ecological system along with all of life, we realize that we have everything to gain by utilizing the energies that are available to us, in the service of the entire biosphere. This means—and I say it knowing full well that it is perhaps the most difficult insight to arrive at—this means that we need to withdraw from the adversarial position vis-à-vis our environment and bring into use the energies of love. These energies arise in the coalescence of body/mind/emotions and spirit. Joined, they become the unitive force which binds together that which in the mind has been separate, and which is able to build on trust an interdependent world.

The trust of which I speak here is not the innocent trust of the child who *must* trust, being dependent upon the mother, the family, and those others who care for it. That innocent trust may lay the foundation for the trust that comes in maturity, but the later trust is the treasure hard to attain, for it comes from the long experience of trying to master the world, and learning at last that the world and the cosmos are in the hands of a greater consciousness than one can ever hope to achieve. Then comes the transpersonal awareness that, indeed, we are all here on earth for a purpose, although the strict meaning of the purpose may not be clear to most individuals. The symbolism of Rodin's exquisite sculpture, which he titled "The Hand of God," expresses it. Resting within the hand is a piece of rock, and from it emerge a male and a female figure, barely formed, but embracing and lying face to face, ready to awaken one another from their slumber with a kiss. The hand of God, in which the rock comes alive, is a human hand. This suggests to me that our transpersonal purpose is to bring the cosmos to life and into the human dimension. We are allowed to serve as the conduit through which this may happen.

13
The Pre-personal Stage:
Emergence

Psychological theories and patterns of human development in the past usually started with the birth of the child or the period of infancy, and concluded when the individual reached a state of maturity in which the desire for personal gratification has been considerably modified in favor of social adaptation and the acceptance of responsibility for others as well as for the self. A degree of personal independence marks the mature individual, along with willingness to cooperate with others for mutual gain and mutual satisfaction. During the past decade or two increasing attention has been given to midlife and the later years of the life-span. Better ways have been found to maintain health and social interaction among the older members of the population. At last, even death and dying, as an important part of the developmental process, have come in for their share of concern. Most of this occurs within the limits of the traditional psychologies and within the paradigm of modernity. There are exceptions in the case of a few people who are working with persons close to death and who are committed to understanding, as well as possible, the dynamics of the crossing-over process and what it means for the human spirit.

Those whose approach comes out of the newer paradigm concern themselves as much with the context of development as with the actual events. The context, as we have seen, is not limited by the individual's existence in the present body, on this earth, between birth and death. The context may be time without known limits; it may appear to stretch back into the inchoate mystery of the past or forward into the still undifferentiated potentialities of the future. Within the context of the new paradigm a human life takes place on a segment of a line of infinite length. Some lives consume a larger segment, some a smaller segment. Each life-span is only a passing moment in comparison with the stretch of time the human race has already covered in the process of evolving.

As I write this, I sense that my work is overshadowed by the nuclear bomb, the collective Sword of Damocles that hangs over all of our heads. It is shocking to realize that while the time line of humanity stretches back hundreds of thousands of years, it may possibly be cut off in an hour or a day or a year or before the end of the present century. Nor am I alone in this. When people sense the presence of a terrible death all around them, many find little incentive to make sacrifices for a better future. The reality of the context in which we are living is that our civilization is at high risk, yet we talk about creating a better context for the development of our children and our children's children. I feel it is absolutely essential to plan constructively for the future, for unless we can envision a context for life just ahead that is worth struggling for, despair will overcome us and make us prey for exploitation.

A quest for knowledge brought us to the point of choice we now face. With increasing speed, science has been unlocking the mysteries of the physical and biological world, the biosphere. Today we know how to kill off every person on earth, and we have the weapons to do it. At the same time, we are learning more and more about how to preserve and enrich human life on this planet, how to conquer disease, how to achieve optimum health, and how genetic engineering can alter life-forms to accord with human needs and desires. Already we have harnessed the energies of the winds, the waves, the tides, and gravity. We have it in our power to harness the energies of love, also. But sexuality, which is the fire in the midst of love, has a will of its own and is not so easily mastered. That is the task for civilization. The task is learning how to keep passion alive and vibrant without becoming enslaved by it. The second fire, sexuality, draws human beings together in hope, and creates union out of separation and new life out of hopelessness. Although the new life is fully dependent at first, its task is to become increasingly individual and independent. The context into which the child is born will play an important part in how the child will develop and the sort of man or woman the child will become. And, since each person re-creates to some extent the world out of which he or she was created, every newborn is empowered at birth to make an impact on the future.

Innocent of what the world is like, the infant emerges from the protection of the womb. In the soft warm darkness the unborn had felt safe, ever since the beginning of its existence as a single cell. Throughout all the risings and fallings of the mother's emotions during her pregnancy and the changes in body chemistry that accompanied them, the placental barrier buffered the infant from the intensity of such changes as would be encountered in the birth process and afterward.

During the final hours of prenatal life the place that had been so friendly suddenly takes on a different character. All at once there is no more room in which to grow, or even space in which to remain. The womb contracts and exerts pressure upon the infant to move along to some other place, to get out! There must be an opening, there must be an exit somewhere! Now comes the valiant struggle for survival. At the last moment of the birth drama, alien hands come to receive the child. Perhaps these hands intervene to draw the tiny body out, to pull the infant through the passage. These alien hands separate child from mother, flesh from flesh. One becomes two. The mother will ask the two crucial questions that birth-giving women have always asked:

"Is my baby all right?"

"Is it a boy, or a girl?"

In every culture, once the fact of survival is ascertained, the next question is the same, for parents know that the course of their child's life will be profoundly affected by its sex, and the exercise of its sexuality.

Every beginning is also the culmination of what has gone before. By the time of birth, some of the most important events in the child's sexual development have already taken place. The future sex of the child has been determined at conception. In the early days of gestation humans are truly androgynous but, depending upon whether the sperm carried a Y or an X chromosome, fetal development proceeds along either male or female lines. The fetus is neuter or undifferentiated during the first six or seven weeks of prenatal life. There are neither testes nor ovaries at this stage, but only undeveloped gonads with the capacity to develop into either male or female sexual organs.

Genital organization takes place mostly between the seventh and twelfth week of gestation. If the fetus is male, the gonad produces a hormonal substance which induces the masculine development of the reproductive system and inhibits its feminine development. In the forties and fifties it was believed that both male and female evocator substances were necessary for human sexual differentiation. More recently, it has been found that the male inductor substance is necessary to bring about masculine development only. In its absence, female development proceeds. This may have some bearing on the differing ways in which males and females experience themselves; for the male has had to undergo a radical shift in his developmental pattern to attain his own sex differentiation, while the female has not had to change significantly in her course of development.

If we are to believe that early intrauterine experiences can leave memory traces on the human psyche, we must ask: At what cost must the male make this early adaptation? Is it a difficult struggle on some deep, primal level? If it is, does it strengthen the male's capacity later on to fight for life in the midst of shifting and changing conditions? Do some males fail to make the adaptation? Researchers have found evidence for the conclusion that they do, for it has been estimated that at the time of fertilization there are three males conceived for every two females, but there are only 110 live male births for every 100 live female births. The boys who survive are, on the average, 5 percent heavier than girls at birth and 1 to 2 percent taller.[1]

Aside from the genital differences at birth, there is no gross visual method of distinguishing the sexes, yet the sexes have been observed to differ in their physiological capacities and in the ways they react to environmental stimuli from birth onward. In addition to differences in capacity and reaction, and differences in reproductive systems, there seem to be inherent constitutional differences of appreciable magnitude. Within the first twenty-eight days after birth about 25 percent more males than females die, on a national average. This ratio of male to female deaths continues throughout life. Although there are typical developmental patterns for each sex, there is a great deal of individual variation within each sex. This is one reason why sexual stereotyping is an inaccurate way of assessing human differences that may be related to sexuality.

Sexual differentiation and sexual development are by no means limited to the reproductive system. They belong to the entire organism, the whole human being. The entire nervous system is involved, as well as other systems. The significance of the brain in sexual functioning is often overlooked. The brain both signals development in other parts of the body and responds to the activity of the total organism. Sexuality, from the very beginning of human life, is far more than an instinctive process; it exists ever and always in the context of consciousness and awareness. Any understanding of the development of sexual differentiation is inextricably bound up with experience and with the response of the organism to its experience. This is why the context of the child's early experiences is so important. The context to which I refer is not only physical space—which I would not want to underestimate—but also the psychological space, that is, the world view of those who will early influence the child.

The reception at birth is the first of a long series of impressions of the world outside the womb that will create the context for what happens later on to the child. The place into which the infant comes after the long and difficult journey is strange and unfamiliar. Birth has been a strenuous effort, but a natural event all the same. It is not a sickness, although sometimes it is treated as though it were. The child who enters this world by way of a sterile and brilliantly lighted delivery room is in for a shock. Many young parents and some health professionals have come to recognize that this may not be the best setting for an infant to be born, especially when no complications are anticipated. Alternative birthplaces are springing up, in hospitals, in birthing centers especially designed for a more family-oriented experience, and at home. Some hospital delivery rooms are being modified to provide a more low-keyed atmosphere. Hospital practices are changing to allow the presence of the husband or other close person at the mother's side during labor and in the delivery room.

We are beginning to re-member, to bring together, some of the older practices which in bygone days welcomed the newborn child into an atmosphere of gentleness and warmth. Dr. Frederic Le-Boyer was instrumental in pioneering his "new" method, which indeed resembles the patterns of our grandparents more than the modern hospital delivery room. In the LeBoyer setting the infant emerges into a place where the lights are dim, voices are hushed, and the entire atmosphere is one of acceptance and love. There is an opportunity to sense the wonder of the miracle of birth, the outcome of an incredibly complex process which has transformed energy/matter in such a way that cells have produced more cells, and all that was needed was present, at the right time and in the right amount, to transform the cellular stuff into a living, breathing, well-formed infant with all its organs and appendages in the right place. The newborn infant is returned to the mother, but this time it is placed on her abdomen, on the body which it had experienced from the inside before. The mother strokes her child; she reconnects with her child. Before the umbilical cord is severed, the child is given time to feel through the skin what touch is, and to breathe in an awareness of being welcomed and being secure. Then the mother gives over the infant to other loving hands to be held and massaged and to be immersed in a warm bath which nearly approximates the conditions of the mother's womb. If delivery has been hard on the child, if it has been long and painful, at least the message is here that difficulties can come to a good resolution and that struggle can be followed by love. The context of welcome into which a child is born may in this way compensate for the trauma of the birthing process.

Participation of the family in the pregnancy and birth can do more than prepare a place for the newborn to enter into. It also can prepare the father, siblings, and other significant people to take responsibility for creating a new context for themselves, in which this new and special relationship becomes a part of their lives. We are beginning to see something like a renewal of the old primitive custom of *couvade*, in which the father went through a parallel pseudo-pregnancy while his wife carried the child. Today's fathers often enter into empathetic relationships with their wives, tuning, in a realistic way, into their experience—even to taking to bed at the time of childbirth and going through something like labor pains of their own. Today, fathers are empathically present with the mothers, often in a spiritual sense. They enter into the birth process by acknowledging its true meaning as the final issue of a sexual union which fulfilled a purpose of nature as well as an aim of human love. When the other children in the family are properly prepared to welcome another person into *their* family— not that *Mother* is having a baby, but that *we* are having a baby— that baby comes into the context of a caring community. Such a child will tend to be more open to giving, sharing, and participating, than one who senses a need to be defensive from the moment of birth. The issue of trust versus suspicion which inevitably emerges at some time in childhood already has a context, a reference point.

When the mother asks, "Is it a boy, or a girl?" she will be informed of the sexual assignment, which has been based on the external appearance of the infant's genitals. How she reacts to this will be, in part, a response to her own rearing and to her own acceptance as female in her own family of origin. Her reaction will also be an effective factor in determining her expectations for this child. Her attitude will be reflected in the self-image that will take form in this child. If we are interested in producing children in our world who will value themselves as individuals and who will not feel limited by externally imposed constrictions, then it is important to give equal value to both sexes, even while recognizing that the sexes are different in certain specific ways. It is no more than natural to take note of the femaleness of the girl and the maleness of the boy, but it is essential that the qualities of neither one be regarded as superior to the other. Whatever the sex, the infant is to be celebrated for its individual essence and for the promise of what it may become.

The myriad of potentialities implicit in the child begin to be explicit with the assignment of sex. This is why it is important to create a balance between helping the child toward a strong identification with his or her sex and instilling a sense that being a member of that sex is nonlimiting. It does not matter so much whether the blanket is pink or blue, or the toys are dolls or air-planes, but the context in which they are placed and the spirit in which they are offered is crucial. "This but not that" is narrowing; "this and also that" is widening. The sex of the child has little to do with the child's valuation as a person. Consequently, belonging to one sex or the other need not be the basis for preselecting the child's toys or activities. If the child is given choices, an opportunity is created for the individuality of the child to express itself.

All this is easier said than done, for many adults have been conditioned to indulge in the kind of behavior that tends to create and reinforce sexual stereotypes. Adults who preserve the prejudices that women can't do this and men are clumsy at that may destroy much of the spontaneity of individual development in their children. Even if parents do not follow the typical pattern of encouraging attractiveness and compliance in their daughters and aggressivity and achievement in their sons, children are still subjected to powerful influences of society outside the confines of the home by people who come into the home and the intrusion of the ever-present media. Parents can, if they wish, supply an effective response to influences that work against the freedom of the individual to move toward self-realization. It is not necessary to accept passively whatever comes into the home by way of television or the conversation of well-meaning friends. Parents concerned with context will raise questions when they do not agree with what is being expressed in their presence. "Debriefing" is essential.

First of all, parents need to know where they themselves stand. If they are frightened and suspicious of others, they will promote an attitude in their children that is either defensive and insecure, or hostile and aggressive. If they are able to trust in the basic decency of most human beings, they will tend to encourage their children to participate in activities based on cooperation and mutual support. The same activity or the same toy can be seen in different lights. The obsession with video games, which children can play for hours, is an example. Sometimes the goal is to "destroy the enemy." "Get 'em," "kill 'em," is the excited cry! A parent can easily shift the emphasis to hitting the mark, to gaining mastery of a skill, to learning how to utilize the machine in expert fashion. How important it is to teach the young that if they can win control over their own abilities, they will have little to fear from strangers. Role-playing games, too, can be structured toward competition and killing. Or, they may be reframed in the direction of forming alliances in order to gather strength for explorations and discoveries that can be accomplished only through cooperation. We plant in our children the seeds of peace or war, of alienation or relationship.

From birth to puberty is a time of self-discovery on a basic level. Stated differently, it is a time of ego formation and ego recognition. At the same time, but on a less conscious level, the child engages in the process of relating to what is non-ego (the rest of the universe outside my skin) and begins to develop attitudes toward the non-ego, the "not-I." A first task of the infant is differentiation from and separation from the mother, as developmental psychologists have shown. Differentiation at this stage means the realization that the mother belongs to the "not-I" realm, that therefore she will be present sometimes and sometimes absent, and that the "I," as infant, cannot control whether she will be close enough to touch and to hold, or away far enough to be out of sight and sound. Tactile contact between mother and child is the keystone of sensory development and relatedness. The feelings that are engendered by the quality of this touching have much to do with the sexual response that will develop later. The receptivity of the child in later life is being tuned by touch just as surely as the ear of the child is tuned by the mother's voice. What happens now does not necessarily determine how the child—when grown—will respond to others, but the interaction here surely establishes patterns that will not easily be disposed of later in life. If the mother accepts her child as lovable, as giving pleasure, as attractive and enjoyable to be with, the child will receive this message about himself or herself. Such messages come through the quality of skin to skin contact more than through words. A feeling of acceptability grounds an infant in a sense of basic worth, which will be a powerful asset in later life and especially in such intimate situations as sexuality provides. If, on the other hand, the infant gets the message that he or she is always doing something wrong, the sense of being ineffective may persist. However, it is important here to say that human beings are always capable of growth and change, and wounds received at an early age may be healed or compensated as the organism by its very nature seeks wholeness.

One of the most important ways to establish the context of relatedness for babies and young children is to demonstrate that parenting is a two-person activity. The model that was so much in evidence throughout the age of modernity was of the mother who spends most of her time at home taking care of her children, while the father goes off to his job in some never-never land, doing things of which the child has no image. He returns weary at day's end when the child is nearly ready for bed. When the mother had to serve as a parental model for both sons and daughters, it was little wonder that her children became excessively attached to her. From her side, child-rearing made excessive demands on her strength and energy, and insufficient demands on her intellectual capabilities. If the mother were overly conscientious in attending to every cry that came from the direction of the child's crib, the child would learn to expect her and other adults to subordinate themselves to his or her needs. If, on the other hand, the child cried too often and for too long a time without adequate response, the infant's frustration could turn to despair and finally give way to a generalized depression. So a mother had to steer a perilous course between too much and too little attention. It wasn't easy for a woman who spent nearly all of her waking hours alone with her preschool-age children. Yet this was the way most nuclear families functioned until the social structures that supported the system began to break down.

The women's liberation movement and hard economic necessity are among the factors that have combined to alter the old patterns. More than half of all mothers of young children now work outside the home full-time or part-time. Some do this out of a desire for living a more rounded life and for developing their capacities and pursuing their interests. Others work because they are single parents and need to support their families. For them the task is survival, rather than expansion of opportunity. There are also increasing numbers of teenage girls—one can hardly call them women—who become pregnant and have their babies before they have received enough education to become self-sustaining. For them life generally becomes a struggle to manage, with public assistance or within an extended family or supportive community situation. The increasing divorce rate along with remarriages and combined families add to the complexity of the social conditions, and the nuclear family in which children remain with their natural parents throughout their growing years is distinctly in the minority. The overriding fact is that many women are in the work force and cannot be full-time mothers. They require the help of the male parent, and most are able to ask for it. In return, these women contribute to the economic support of the family. Possibly the most important contribution of the women's movement to the family was the beginning of a redistribution of parental responsibility, with fathers becoming more active. So, in an unexpected way, the balance began to be restored in the two-parent family, a social unit which in the recent past had often existed in name only. This has affected the perception of what being male or being female means today, and earlier self-images are being called into question.

I have been reflecting for a long time on the relationship between the inner nature of man and woman as it interacts with the roles which they believe society expects them to play. It seems to me that there are intrinsic differences between the functioning of the sexes in relation to their emotional, intellectual, physical, and spiritual needs, and also that there are other differences between the sexes that cannot be said to be intrinsic. The latter are learned, in the inevitable process of repeating behaviors that result in responses that give us pleasure and inhibiting behaviors that bring about pain and suffering. So we are male and female and there is something nonnegotiable about that, but there is a great deal that is negotiable about the characteristics and the roles we learn that result in the exercise of our masculinity or femininity.

It seems to me that Jung understood this distinction when he looked to archetypal sources to describe the intrinsic nature of the two sexes. Familiarity with the mythologies of times and places other than our own allows us to look with a fresh eye at images created in other societies to express what people knew inwardly about sexuality, and about maleness and femaleness. Jung wrote out of his personal experience of the mother as she existed in a small Swiss town at the end of the nineteenth century. His was the conventional rearing common to most Western Europeans and Americans in the waning days of the old paradigm. He wrote about his images of the feminine as various manifestations of the mother archetype, appearing first in importance as personal mother and grandmother, stepmother and mother-in-law; then, any woman with whom a relationship exists—nurse, teacher, or perhaps a remote female ancestor. But he also knew about mothers "in the figurative sense," to which category belong the goddess, and especially the Mother of God, the Virgin, and Sophia, the symbolization of feminine wisdom, as well as the siren, the prostitute, and the consort of Satan. Many variations on the mother archetype are to be found in mythology. The myth of Demeter and Kore, for example, tells of the mother who reappears as a maiden, that of Cybele and Attis portrays the mother who is also the lover to her son. Jung suggests that symbols of the mother appear as representations of our longing for redemption: images of Paradise, the Kingdom of God, the Heavenly Jerusalem. Her sheltering presence appears in church, university, city, woods, and earth, in caves, wells, the baptismal font, or in vessel-shaped flowers like the lotus. As fertility, she is a plowed field, a garden, a cornucopia. All of these images are symbols of the feminine, of those multiple manifestations of the archetype which he called "anima."

What a man is, is characterized by his difference from woman; he is what a female is not. He is hunter of the woman, progenitor, father, patriarch. He is King of Heaven, wielder of the thunderbolt: he is Zeus and Wotan. He is stern and loving father to the son: Lord to Jesus, Daedalus to Icarus, David to Solomon. He is warrier and hero, lusty and in love with danger. His symbols point to phallic power: the sword, the cannon, the tower, the trajectory, and the plow. All these and more are manifestations of the archetype of the masculine.

During Jung's formative years, the archetype of the feminine was being systematically repressed from masculine consciousness in the Swiss culture, just as—in embryo—the physical aspects of the female reproductive system had been inhibited from developing in the male. By the age of sixteen most boys were enrolled in either technical or scientific schools, or apprenticed to trades-people, while most girls were learning domestic science in the *Frauenbildungsschulen.* Consequently, it is not difficult to imagine why consciousness was male to Jung, and the unconscious represented itself in the male psyche as female. It flowed from this that it was correct to characterize worldly or intellectual knowledge as masculine. This means knowledge that leans heavily on the thinking function, upon clarity, discrimination, and logical reasoning. In a world in which masculine consciousness was dominant, and feminine consciousness considered to be imprecise, vague, and undifferentiated, relying more on intuition and feeling than on thinking, it was natural that the so-called "feminine" aspects that might be present in a man would tend to be undervalued and would suffer through neglect, lack of respect, and disuse. For Jung, and for men of his time and place, these feminine qualities were rarely recognized when they appeared in the psyche of the man, but readily accepted as natural aspects of the feminine.

Yet the reality is that both men and women must be androgynous on some very basic level, having been conceived out of a conjunction of opposites, sperm and ovum. Even in Jung's day it was not possible for an individual altogether to deny the presence of the contrasexual part. Awareness of the contrasexual meant awareness of the mystery, the aspect of oneself that is hidden deep within and appears as an image of the soul. This soul-image appeared as feminine in a man, and was called the "anima." In a woman the soul-image appeared as masculine, and was called the "animus." When a man projected his inner image of the feminine —his anima—onto a woman, the attraction or repulsion could be immensely strong. This affect created the passion in relationships. The resulting symbiosis generally held people together in marriages through a strict delineation of tasks and roles and a division of labor. Few men would do "woman's work" willingly, and the woman who went out into the world to do anything but the narrowly specified women's jobs was looked upon as not feminine. If married, she did discredit to her husband, for typically a woman of middle class only worked outside the home when her husband could not support the family adequately.

The very qualities in the opposite sex which attracted a partner, those which were different from one's own and so desirable, were the ones which eventually became a source of misunderstanding in intimate relationships. This is because fundamentally people are far more androgynous than they recognize. The contrasexual asserts itself regularly, even if this is not consonant with one's own expectations or those of the partner. Men, until fairly recently, expected the women to whom they were close to behave in the traditional ways. This meant to provide companionship, to take care of home and children, to provide a social context, and to be readily available as sexual partners. Many women found these expectations limiting and constricting. At the same time, women also expected men to behave in traditional ways, which included supporting the family, handling the mechanical aspects of the home's functioning, establishing the social status of the family, and staying faithful to the marriage vows. While men admitted it less often, because men's complaints might be interpreted as a sign of weakness, they also found their roles limiting and constricting.

What has been happening, it seems to me, is that the archetype of the contrasexual that Jung saw as a deeply unconscious psychic factor is no longer so unconscious as it once was. The shift began with the emergence of a more dynamic consciousness in women, but it has been swiftly followed by reciprocal changes in the consciousness of men. No part of a system can be radically altered without all other parts of the system being affected. This is clear enough when we consider that today we are aware of being members of a world community in which all persons and all natural forces are bound together in an ecological interdependence. We experience this universal reality in our own lives as we live consciously with knowledge of the interdependence of man and woman, and of the masculine and the feminine consciousness.

When women found themselves with more freedom from the grinding responsibilities of an earlier day through the advances of biotechnology, they had time to become dissatisfied, and to imagine what they might be if only they could begin to use parts of themselves that had lain dormant for so long. In my own early exposure to the teachings of Jung, I had gained courage to assert that part of my personal essence that had been identified as "animus." At first I heard that women who were "animus-possessed" were opinionated and demanding, prone to intellectualize and devoid of feeling. This was painful to absorb, because I knew from a place deep inside myself that I had to exert every last bit of energy I possessed if I were to break through the bonds I had fashioned for myself. I had accepted my limited role as a woman because I was committed to the concept that my husband needed my emotional support but not my intellectual competition. And yet there was this small boisterous child in me struggling to get out; and when he did, it was with more vehemence than patience. It took a long time to bring up the undeveloped animus to a reasonably presentable state, where he would not put people off with his stubbornness and rigid refusal to remember his limitations.

It was only later that I saw how Jung had encouraged woman to raise the animus to consciousness and to allow this aspect to function in freedom, yet without obliterating the feminine aspects of her nature which belonged to her biological heritage. I saw how many of the analysts whom Jung had personally trained were women of high intellectual caliber. I think of some of them now: Barbara Hannah, a painter, well versed in classical literature when she first came to Jung, with strong views and strong ways of expressing them; Jolande Jacobi, a powerful matriarch whom Jung pushed to the limit by refusing to train her until she had her doctoral degree; Marie-Louise von Franz, a Greek and Latin scholar, and brilliant in her capacity to synthesize knowledge from a seemingly infinite variety of sources; Aniela Jaffé, interpreter of literature, art, and parapsychology, and deeply attuned to Jung's inner psychic processes as well as to her own; and my personal analyst, Liliane Frey, whose discriminating intellect remained in the background as she gave her warmth and understanding to women who, like myself, were making their first tentative steps on the path of individuation.

In his way of working with men, Jung also created space for the expression of the creative sides of their nature. He offered respectability for the development of introverted intuition in the male, and he showed how the anima could act as *femme inspiratrice*—as

Beatrice to Dante—to lead him into realms that had little to do with the typical male role. Jung knew enough about the hero's journey with its commitment to great accomplishments, to fame and fortune. In his work with men he placed far more emphasis on the night-sea journey, the lesser-known voyage into the depths of their own souls where the treasures lie.

When I came back to the United States in 1964 after my years of training in Zürich, I saw that the shift in the quality of consciousness that was occurring far exceeded Jung's anticipations. Not only were many women recognizing their inner masculine aspects, they were turning themselves inside out to give the animus full permission for expression in the world. Many men were able to respond to this challenge by entering into a freer relationship with the anima, which is to say that they were allowing themselves to express their feelings and their more tender sensibilities.

These men and women pioneered in breaking down the sexual stereotypes by refusing to live according to the old established patterns. Open to change, they made the old boundaries permeable. They had begun to find, in relationships with members of the opposite sex, that much could be learned about the partner by cultivating their own contrasexual aspects, making it possible for animus and anima to function as openings through which the unconscious could manifest. For the unconscious, in Jung's theory, was by definition *something other* than consciousness, and the purpose of the inner work of analysis was to establish a working relationship between the ego and the unconscious. If, then, a woman's masculine aspects were unconscious, she had as her individuation task the drawing up of the animus out of the unconscious depths, freeing him from the illusory aura created by the projections of unconscious contents, and integrating him into her ego consciousness. She had to come to terms with this other aspect that had been a part of herself but previously was not acceptable to consciousness. The converse was equally true for the male; his task in individuation was to integrate the anima into his conscious functioning. Because the unconscious was deep and unfathomable, its contents could never be fully integrated, and so the task was not one which a person could expect to complete in one lifetime. It was more in the nature of making a commitment to the process of bringing together those aspects of being which were essentially different and which operated with different objectives.

This issue caused me the greatest difficulties. I could not accept Jung's position that consciousness and the unconscious were distinct and separable. I am able to understand that in a historic time when the existence of a mysterious realm beyond the awareness of ego was new to the field of psychology, the unconscious must have seemed alien and forbidding. Furthermore, in a society in which social norms determined the concepts of the human potentials and human limitations, admitting the so-called "inner masculine" into awareness must have seemed a formidable task to woman, and the converse equally formidable to man.

My own experience, however, told me otherwise. I had long known that I felt at peace with myself when I rejected certain tasks whose only raison d'être was that they were expected of me because of my particular role in society. When I forced myself to play the part of an extraverted and banal female occupied solely with supporting various male egos, I generally wound up with a migraine. Nor was it that I had ever considered myself less than womanly. Gentleness and empathy have always seemed to me admirable virtues to strive for, and I feel perfectly at home in a nurturant role. But I have long been aware also of an impulse to move out into the world and to plant my seeds—which exist in the form of a number of projects designed to have impact, however small, upon others. I do not feel any dichotomy within myself as a consequence. In the past, before I moved out of the traditional housewife role, it was different. Reflecting back upon those times, it seems to me that the dichotomy was imposed first by the stereotypes of the culture and second—and even more important —from within myself, since I had internalized those stereotypes. But the real person that was I never felt split in the depth of being. At heart I knew that I was one androgynous being psychologically, yet perfectly at home in my female body.

I can see now that whatever problems I had on that score were the outcome of living with an essentially dualistic model of consciousness, which was perfectly consonant with the paradigm of modernity to which I was heir. But it did not correspond with another level of my knowledge. This other level was based neither upon what I had been taught nor upon what I had assimilated from the culture but came, rather, from a source which was only gradually beginning to be activated in me. That source was intuition. Intuition, as I am using it here, means the direct access to unconscious data by means of a nonfocused scanning which does not impose preconceived notions upon what it perceives.

Disquietude with Jung's dichotomization of masculine and feminine consciousness came to me well after I had reached midlife. While sexuality was no longer so urgent a need for me, the energies of love—which seek union with someone or something beyond the realm of ego—were essential for my existence. I began to see in the process of analysis an effort to organize and systematize the structure of the soul according to a preconceived design, which clamped down on its spontaneous expression. I felt as did Blake, when he wrote:

> Why wilt thou Examine every little fibre of my soul
> Spreading them out before the Sun like Stalks of flax to dry[2]

In the years since the issue of the dichotomization of the sexes and sex roles first caused me to take issue with Jung, I have taken much time to reflect on the meaning of my discomfiture. It now has become clearer to me. In my own life I had come upon the watershed when the old paradigm no longer worked and there was a choice as to whether to retreat from the painful disequilibrium that I felt, or to stand the tension of the opposites, hoping for a resolution of the problem and a reconciliation of the disparate aspects of the psyche.

I did not retreat from Jung but, rather, took a step in a direction that, as I now see, he was moving toward in the last years of his life. Jung used the term *transpersonal* to describe levels of the unconscious that were not specific to any individual but were shared by all. He used the term interchangeably with *collective unconscious* and yet, from my present perspective, there is a perceptible difference in meaning. The collective unconscious is that vast pool of the unknown, the unknowable and the not yet known, out of which the infant's consciousness of itself emerges.

It is also a reservoir of the history of the race, hence a source of knowledge. The transpersonal unconscious is the realm beyond consciousness, but capable of becoming conscious—through specific processes designed to remove obstructions to the flow between realms, or through direct revelation. The latter term is not used here in a theological sense but in the sense of something suddenly being revealed, as when a cloud is swept across the sky and all at once the moon is shining. Because the realm of the transpersonal includes an ego that has been fully developed over time but goes beyond that ego into a wider consciousness, we can speak of the transpersonal unconscious as the *superconscious*. The vastness of the superconscious is as hard to imagine as that of the Jungian concept of the collective unconscious. The difference lies in the way each relates to the ego. The collective unconscious is the *source of ego development* and the transpersonal unconscious, or superconscious, is the *goal of ego transcendence*. When consciousness is in a state that transcends ego considerations and ego functioning modalities, we may speak of the superconscious aspect of the organism. This is effective only in the latter stages of a person's psychological development, although glimpses of it may appear earlier.

In his essay "The Stages of Life,"[3] Jung interpreted the psychological meaning of the pre-personal stage of development. He likened the unconscious, instinctive mind of the infant and very young child to that of primitive man. Consciousness in the child, as in the primitive, arises not out of logical process, but out of an inner knowing. As I have suggested, some of that inner knowing consists of the not-yet-forgotten remnants of what has gone on earlier; around birth, perhaps before birth, and possibly even before conception. I cannot know for certain, but I do not feel ready to reject the possibility that this foreknowing may be more extensive than we imagine. Just as the Dreaming of the Australian tells him of the spirit-child that has taken up residence in his wife's womb, so the preverbal knowing of the child appears as though out of nowhere, because adults have forgotten the source. If you watch a very young child carefully, it is not difficult to observe the dawning of an insight, of a recognition of something not hitherto perceived. Consciousness arises as the child's perception links up with an already existing context. When this happens, it is a pleasant experience for the child. Since the child is young, no one expects it to do anything as a result of the perception—it is simply enjoyed for itself. I suspect that is what the special secret smiles of babies are about, but of course this is only my fantasy.

A primary task in the years between infancy and puberty is the freeing of the child from an original and archaic identification with the Self. The identification with the totality of existence is unconscious in the very young child, who is so immersed in the world (as it was in the womb) that it does not experience itself as a separate being. In this archaic world the infant is moved by forces of nature as expressed in bodily needs, feelings, and instinctual behavior. From total dependence upon the magical powers of the parents and others in the environment who provide whatever is required and who protect the child from danger, the child will move out, hesitant at first, into experiments which will define him or her as a person. Limits as to what can and cannot be done will be discovered. There will be rewards for cooperating with a system that belongs not to nature but to society. Throughout childhood a largely unconscious battle is fought between the natural impulses toward self-preservation and growth in accordance with an invisible "blueprint," and the civilizing influences which would educate and train young people to assume appropriate roles in the particular social order to which they belong. The archaic tendency is to respond instinctively to the innate guiding patterns; the civilizing tendency is to adapt to rules and customs imposed from outside the organism.

Jung distinguished three stages in the course of pre-personal development. In the first, the infant is merely recognizing and knowing. This is a generalized, anarchic, and chaotic state. The second stage is marked by the development of the ego complex, the sense of "I-ness." This is initially monarchic—"I am the ruler of all I survey"—or monistic—"I am all there is." The third stage is the divided or dualistic state in which the child begins to discriminate between "I" and "other."

In the first stage of the pre-personal, the infant's life is largely governed by the instincts. Put in a more dynamic way, the instinctive knowing of the child propels it to proceed along the perfect course that it has been following since conception, developing in the right way at the right time without working at it or needing to make decisions. The sureness of an infant's instinctive behavior is awesome. Consciousness moves forward when infants begin to discover their own bodies. Realizing that they have some control over those five-fingered appendages that stretch out before their eyes is the beginning of the formation of the ego complex. "I am something, I can move, touch, scream. I can rule myself. I am fully in charge!" What a wonderful feeling. So the second pre-personal stage begins.

The euphoria lasts for varying lengths of time and, of course, it recurs frequently, but usually the grandiose self-concept is considerably diminished the first time somebody tells the child, "Oh no you don't!" The child's powerful instinctive drive runs head on into opposition from the forces of society, as embodied in the initial caretaking persons. Sooner or later the dawning of consciousness chases away the unconscious joys of infancy. The increasing light of consciousness creates problems. These are the gifts of civilization. The psychic processes of the growing child are made up to a large extent of reflections, doubts, and experiments —all of which were foreign to the infant. Jung said that the growth of consciousness creates problems that did not exist in infancy. "Instinct is nature and seeks to perpetuate nature, whereas consciousness can only seek culture or its denial."[4]

The third pre-personal stage involves the physical separation from the mother, from the paradise of the unconscious. This is an act of consciousness which introduces dualism into the psyche of the child. The mother is no longer always available to the child; more and more often she is "out there." She begins to impose restraints upon her child, but these do not create an inner separation in the child. The restraints are either submitted to, or circumvented, while the child remains relatively placid and centered. This is because the child at this stage does not yet know inner tension. Tension only arises when the external limitations become inner ones (superego), and one impulse is opposed by another. A certain amount of tension is necessary in order to help the child develop resilience. Too much softness and acquiescence on the part of parents does not foster initiative on the part of the child; too little tenderness brings about a sense of isolation.

The tasks of the pre-personal stage of development, including its three phases, center around increasing the child's self-awareness and enabling the child to create and sustain relationships. The responsibility of those who care for young children is to provide a stimulating atmosphere in which this can take place, and to teach them more by example than by precept. The modeling that is suggested here does not come out of deliberate planning, but out of an orientation which recognizes transpersonal consciousness as the purpose toward which the psyche naturally yearns. The danger is that the acculturation process may get in the way of the natural development in consonance with the inherent patterns in nature and the psyche.

A delicate balance is to be maintained as the child emerges from the unconscious Self. Adaptation to social norms is one side of the development. The other side is to learn to recognize transpersonal signals which guide the process of individuation toward the realization of the specific character of the individual within a wider context than the merely personal one. One aspect of adaptation to social norms during the pre-personal stage is the formation of a strong gender identification. This provides the needed foundation for ego coherence and for ego tasks. A positive self-image can only be achieved when the child is fully accepted for being a girl or a boy. This involves accepting obvious sexual differences simply as what is given, with both sexes being equally valuable in the eye of nature. Corollary to this is that no skill the child wants to learn should be excluded on the grounds of being gender-inappropriate. Each young person needs the challenge of testing the boundaries of what is possible.

Awareness can be encouraged in the child by adults who are themselves aware, and eager to share their perceptions. Sensory awareness is one of the first and easiest things the child can learn. Adults can draw attention to sights and sounds, to textures and colors, to heat and cold; they can encourage the pleasure of touching persons and things with their children in order that children may know what they are through direct experience rather than through being told about something. In this way children learn to trust themselves, to know what they know and not to be easily dissuaded from the evidence of their own senses. Sensory awareness, when extended to children's awareness of their own bodies, serves to place a value on the body as the vehicle in which each person's essence is contained. Enjoyment of the body as something which gives and receives pleasure is important to growth. If the body is respected by adults, the child will value it and care for it.

During the pre-personal stage of development, children are attempting to form a picture of the world and of their part in it. One of the most important things that will happen in the prepubertal years is that children will discover what it means to be a boy or to be a girl. Maleness and femaleness are fundamental aspects of the child's identity. It is not necessary to reinforce sex differences. They will become apparent without our help, simply because they exist, in human beings as in all other animals. It is not necessary to tell a bull how to be a bull and a cow how to be a cow—it is part of their nature. Sex and gender are part of human nature as well. If we do not obstruct the natural development of children, sex-appropriate behavior will usually occur as a matter of course. Girls need only to be told that they will grow up to be women, and that women can have babies and nurse them, and boys need only to learn that they will grow up to be men, and can become fathers. They do not need to be informed about any limitations based on sex and gender, because in reality there are no intrinsic limitations. It is quite true that, on the average, males grow to be taller and heavier and stronger than females, and it is true that, on the average, females tend to learn verbal skills at an earlier age. Much has been studied and written about the development of sex differences. In some studies these differences have been minimized, while in others they have been emphasized. An overall conclusion could easily be that while there are differences between the sexes, the differences between individuals within either sex are far more remarkable. After all, we are concerned with individuals and with individual differences, because, finally, that is what humanity is—a collection of individuals.

The way that children are conditioned determines to a large extent their sex-differentiated behavioral patterns. Biology determines what a male or female can do, sex-differentiating conditioning sets arbitrary limits on biological givens. For example, boys are encouraged from an early age to play outdoors, to explore farther from home, and they are rewarded for bravery and risk-taking. Girls are generally more closely watched, kept closer to home, and encouraged to be helpful and to look pretty. Boys' games and toys are designed to develop competitiveness and aggression, while girls' games and toys encourage nurturance and empathy. The activities of childhood are rehearsals for the activities of the adult. Parents can break down the barriers to the actualization of the total personality of their children simply by refusing to establish limits which have no basis other than gender.

If it is seen as desirable that sex be experienced in a loving context, then enjoyment of the body needs to be associated with loving relationships. Children need to see themselves early in reciprocal relationships. It is easy enough to reflect with children about how their behavior affects their world, and how their world affects their behavior. Children may learn to be totally passive and reactive, following the television viewer model. But if they are encouraged to recognize how they can create responses in others, they can begin to create their own context—the context in which they wish to live.

Children have needs to express hostility and anger. When there are passionate disagreements, children need permission to face them directly as issues to be confronted, with confidence that it is possible to find resolutions. The energies of love are often blocked by unexpressed anger; acknowledging the distress is a first step toward dissolution of the block. Humor is a good way of resolving differences also, especially in laughing with, and not laughing at the other. Learning to harness the energies of love begins with careful listening, attending to another person, whether child or adult, while at the same time claiming the space one requires for oneself.

These are a few of the tasks of the pre-personal stage of growth. I have not been too explicit about the ways in which they are to be executed because each family, each household is different. It is the overall context of understanding that is important, for the context is like a vessel into which every social unit pours its special contents.

Traditional developmental theories have emphasized, and to my mind overemphasized, the degree to which adaptation to surroundings and intellectual growth go hand in hand. It is generally accepted that all animals assure their survival by demonstrating their fitness to adapt to the particular environment in which they live; however, it is easy to forget another tenet of Darwin's theory, which asserts that it is through the mysterious leap of a member of a species into a different form from that of its parents, a mutation of the ancestral form, that new and sometimes more highly developed strains come into existence. These latter seem capable not only of being shaped by circumstances, but also of being able to take a part in shaping them. In human development, this translates into the importance of preserving the eccentric, the fantastic, and the creative capacities even while young people are learning to adapt in order to survive. The unique characteristics of the individual can be accepted with a sense of wonder, and the whole context of life is re-membered when we understand, and help our children to understand, that these gifts are a sacred trust and that they carry with them the obligation of stewardship.

14
The Personal Stage:
The Rise of Ego Consciousness

Personal power is the goal of ego development. The very word *power* carries with it mixed connotations. Power is eagerly sought after in our society, yet the "power drive" is often seen as morally reprehensible and destructive of the finer sensibilities. I was discussing my own mixed feelings about the connotations of the word *power* with a French woman, who saw the dilemma immediately. "In English the word is so gross, so undifferentiated," she remarked. "In French we have two words for power, *le pouvoir* and *la puissance*. The first, in the masculine gender, is the power that has to do with command and authority. The second, in the feminine gender, has more to do with strength and influence. You see, both words express power, but the shading is quite different."

The child becoming a youth is faced with the necessity of coming into power, and the tendency to resist this by all possible means. There is a strong backward pull, a clinging to an earlier stage of consciousness in which the child is largely self-centered and used to being supported emotionally and cared for with respect to physical needs. There is a strong pull to remain unconscious of social responsibility and conscious only of the developing ego, to reject the strange or to subject it to the will. There is a resistance to forces in and around the young person which would involve him or her in the world. With all this, there are also physical changes occurring in the prepubescent youngsters that force upon them the necessity of accepting the new and strange within themselves as "also I." They experience a disturbance of equilibrium, caused in part by the activation of sexual energy.

Puberty is a time when nature rouses herself with full vigor and turns brains and hormones into powerful forces that alter consciousness as much as they alter the physical body, its capacities and functions. Societies which did not make a sharp division between the rational and the nonrational aspects of life regarded puberty as a time for propitiation of the gods. Initiation ceremonies were held to ensure that the awesome powers inherent in the activation of sexuality would not be allowed to run amok, but would function under the blessing of the extrahuman forces of creation in accordance with nature's design. From ancient times until today, in places where puberty rites remain a part of the culture, ritual practices give proper weight to the recognition that young people are entering a state where they will become sexually active. There is full awareness that this marks a time of life in which the sexual behavior of the young person is a matter of serious concern to the social group, since it will determine in many ways the future of that group. In special and often secret ceremonies limited to members of one's own sex, the sexual identity of the participants is tested, confirmed, and celebrated. For girls the appearance of menstruation makes it clear that the time is appropriate. This sign of maturation is honored by initiating the girl, either alone or with her peer group, into the mysteries of the feminine. In one way or another the older women will see to it that she becomes aware of the deeper meaning of her sexuality. She learns the rules and restrictions that place limitations on her sexual activity. She may be instructed in ways to make herself pleasing as a sexual partner to a man. She will be informed about the role she will be expected to perform in the particular society in which she lives. She will be told what her obligations to her family will be, and also in what way she will serve the will of the gods—which is generally interpreted in terms of accepting authority and submitting to it.

The advent of sexual maturity does not announce itself with so clear a signal to boys as it does to girls. Therefore, in these ritually oriented societies, male youths have to establish themselves among their peers and their elders, and demonstrate that they are no longer boys, but ready to assume the responsibilities and privileges of manhood. The youths are removed from the mother-world environment and placed in an exclusively masculine setting for the puberty rituals. The individuals must demonstrate their prowess by undergoing painful and dangerous trials demanding a display of unusual courage. These initiatory proceedings may include fasting, self-mutilation, or any other trial or sacrifice that may be demanded in order to demonstrate that sexuality is a vital aspect of life and not something to be taken for granted, or played with, as in the more rationally oriented societies. Elaborate ceremonies are entered into, to affirm the strength and potency of the male sex.

These practices around puberty, which we tend to consider as archaic, serve to prepare the young people for participation in their communities as consciously functioning members of the collective. For them, the development of what we call a "personal ego" is not important in the same way as it is in the more sophisticated contemporary societies. In those groups which are closer to nature, custom, and tradition, where the fear of the gods is never far from awareness, ego development is closely connected with the manner in which the individual's activities contribute to the security and welfare of the group. Heroes of the pre-industrial societies were those who led or protected their fellow members, who were willing to sacrifice themselves for the larger system to which they belonged, and to submit to the will of the gods even when this could mean their personal annihilation. The source of this heroism, or of the cooperative spirit on the part of the unsung heroes who simply did their duty, was the pervasive tribal ethic, the spiritual practice—if you will—that made all members brothers and sisters under the eyes of the unseen rulers of their world. Facing the power of nature and often nature's cruelty and disdain, they were prepared to struggle for survival. They were aware, with that deep and inward knowledge that comes from being fully present to one's surroundings, that survival could never be the product of one person's exploitation of the collective. They knew that strength lay in a well-functioning systemic organism—although such concepts would have meant nothing to them if presented verbally. But in seasons of plenty—whether at harvest time or after the kill of the wild beast—they knew how to distribute the food supply and to preserve what would be needed in time of hunger.

They also knew the value of human resources, and so the community took charge of the customs and practices around sexuality. While there have always been great differences among social groups as to what kinds of sexual behavior would be socially approved, the common factor to all was that the young people clearly understood the guiding principles under which their particular group operated, and what their personal responsibilities were expected to be with regard to these principles.

With us, it is quite different. We are hard put to discover where the puberty rites of Americans are today. Among some of our religious groups the arrival of puberty is marked by a ceremonial "confirmation" but, strangely enough, the vital sexual component of the pubescent consciousness is obscured by the quasi-spiritual component of the ceremony. The parties and presents that follow suggest that puberty is a personal achievement instead of a transition into another stage of life with a new potency and all its associated responsibilities.

"Concerning the crucial issue of sexual awakening," Robert Lifton writes, "our society lacks not only formal ritual but any structure or pattern suggesting that the issue is being recognized and addressed. Experiencing strong bodily impulses, and faced with conflicting social messages of prohibition and encouragement, adolescent individuals and groups must continually improvise around their sexuality. The results vary from a new sense of vitality and liberated growth to mixtures of fear and guilt, despondency over failed performance, and deep confusion."[1]

In our time there seems to be a curious admixture of sexual innocence and sexual experience among the youth of our country. Ill prepared for the demands and responsibilities that go with mature sexuality, they grow up in an atmosphere overheated by aggressive and seductive fantasies having to do with intimate relationships. The curiosity of youth is titillated but rarely satisfied by the agencies in our society that stand to profit from a frenzied search for sexual excitement. The search is addictive, too, for what excites today becomes banal tomorrow. Always there is a demand for something new, something different, something higher than high.

When this energy is not channeled into responsible behavior, ego development may regress in the direction of pure instinctive sexuality. Naturally, there is much hue and cry about all this. Some angry parents insist that sex education is bad, because the more youngsters know about sex, and especially about contraception, the more likely they are to engage in promiscuous relations. These parents favor withholding such information from their children and letting them know that they will have to accept the consequences—no abortions—if they "mess around." Other angry parents, on the opposite side of the fence, insist that young people are going to experiment with sex no matter what their parents say about it, and they may as well be prepared so that they can avoid the unwanted results (pregnancy and venereal disease) of their sexual experience. It appears to me that the issue goes far beyond the questions raised and the variety of solutions offered, all the way from ignorance and fear to sex education, contraception, and abortion. Parents, educators, and other adults will need to address themselves to the more fundamental questions regarding sexual precociousness and promiscuity. Norman Cousins, in an essay titled "Being Healthy Is Not Enough," addresses the issue squarely: "Obviously none of these problems [violence, drug abuse, and pregnancy in teenagers] sprang into being overnight. They are the result of a wide range of interactive causes involving many segments of our society. *They do not exist outside ourselves but are the reflection of internal weaknesses and defaults* that have been accumulating over a long period of time. It is a serious error to suppose, therefore, that the total situation lends itself to a quick fix. The corrective changes will come about, as they have come about in the past, when enough people decide to take personal responsibility. Before we celebrate the conquest of many diseases in the United States we have the obligation to show progress in the conquest of violence and moral breakdown." (Italics mine)[2]

Violence and aggression are responses to fear and rage. The exploitation of others for the sake of making money is a response to overweening greed. Incest may come of selfishness, numbness of feeling, frustration or alienation. But these are just words; they cannot begin to express the pain and sorrow of those who commit the antisocial acts and those who are the victims. The forms of expression may be sexual in nature, but for the most part they are not primarily grounded in sexuality but in a whole complex of disturbed relationships of the ego to the world and to the self-image. It is not that sexuality is expressed through violence, but that violence and other destructive impulses are expressed through sexuality. The disordered ego personalities with their disturbances of the creative and potentially harmonious aspects of the psyche require attention. Treating these individuals as sexual misfits does not begin to answer to their needs. They must be treated as whole persons, which means not only to attend to their individual needs, but also to deal with all those places where they interface with the social order of which, although unwelcome, they are still a part.

Today there is hardly any city in our country, from the Halls of Congress to the Tenderloin district of San Francisco, where sex is not exploited for financial gain, where drugs are not abused in connection with sexual activity, and where violence does not take sexual form as an expression of aggression. In a nation that is as willing as we are to spend an enormous proportion of our national resources on the manufacture of weapons which have no purpose other than to destroy human life, it is not surprising that people have become alienated from their feelings. Where there is much poverty and deprivation, where many young people cannot find employment, one would expect depression to be the prevailing mood. With housing in a state of decay and people unable to afford even to keep their shabby dwellings warm, where schools are run down and inadequately staffed, a general lethargy threatens to overcome. But the human spirit does not give up so easily. When it cannot find a good situation, the spirit does the best it can with what it has. And so, in the sections of our large cities where the environmental conditions are the worst, sexuality is the fire that keeps hope alive and makes life appear to be worth living—if only for brief intervals of human touch and gaiety that break into the chilling succession of nights and days.

When the heart is hungry, an offer of sex is misconstrued as a promise of love. Men and women, eager for human connection at whatever cost, may allow themselves solace in sexual relationships wherever they can be found. There seems hardly any way to persuade young people who feel they have little going for them in the world that they will be better off postponing sexual relations until they are mature enough to take on the commitments and responsibilities that come with procreative sex. Most young people do not expect or wish to become parents when they first become sexually active. But many do become parents, that is, biological parents, whether or not they are capable of doing the parenting that is required.

And so the cyclic process of human development takes another turn, and the children have now become parents with children of their own. But not all follow the expected development so neatly laid out by the developmental psychologists as "normative." Social practice has raced ahead of theory, which, inevitably, is built upon the social practice of the past. The ego development of the individual does not necessarily conform to the rules of the past in its search for personal power. Where a generation or two ago the influence of the parents was of prime importance in transferring the values of the culture, today the parental influence is only one among a number of important factors that shape the consciousness of the child and influence the course of its ego development.

A clearly stated series of developmental steps was set forth by Jane Loevinger in the mid-sixties, and was discussed in Chapter 3. How has this pattern changed? In considering some of the ways in which this scenario has shifted and ways in which ego development may have failed to negotiate the transitions to the higher stages projected by Loevinger, it will be useful to review briefly her stages in the context of the eighties.

The presocial, symbiotic stage of infancy is not so much limited to the mother-child relationship as it once was. At best, parenting is shared, with the father and other members of the family taking important caring roles. Early socialization in the child is encouraged; sometimes it is necessary when the mother is employed outside the home. The quality of this infant care is of utmost importance. Unless it approximates that consistency and constancy which in the past a mother has been expected to provide, the child's sense of security is endangered for the time ahead.

The child who has had little opportunity to enjoy the oceanic

comfort of a placid home, with the mother's presence and attention an ongoing reality, will enter the *impulse-ridden stage* without the undergirding of knowledge that the beloved and caring
person will be present no matter what. Instead of allowing the
normal, healthy oral drives free expression, and instead of the inevitable response of being nurtured and held by the mother, the
infant faces premature restrictions and pressure to conform to the
needs of others. Instead of the impulses reaching a certain level of
need and then being satisfied, the infant may at times have to give
up the hope of being heard, of being attended to. A subtle form
of hopelessness may cloud the infant's consciousness. This will be
noticeable from the infant's crying, excessive sleeping, and lack of
interest in the environment. The infant will not reach out to be
picked up when mother or another person approaches, nor will its
eyes dart about searching for people or things that promise pleasure.

The *opportunistic stage*, which follows in Loevinger's
scheme, corresponds with the Freudian anal stage in some respects. It has to do with the anticipation of reward and punishment and the child's ability to gain control over impulses in ways
that will avoid punishment and reap rewards. Toilet training is
the classic example here. Gaining the ability to give or withhold
behavior that adults desire, and thus manipulate adults, represents
an important stage of ego development. In environments where
the adults have not transcended opportunistic ways of functioning
but see everything in terms of who gets what and how to manage
to get as much as you possibly can, the child's ego development
can, in important respects, become fixated at this level. In opportunistic sexuality, the energy is directed into manipulating the
other person into fulfilling one's own sexual desires. Presenting
oneself as attractive to the potential sex object will be seen in
terms of making conquests, not relationships. The use of energy
primarily for personal gain, without concern for the others involved, not only leads to sexuality alienated from any feeling resembling tenderness or affection, but also prepares the scene for
the exploitation of the sexual instinct which is endemic in contemporary life.

The *conformist stage* normally follows the opportunistic

stage, and usually is the stage of the young person entering puberty. Whether the earlier stages have been experienced in satisfactory ways and then transcended, or not, will determine to what
social group the young person will conform—but, in any case, peer
pressure will be a vital factor in determining attitudes and behavior. In the conformist stage, the individual recognizes the power
of the collective to set standards and to inform people what their
personal and social obligations are. The formation of a strong gender identity is high in importance to the young person attempting
to define himself or herself in relation to the collective.

From birth, when male and female infants could scarcely be distinguished from one another without examining their genitals,
until the time of puberty, sexual differentiation has been going on
at many levels: physical, emotional, social, and behavioral. These
developmental changes have come in for study since the beginning of the women's movement in the early sixties. The increasing
involvement of women scholars in the study of sex differences and
sexual differentiation reflected women's efforts to justify their
claims to parity with men in employment and professional life.
The research covered the period from early childhood to adulthood. Some of the findings are important here in that they suggest
possible reasons for the differences in functioning between boys
and girls. They raise questions concerning the interface between
innate and instinctual aspects of development, and the institutions of the culture. It was shown, for example, that girls test
higher on general intelligence during preschool years, while boys
test higher in intelligence during high school years. The tests supposedly have no sex bias, but interpreters disagree about this. Also,
the higher scores of boys may reflect the possibility that the higher
dropout rate among boys produces selectivity. On the other hand,
the lower intelligence of some boys may account, at least to some
degree, for their dropping out of school. In verbal ability, in the
preschool years girls say the first word earlier, articulate more
clearly and earlier, use longer sentences and are more fluent than
boys. By the time of elementary school there is no longer any sex
difference in vocabulary. Girls tend to read sooner and better than
boys, but by age ten boys have caught up. Is this a function of intelligence, one may ask, or is it related to the fact that little girls

tend to stay closer to their mothers and to have more exposure to adult language while boys are more likely to be engaged in active outdoor play? Again, girls count sooner, but all through school there is no consistent sex difference in arithmetic computation. In high school and college men do better in mathematics. In areas of creativity, boys tend to do better on problem solving and restructuring when there is a large perceptual component, while girls do better on problems that require verbal reasoning.

Some interesting observations have come out of research in which intellectual performance is correlated with personality characteristics. In boys, impulsivity, aggression, and competitiveness seem to inhibit intellectual performance, while in girls these same personality characteristics seem to facilitate intellectual performance. Again, we ask, is this an innate difference? Or are boys so well rewarded for, say, excellence in sports that they are not so highly motivated to concentrate on studies, while girls need to use their extraverted energies to come to grips with the demands of the external world, represented by the school?

More questions are raised than answered in studies such as these. To what extent do people respond to having been trained in socially defined sex-appropriate characteristics, and to what extent is behavior based on a substratum of biological determination with which environmental input must interact? What is the role of hormonal sensitization during the prenatal period in contributing to sex-appropriate behavior later in the life-cycle when these specific hormonal concentrations are no longer present? How important are variations in physical size? How important is the anticipation from childhood on that the female does the bearing and suckling of children? To what degree are these perceptions generalized to similar activities? How do they become institutionalized into occupational roles and other cultural prescriptions? To what degree may the long history of reinforced dependency for women be responsible for the reported female "conformity"? Once sex roles were based on evolutionary necessity, but now they have become highly elaborated cultural products, says one researcher. This seems to reflect a consensus of the researchers in the field during the decade of the seventies.

Whatever the factors have been that contributed to the increasing divergence between the sexes in childhood, it is clear that at no time is a girl more feminine or a boy more masculine than when they are turning into young women and young men. Even if, in our times, the casual dress and manner of females seems to belie this as they put on blue jeans and go without makeup, it is clear that they are not the least bit interested in being mistaken for males. In a way, it is a preposterous protest against defeminization, for the young women carry themselves and behave in feminine ways, and can turn into magical butterflies at a moment's notice when the occasion is ripe or the right person comes into view. They enjoy becoming women, and all the more so because, in these days of increased opportunities for women, they have more of the freedom to express the many facets of their natures than any generation of women has had since the days of the ancient matriarchal civilizations. If they have managed to get through the perils of adolescence in reasonably good shape without any serious traumas, their attention turns toward attracting the man with whom they will hope to have a serious committed relationship. However free they feel about their ability to choose a person with whom they will share closeness and intimacy, many unconscious factors are operating that will affect the determinations they will make as women. For finally the woman, being the receptive partner, will have men present themselves to her, and she will either accept or reject each one, depending upon some indefinable feeling that rises up within her. The male takes the risk of being rejected every time he approaches a female. Problematic feelings that may have originated at any time from infancy on are often reexperienced in the process of becoming mature and fully conscious.

In speaking of sexuality here, I am using the broadest connotation of the word, meaning essentially everything that belongs to the erotic realm of human relationship—the ways men and women regard each other, the ways they care for each other, how they share their lives in deeply personal ways, their enjoyment of each other's companionship and supportiveness, the physical and spiritual affirmation that comes from the tender touch of skin to skin. Within this broad spectrum is the act of sex itself. Its importance comes from its fulfillment of the totality of sexuality more

than for itself alone. The emotional connection between lovers ignites a spark that warms the spirit. It is terribly compelling; it
knows no reason; it draws people together and casts a spell over
them. No one knows exactly what it is that brings about the great
heat of passion, but no one can mistake it when it appears.

As young children, most of us played more or less indis-
criminately with members of both sexes. As we approached puberty, or perhaps when we were well into that transition, we were
for the most part more compatible with members of our own sex.
It is so much easier to be close to someone who is rather like yourself. A boy knows how to please another boy, and there is much
that can be shared. It is the same with a girl. Usually, there is a
period of extreme closeness with one or more members of one's
own sex. There may be some sexual exploration during this period,
some learning about one's own sexual response and some comparing that with what other members of your own sex are experiencing. Curiosity will be satisfied, since even if young people have
been taught as much as possible about sex in these growing years,
they will still want to experiment on their own and discover for
themselves how to manage the mysterious feelings that arise in
them. This kind of experimentation is not particularly threatening
because usually the people involved already have proved themselves as friends, and since they are feeling the same kinds of feelings, there is little to fear. Left to themselves, these youthful rehearsals for adult sexuality run their course, and the young people
become ready to move on to the greater risk, that of heterosexual
exploration.

It is not a very easy bridge to cross, as most of us may remember. If something disturbing has occurred in the course of homo-
erotic play, a barrier may have been created in the way of further
exploration in the realm of sexuality. In the face of such barriers,
sexual energy may be turned back, and the person may look toward the mother-father world and the ways in which sexuality was
expressed between the parents in the home. What sort of models
did the adults provide for the enjoyment of intimacy? Were they
caring and considerate, helpful to one another? Were they supportive in difficult moments? Were they forgiving, or were they
more often stern and judgmental? Was the same-sex parent the

dominant one, or was it the opposite-sex parent? Did the growing child see stability in man-woman relationships, or were such relationships fraught with uncertainty and the fear of dissolution?

The answers to these questions do much to condition the developments in the next stage, the *stage of self-awareness*. When the first romantic encounter occurs, the ego personality may find itself between the urge for a fuller expression of sexuality and the need to protect and preserve itself against rejection on one hand or invasion on the other. The driving force of nature must contend with the braking power of lessons learned from parents or from personal experience. Some people become fixated in an immature form of sexual expression, playing with sex as a kind of sport without any intention of establishing a relationship with a person. But most become sufficiently confident of themselves and of their gender identity to cross over into the brighter realm of "being in love," with all the fantasy and romance that state brings about. This is the time of eternal spring, of poetry and tender feelings. Everything seems wonderful and full of promise. It is the time when the beloved person feels like the one, the only one, who can make the lover feel complete. It appears that before, the lover was only half a person, an echo chamber for his or her own thoughts and those of others. But now there is deep resonance and a feeling of harmony and balance. The lover has found a love object in the other, and a connection can be made.

The establishment of a relationship that entails mutual commitment is an important step toward psychosexual maturity. It means often giving up a wide range of options in favor of focusing on a primary relationship which will serve as a keystone to other relationships and to other dimensions of living. Relationships that are based on self-awareness help the individual to place personal needs in the context of the needs of the other. Personal values are enunciated in love relationships, and if they are accepted by the partner then there is impetus for replacing group values with values of one's own. When these values are accepted and supported by the other in the relationship, the ego is strengthened and its energy is freed to be more active in the world. Inner doubts can be talked about, the problems shared. In intimate relationships it is possible for each to be vulnerable and to show weakness as well as power. Naturally, each person holds expectations that the other person will respond in ways that will be helpful and furthering. The expectations are often not realistic, especially when they come not from knowing the loved person but from projecting one's own unconscious aspects onto the other. We are likely to be attracted to people who are different from ourselves, who seem to fill the needs for which we are longing and compensate the lacks in our own development. We want the other to make us whole, and that is why the first fire of romance brings about an inner feeling of completeness. The partner takes on the qualities of the anima, the unconscious image of the inner feminine, in whatever form he needs her to fill out his own personality or, in the case of a woman, the beloved is dressed in the appearance of her animus, the one for whom she has waited and who she believes will bring her what she desires.

In the course of living together and coming to know the partner, it becomes apparent sooner or later that the other is not the person who was imagined. When the other's humanness pokes its way through the cloak of illusion, self-awareness is put to the test. Does the individual know what belongs to his or her own unconscious fantasy and what really belongs to the partner? Are the two willing to do the hard work of sorting out the personalities from the projections and to look at themselves and their partner with a fresh eye, and accept what they see? If not, the relationship will begin to deteriorate, although appearances of relationship may continue intact for a long while. This is a time when persons unwilling to face the dissonance between their expectations and what they have found in relationship now begin again to seek the fulfillment of their fantasies elsewhere, openly or in secret. Faithlessness to the commitment to the partner, while pretending that things are going well enough, is possibly the most damaging blow to the partner's ego. When two individuals have been close in body, mind, and soul, there is something in one which knows when the other has broken the trust—and yet consciously it is often difficult to admit that one knows. And so there is that subtle undermining that happens, like standing on quicksand that is just beginning to give way and draw one into the depths. Self-awareness is not enough to sustain a relationship. The ego must move on to the next level.

The conscientious stage may be the first step in the passage from the ego stage toward the transpersonal stage, but it is by far not there yet. The possibility of transcending pure ego concerns arises here. Personal values by now are internalized; they no longer have to be fought for but are taken for granted as self-understood. People are able to be self-critical, to recognize their role in relationship disturbances. By this time they have a sense of long-term goals, and the patterns by which they hope to achieve these goals are fairly well established. If the previous stages have been successfully negotiated, the person by this time is making progress on the ladder of worldly success, and also has established and is maintaining a family, if that has been part of the life-plan.

When being in love has run its course, there is a chance for real loving to enter. Real loving requires that one believe in oneself enough not to fear dissolution of ego integrity if she or he gives space to the other's individuality. Real loving cares for the other's well-being and supports the dynamism of the other's growth. Real loving means giving up the hope that the other will fill out all those parts missing from one's own wholeness; it means giving up dependence upon another to fulfill what one cannot do for oneself. Loving opens the door for each person to reclaim that part of himself or herself that has been held in abeyance while he was trying to fit the image of the "ideal male" as transmitted by his parents or peers, and she was trying to fit the image of the "ideal female."

The individualistic stage marks the highpoint of ego development, according to the schema of the ego psychologist. Not everyone arrives this far. The stage is marked by a desire for emotional independence and self-expression. It frequently involves serious questioning of the mores of modernity and even rebellion against them. But the philosophical system that characterizes the paradigm of modernity still rules the individualistic stage of ego development. The person has by now freed himself or herself of the necessity to conform to the old patterns of behavior. All sorts of new and creative life-styles are tried out. In the effort to achieve "self-realization," the personal ego is in the forefront of consciousness. The person may be striving to discover the limits of his or her capacity, and this occurs more often than not at the expense of relationship. The possibility of being "independent" and not needing others is especially seductive. At this time marriages fall apart, families are dispersed, and individuals try to go it alone like the typical American cowboy hero.

I suspect that this individualistic urge was one of the important factors in the initiation of the movement that came eventually to be known as "women's liberation." Woman's role had long been defined in terms of her relationship to a man. This was true of not only the wife and mother, but also the woman in the business or professional world, who was expected to play the supportive role in a male-dominated environment. Her own identity under these circumstances was not clearly differentiated—she never knew who she might be or what she might attain as an individual because she rarely functioned in the context of her own individuality.

The women who started the movement were strongly individualistic. Those who followed them discovered that attempting to transcend the stereotyped sex roles was incredibly difficult and demanding. So many vested interests would be threatened by the radical changes that would ensue if women ever approached social, political, and legal parity with men. It was not to men's interests in general for women to forsake their supportive roles and to begin to develop their own latent capacities. Not only would they withdraw their energy from the male endeavor, but they might even come to expect a situation in which they would be supported toward their own goals—where support would be mutual and independence would give way to interdependence. Most men saw this as a losing proposition for themselves, while some women saw it as a prospect from which they would gain more than they lost. However, the women who saw the exciting possibilities in the women's movement that its early leaders talked about were far from a majority. The free and independent woman could be nothing but a threat to the woman who remained in a dependent relationship. The "new woman" was seen as more attractive, sexually freer, more mobile, more intelligent, and more self-seeking than the traditional woman; hence the new woman was not exactly

cheered by her less adventurous sisters. It took a long time for
many women to see that they might gain their individuality without losing everything else that was precious to them, and many
women have yet to see this.

15
Transition:
From Personal to Transpersonal

The rise of the new feminine consciousness did much to upset the already uneasy balance between the sexes. This is not to say that sexual relationships had necessarily been happier in the past, but marriages were more stable when the expectations of both partners were clearly defined and husband and wife roles were more distinct and socially approved. Marriage and other committed relationships usually provided a framework within which love could be expressed, without people being paralyzed by the residues of this pre-personal fear. They were better able to put their negative emotions aside when the sexual relationship was new and satisfying, and when there was the promise that the two would share the responsibility for bringing up issues that needed attention and working on them together. Nevertheless, the old inhibitions often remained unresolved at the most fundamental level because they could not be worked on, since they had slipped below the level of consciousness. In times of stress, or during periods of particularly rapid psychological growth, the channels between consciousness and the unconscious would widen and the buried emotions would rise to the surface and become conscious. This would occur inevitably when the partners' growth would take them in different directions. The old fears would then return. Each person would be concerned either about losing the other person, or about the other's placing limitations on the new growth. To avoid these constrictions, the person who felt threatened would withdraw emotionally from the partner. Various kinds of difficulties in sexual function would appear, and successfully create distance between the partners; or one person's sexual indifference would create frustration on the part of the other who desired more sexual contact.

The women's movement has drawn attention to disturbances in sexual relationships on a scale that has not been seen before. When women found their voices they began to communicate with each other, and sometimes with men, about their dissatisfaction with their most intimate relationships. They discovered that they were not alone. The conflictual feelings they had—between the emergence of their individuality and their desire to improve their relationships—they found were being experienced more generally than they had imagined. In fact, these kinds of conflicts were surfacing wherever the traditional family system was being threatened or where it had given way to alternative styles of relationship. Their concerns were reflected in a whole new genre of literature and media presentations offering suggestions for more and more ways to expand the varieties and pleasures of sexual experience. Sexuality was portrayed as a never-ending series of exciting adventures, romantic seductions, and emotional roller coasters featuring intrigue, passion, and mystery. Many people who had been living relatively normal lives, holding jobs, supporting and rearing families, began to regard their own sex lives as falling below the standards for sexual activity as they perceived those standards. Whereas in the past, women who were economically and socially dependent on their husbands did not expect also that sex would regularly offer them ecstatic delight, the more independent women were no longer easily put off. Active in the world and informed about sexual matters, they formed their own expectations. Rather than suffer in silence when they did not feel sexually fulfilled, more and more women decided to do something about it. They sought help where it was offered, bringing along their husbands or other partners.

"Sexual dysfunction," as these difficulties came to be known, are treated in married couples more often than nonmarried couples. This is possibly because of the commitment that marriage implies: to stay together and attempt to resolve any difficulties, if at all possible; while in other sexual relationships there is less incentive to remain in a relationship when it is unsatisfactory sexually.

Over the years since people began going to sex therapy clinics for help, the presenting complaints have changed. At first, the preponderance of problems for which men came into treatment were impotence, or premature or retarded ejaculation. Women typically came because of lack of sexual responsiveness, vaginismus (muscle spasms that make intercourse impossible), dyspareunia (difficult or painful coitus), or inability to reach orgasm. These problems were primarily physiological, often caused by ignorance about sexual techniques, by tensions that were the residues of early prohibitions around sex, and by a general lack of experience. In addition, there would be the emotional factor of disappointment when the expectations that sex would be somehow magically transporting failed to be realized.

As the public became more willing to accept sexual dysfunction as a disorder that could be remedied, a spate of the explicit sex manuals appeared, detailing every sexual technique. Help came also from family doctors, psychologists, marriage counselors, and from friends with whom such matters could be safely shared. With the increase of information about sex, many couples were themselves able to overcome such problems as premature ejaculation and inability to achieve orgasm. The people who determined to undergo sex therapy, then, were those with more pervasive problems, involving not only the sexual aspects of their relationship but often the entire relationship.

Sex therapy programs have been instituted by the outpatient services of many hospitals, and sex therapists in private practice established treatment programs as well. It often happens that following "successful" results around the symptoms, the deeper problems in the relationship reveal themselves. Impotence in a man or frigidity in a woman may turn out to have been an adaptive coping mechanism for keeping the partner at a distance. The real situation was that the person, consciously or unconsciously, felt that the partner was or could be a threat to the stability of his or her own ego, in the open and vulnerable area of sexual intimacy. To explore the basis for these feelings is quite a different matter than dealing with the mechanical aspects of sex.

In the pathology/treatment model, the condition of apparent lack of interest in sex acquired the rather pejorative diagnosis of *inhibited sexual desire*. Both married and single patients suffer from all of the sexual disorders but this one, while *every* man who has sought treatment for inhibited sexual desire has been married. The inescapable implication is that women, freer now to express their sexual needs, are insisting that their partners who cannot satisfy them seek professional help. The recent shift of focus in sex therapy clinics has been from dysfunction to dissatisfaction. Currently some doctors are reporting that inhibited sexual desire is the number one cause of applications for sex therapy.

It has been suggested that there is a lot less sex in many marriages than people commonly suppose. Investigation into the frequency of sexual relations has shown that almost a third of all married couples have intercourse as infrequently as once a month, or even less often. Once the frequency of intercourse begins to diminish, it becomes more and more difficult to approach the partner, and finally efforts are given up altogether. The energy that used to be available for sex dwindles, or is expended in other directions.

When couples are asked in sex therapy what they believe are the reasons for the lack of desire, they talk of not having enough time, or not being able to communicate with each other, or that their sex life is no longer interesting. These superficial reasons often cover emotions that have been buried under mounds of indifferences. Sometimes it is possible to bring these emotions out. Sometimes the people retreat for fear that the explosion that might follow their exposure would be more destructive than simple, slow stagnation.

In my experience as therapist I find that sometimes these truths can be better reached in individual psychotherapy. The protection of this private and confidential therapeutic alliance makes it possible for people to reveal what cannot be said in the presence of their partners. Sometimes their reticence stems from a genuine and loving concern for the preservation of the partner's own integrity. For example, a woman who had grown away from her husband in the course of her own development was no longer able to accept his crude and insensitive treatment. She did not feel he was either capable of changing or motivated to do so, since he was not dissatisfied. She was committed to remain in the marriage because she believed strongly in the importance of maintaining a stable home for her young children, so she resolved the problem within herself by withdrawing from the physical part of the marital relationship. Another case, in which the man was disinterested in sex, seemed to be related to his preoccupation with his work, which demanded a great deal of creativity from him and which he loved passionately, as one would love a woman. His wife did not interest him nearly as much, so he poured his energy into his work and into relationships with people in connection with his work. He was perfectly happy but his wife was miserable, and this precipitated the wife's requesting sex therapy. One might have asked why this man remained with his wife. He enjoyed the comfort of his home, his children, and the relief from the steady pressure of work. He provided materially for his wife, was kind to her, and made absolutely no demands. He couldn't understand why she should be dissatisfied.

There are couples where the anger runs deep, where husband or wife has unknowingly re-created earlier traumas, and there is no rational way to come to terms with the emotions they generate. Or, the marital partner turns out to resemble the opposite sex parent in ways that were not understood in the first fiery expressions of love. But, when intimacy becomes habitual, the ancient prohibition of incest clothes itself in the guise of indifference, and creates the distance that is needed. Again, sexual desire may be withdrawn from the partner because it is being directed elsewhere; there is another lover toward whom the energy of life flows more freely. For some, it is possible to love truly more than one person, but intimacy of the sexual body cannot so easily be shared. For others, it is guilt which inhibits sexual expression.

Sometimes a couple concerned about "inhibited sexual desire" inquires as to what is the normal frequency of sexual relations. Naturally, there is no general norm. If both partners are content with intercourse five times a week, that would be normal for them. If both partners wanted intercourse no more than once a month, or once in six months, that would be normal for them. But when one person's needs call for sex at more frequent intervals than the other's, then the difficulties arise. Understanding that this discrepancy commonly occurs may help considerably. When sex becomes an obligation, or a way of proving love, not wanting sex may be interpreted as not caring sufficiently about the other person. Is there under this hurt a secret disappointment that the partner has not acted in a way that corresponds to the image in the mind's eye of the other? Is there a hidden resentment that he has not performed as she imagined he would? Has he failed to provide for her the level of fulfillment that she believes she is entitled to? How often, spoken or unspoken, is the perception "my partner has failed me." Along with that may come the deeper wounding of the ego which one performs upon oneself by giving way to the feeling, "Therefore, I must be inadequate, I must be worthless. There is nothing I can do." Hopeless and helpless, the partner who has been cast aside suffers a severe deflation of the ego. At such times the individual feels shaky and ungrounded. The ego gains for which the person has worked so hard now seem ephemeral and the social adaptation that the person has achieved at such great effort now seems meaningless and without value. The individual finds that he or she is not in control of the powerful forces that rule human relationships.

Everyone experiences such shattering crises at one time or another, if not in the context of sexuality, then in some other context. Whatever has mattered most in life seems to fall away. The ego personality is bereft and the self-image begins to crumble around the edges. This is an utterly crucial moment in the development of the person. It is not possible to be the same person one was before the catastrophe. There is no way to stay in a position which no longer exists in the dimension of matter or of spirit/psyche. A radical change must take place, and there are two possible directions for this to happen: regression in the direction of the pre-personal, or progression to another level of consciousness in the direction of the transpersonal.

Jung had written about the "persona,"[1] that adaptive mask we show to the world so that people are able to define us and relate to us. Each person protects the ego with this covering which smoothens the way in interpersonal relations. The catastrophes that separate us from the beloved person or from others upon whom we depend for nurture and support, and the catastrophes which destroy our self-image vis-à-vis the world, annihilate this persona, leaving the ego defenseless. One possibility of coming to terms with the damage is, in Jung's words, a "regressive restoration of the persona." This occurs with the collapse of the conscious attitude. "It always feels like the end of the world, as though everything had tumbled back into original chaos. One feels delivered up, disoriented, like a rudderless ship that is abandoned to the moods of the elements. So at least it seems. In reality, however, one has fallen back upon the collective unconscious, which now takes over the leadership . . . But once the unconscious contents break through into consciousness, filling it with their uncanny power of conviction, the question arises of how the individual will react. Will he be overpowered by these contents? Will he credulously accept them? Or will he reject them? (I am disregarding the ideal reaction, namely critical understanding.) The first case signifies paranoia or schizophrenia; the second may either become an eccentric with a taste for prophecy, or he may revert to an infantile attitude and be cut off from human society; the third signifies the *regressive restoration of the persona*."[2] In this last reaction, the individual avoids further risks, tries to patch up the damaged social reputation within the confines of a much more limited personality, and refuses to be again placed in a vulnerable position. Clearly this is a return toward the pre-personal state, toward a collective unconscious which is represented by more archaic forms and images. The individual spends much time reverting to the past in thought, living a life of useless regrets, identifying with the antiheroes of myth and history.

The other possibility to which Jung alluded, the "ideal reaction, namely critical understanding," suggests that the best that Jung could hope for as a result of the deflation of the ego and the loss of the persona was some learning from the experience, some insight, and eventually a reestablishing of the ego. The optimal result, over time, would be an even better adaptation to the circumstances of life and an improved capacity for self-criticism. Ego defenses would be shored up, and the person would regard himself or herself as "autonomous," which is to say relatively self-contained and independent of the views and opinions of others.

(This would correspond to Loevinger's *autonomous stage* of ego development, a stage few people reach.)

A radically different approach to the ego crisis leads in the direction of the transpersonal. This is most likely to occur when the ego that has once been powerful and strong is suddenly stripped bare of its protective persona. Instead of despair and alienation, or after a period of despair and alienation, the person "sees" with the inner eye that the catastrophe has occurred on one level only, the level of pride and attachment to persons or objects or to a way of life. One sees that salvation rests not in any person or object or way of life to which one has become attached, but in freedom from the attachment. This means that one can love, and let go, for loving has become more important than holding on. With this freedom comes the paradox that we are almost nothing in the grand scheme of things ("What is man that thou art mindful of him, and the son of man that thou dost care for him?") and that we are also the carriers of life and hope, of civilization and of the energy of love which binds it all together ("Yet thou hast made him little less than God, and dost crown him with glory and honor") (Psalms 8:4).

One begins to realize that the cataclysms of personal life, though real enough, are not the alpha and omega of Life itself. They belong to the world of small knowledge. Personal tragedy may signal the diminishment of the ego; but if this can be accepted as being part of the nature of things, the trough that follows the wave, the ego may be able to find a new place in the larger scheme of things. Then one need no longer be rigidly bound to the old paradigm—although it is useful for negotiating some of the practical aspects of everyday living—but can incorporate the old necessities into the new possibilities. One is made free to explore the realm of the new paradigm and, because it is still in formation and will be for a long time, one is able to explore uncharted fields aided by the intuition that one can learn to finely tune. Great Knowledge is what will be sought after.

The transition to the transpersonal is not a one-way street. The suffering ego more than likely will waver between the regressive and the progressive movement, glimpsing some of the possibilities of the transpersonal realm, losing nerve and retreating into the pre-personal, swinging back and forth, and perhaps returning to the ego position after a time with some residual tendencies to move in one direction or the other, as though the pendulum were slowing down. The collective unconscious was the original matrix of consciousness, out of which the thinking process of the individual emerged; thus it forms the foundations of consciousness. The archetypes and images of the collective unconscious give rise to our patterns of thinking and behavior, often dominating us so that we do not know why we do what we do. The introspective process, as in analysis, leads us back to unravel some of the hidden factors that exert powerful influences upon us and hold us in thrall. The introspective process involves, above all, finding one's way through the mazes of the collective unconscious, discerning what in one's life is personal, and claiming it, and knowing what belongs to the collective.

The process of self-reflection also concerns itself with the purposive aspect of the psyche. Patterns of development, as we have seen, reach back into the distant past for their origins, not only to the infancy of the person, but also to the time before birth and, as far as possible, to the historical and mythological patterns common to the human species. These all combine to give direction to the psyche, and the linkage of past-present-future can be understood as an essential reality that gives shape and substance to the life of the individual. Each person's uniqueness is the product of the innumerable effects of the past impinging upon the present, as the person develops and interacts with the environment and its teachings.

Unlike the collective unconscious with its setting in the remoteness of time, the superconscious faces onto an eternal and expanding present. The psyche's thrust toward the superconscious, which is the foundation of the transpersonal realm, is not so much backward and inward, as in analysis; rather, the thrust is outward, expanding as concentric circles ripple, disturbing the surface of the pool into which a stone has been dropped. The superconscious is coexistent with the knowledge of the ultimate reality, the "Absolute" which has no name, neither can it be described. It encompasses the collective unconscious, yet it is beyond form or even the possibility of form. It is pure consciousness, of which

human consciousness—even in its highest forms—is merely derivative. At the same time, there is given the possibility that the
human being can be a channel for the superconscious. This may
come about when people begin to recognize who they are—on a
transpersonal level.

The transpersonal way is not to focus on the pathology or, in
other words, on the emotional response to the pain and suffering
which is the heritage and the fate of every individual at one time
or another. It is a way of getting free of the belief that by our own
power we can keep ourselves intact; that we can avoid annihilation. It is knowing that, of the many forces that affect us every
moment of the day and night, only a few lie within the absolute
dominion of the ego. The others can overtake us at any time. We
need to accept that, and be prepared for it. Anyone who has lived
awhile has met with those winds of change in the universe that
remove us from the steady, predictable course of events and toss
us about in ways over which we have no control. A child is killed.
A city is flooded. A friend goes mad. We become seriously ill. The
plans we made yesterday cannot be carried out. We have tasted of
annihilation. What can we do?

Once we have known that taste, and known that it will come
again and again until we die of it, there is no sense in hanging on
to the fear. It will come, it comes, and in its own time it carries
away the ego that we know in this life as our identity. So all this,
for which we have struggled so much, is ours for only a little time
at best, and cannot be preserved beyond that. Why should we try
to hang on to quicksilver when it will not stay in our hands? This
awareness is truly liberating, for if we know that we cannot keep
ourselves to ourselves, then we can freely give ourselves in human
relationships. As ego personalities, we are incomplete. We are
fragments of the human community, yearning for union. When
we acknowledge this and act on it, we can approach wholeness.

16
The Transpersonal Stage:
Uniting the Fragments

We are able, at the transpersonal stage, to see life whole. No longer do we limit our seeing to the fragments of self and others as isolated entities capable of autonomy or self-sufficiency. No longer do we regard power as a magic wand, a great manipulator that humans can use to achieve superiority over others who are less powerful. We begin to understand what it means to say, "We are all One." It is an affirmation of the union between the divine and the human principles, a union which exists on a profound and basic level and underlies every plurality that exists on the level of manifestation. The transpersonal perspective allows us to remember that Great Knowledge exists, that it is ever-present as an overriding consciousness in which we are contained, even while we make our peace with the world of small knowledge, of multiplicity.

Oneness means to us, as we reflect from this perspective, that there is no separation between the Divine principle and human life. As in Michelangelo's noble and familiar image, the creative spark flows from God's fingertip to Adam's, and human beings enact what is ordained for them. This passing of the spark from God to man may be seen as an act of love. In the most subtle sense it may contain the essence of sexuality as well, for the fire that passes from the One to the other is fully generative; it brings humanity into being.

Out of the one come forth the many. This is the theme of creation mythology the world over. First there is the Creative Power, drawn in the imagery of the culture to which the story belongs. Among the Greeks it was told that there were no human beings until the Titan Prometheus, with the consent of Athene, formed mortal men out of water and clay. Prometheus had been present and assisted at the birth of Athene from the head of Zeus, hence she was indebted to him for her existence. She breathed life into Prometheus' creation, for life comes only from the Divine source. Also, the Goddess of Wisdom taught Prometheus architecture, astronomy, mathematics, navigation, medicine, metallurgy, and other useful arts. Prometheus so loved mankind that he passed on all his knowledge to them. He had given fire to mankind, after having stolen it from the gods, by lighting a torch at the fiery chariot of the sun, breaking off a fragment of glowing charcoal and carrying it off hidden in the pith of a giant fennel stalk. It is said that this is why, to this day, the Greeks carry fire in a fennel stalk.

This first fire led indirectly to the gift of the gods to mankind in the form of Pandora. Zeus sent this first woman to Prometheus' brother as a vengeful act, because of his anger against Prometheus. With Pandora, he sent a box containing all of the world's troubles. Despite Prometheus' warning, curiosity triumphed over obedience and Pandora opened her box, disseminating its contents throughout the world. In spite of her inquisitiveness and willfulness, mankind loved and united with the feminine that is woman. Along with love came sexuality, the second fire, which ignites the energies of love.

Teilhard de Chardin has written:

"Considered in its full biological reality, love—that is to say the affinity of being with being—is not peculiar to man. It is a general property of all life and as such it embraces, in its varieties and degrees, all the forms successively adopted by organised matter. In the mammals, so close to ourselves, it is easily recognised in its different modalities: sexual passion, parental instinct, social solidarity, etc. . . . If there were no internal propensity to unite, even at a prodigiously rudimentary level—indeed in the molecule itself —it would be physically impossible for love to appear higher up, with us, in 'hominised' form. By rights, to be certain of its presence in ourselves, we should assume its presence, at least in an inchoate form, in everything that is . . . Driven by the forces of love, the fragments of the world seek each other so that the world may come to being."[1]

Love's energies have the capacity to move us from the personal to the transpersonal stage of life. Transpersonal love is the love that goes beyond ego, beyond the needs of the individual, beyond anything that is narrowing and possessive. Transpersonal love unites the personal ego with the larger Self, and allows us to experience the flow of the energies of the universe in and through our own beings. But in human experience the ego personality feels frail indeed, when facing the powers of nature in which the Self is manifesting. How to live with the forces that cannot be encompassed by the ego is a difficult question. Answers cannot come from reason alone, although reason has surely helped to harness some of the energies of nature. Still, we often stand at the rim of knowledge, and there answers do not stem from reason alone. Sometimes meaning arises from an inner knowing that may clothe itself in the images of dreams.

A woman told me of a dream in which she was at sea in a small boat when a terrific storm came up. The waves were as high as mountains. They tossed the craft up and down at a furious pitch. She clung to the mast, feeling every muscle tense, until the agony was so great that she had to let go. Instead of dying, she leaned back into the sea and became a great wave. Completely relaxed now, she felt the power of the water surging through her being as she rose and sank and rose again. Then, as suddenly as it had begun, the storm subsided and she was back in her little boat again, and the sea was smooth once more. She had given herself to the sea; she had transcended the conflict between life and death, and she had entered the space of oneness with all there is.

To move deliberately and consciously to a stage beyond ego requires a willingness to let go, to give up what has been most valuable and most comforting in life, and what has promised the greatest rewards. The high point of the ego stage, as we have seen as we reviewed some developmental theories, is the achievement of a sense of independence and personal autonomy. One has learned to depend upon oneself and one's own judgment to find a way in the world. After much experience, and learning from the experience, we find out who we are and we present an image to the world that more or less represents our self-image. I am that, we say, rich man, poor man, beggarman, thief. We take our place in society, fill a role, become known by our reputation. Whether or not we are successful in the world's eyes, most of us struggle to maintain that image. We know only too well that the image has its flaws, but at least they are flaws we have learned to live with. As for growth and change, we are prepared to use our intelligence and guile to pursue ends that will improve our situation and demonstrate our competency. This is what the world rewards, as we have learned.

The self-images that we employ to negotiate our way through the world represent parts of our being, but surely not all of it. We present ourselves as conscious human beings moving in the world as women or as men, performing the functions that are consonant with our role in life. We know that we are far more than this, and that we draw upon resources from the contrasexual side of our nature to experience ourselves more fully and our lives as more whole. The transpersonal view allows us to unite the opposite tendencies within ourselves, to integrate energies which flow in different directions into a dynamic system. The natural energetic systems, which in our culture and others have been identified with the masculine principle and the feminine principle, or with yang/yin, suggest the active, probing consciousness on the one hand and the receptive, containing, conserving on the other. This seeming dichotomy is as old as creation. The archetypal qualities of the energetic forces that we experience continuously are expressed in the symbolic language of Genesis 1:14–19, where energy, as light, is given the form of the sun and the moon:

"And God said, 'Let there be lights in the firmament of the heavens to separate the day from the night; and let them be for signs and for seasons and for days and for years, and let them be lights in the firmament of the heavens to give light upon the earth.' And it was so. And God made the two great lights, the greater light to rule the day, and the lesser light to rule the night; he made the stars also. And God set them in the firmament of the heavens to give light upon the earth, to rule over the day and over the night, and to separate the light from the darkness. And God saw that it was good. And there was evening and there was morning, a fourth day."

If we are to understand this as a psychological statement, then the light which is given by these two lamps set in the heavens can represent two kinds of consciousness. When we allow our imagination to go with these symbols, we see that although one rules over the night, or lesser consciousness, and the other over the day, or greater consciousness, there are nevertheless times when both sun and moon can be seen in the sky. Even when only one can be seen, we know that the other is present, even though it is invisible. We also know that at dawn the sun moves into the dominant position, and the moon recedes, and at twilight the opposite comes to pass. So, in the human psyche, the sun-consciousness has its day and the moon its night, and our charge is to learn to live in the light of each one and value it for its own special way of being.

Out of the nonmanifest unity that we call God, we have taken the manifestations and used them for symbols to bring us closer to perception of the hidden order that rules over us. The progressive creation of human life depends on the union and separation of male and female in a drama that is being perpetually enacted. When we lived altogether in the framework of the Cartesian-Newtonian paradigm and our consciousness was subject to it, we were engaged in the analytical process of separating out and making distinctions between male and female. We were not satisfied with anatomical and functional descriptions but found it necessary to designate behavioral characteristics as masculine and feminine, corresponding to the biological sex. We needed guidelines for rearing children so that they could identify themselves with their sex and its functions and, beyond that, with the sex roles that would help them to adapt to the social structures of their environments. Throughout human history, the degree of psychological differentiation of men and women on the basis of sex has varied greatly, from the old matriarchal civilizations of ancient times, to the small agricultural communities preceding the industrial revolution when there was relatively little differentiation of sex role, to the sharp separation of concepts of masculinity and femininity which came into prominence after the industrial revolution, and to the emergence of a new kind of cooperation between the sexes in the working world.

In the days of Freud and Jung, "feminine values" were relatively easy to categorize. The feminine values were those that had to do with nurturance, emotionality, passivity, and submission. These designations came from the psychological theories of men, so there may be some masculine bias here, but nevertheless they did reflect ways in which women's functioning had been limited before the advent of the technology that offered women reproductive freedom. Once these limitations were lifted, women were able to develop areas of their personalities that had been dormant before. They faced new and different demands as they began to take significant responsibilities in what had previously been considered "man's world." They discovered the presence of another order of consciousness that was available to them, if only they had the courage and the stamina to make full use of it.

In women's studies, the new field of scholarly research, it was demonstrated that many of the qualities of personality which had long been associated with the sexual stereotypes of "the feminine" belonged to the male psyche as well, and that many of those qualities that used to be ascribed to males exclusively were, in fact, also components of the psyche of women.

The term *androgyny* came into common use during the seventies to account for the interplay within one person of two sets of qualities that had formerly been designated as "masculine" and "feminine." Psychological tests were designed that justified the observation that certain individuals frequently utilize the qualities attributed to both sexes, while others follow the more or less traditional patterns associated either with masculinity or with femininity. I embarked on a study of persons who apparently were able to transcend the cultural stereotypes and incorporate. whatever attributes they needed from a psychological repertoire of diverse modes of thought, feeling, and action. In my investigation of androgyny, I traced the roots of this ability—to blend the distinct kinds of energies that are associated with the masculine and the feminine nature—over the centuries and back to their beginnings in myth and legend. I discovered that many of the qualities which seem to us representative of the "eternal masculine" or the "enternal feminine," because we have made rigid stereotypes of them, have, in fact, been undergoing continuous transformative processes. Sometimes these shifts would occur with great drama and intensity, as when the Hebrews invaded Canaan and immediately attempted to demolish the goddess-worshipping cults that they found there and establish in their place the dominion of the Father-God. Sometimes they changed more slowly with gradual cultural developments.

My view of androgyny[2] was not bound by the descriptions of qualities of personality or modes of behavior reported in the psychological literature of the time. I addressed myself, rather, to seeking out an awareness of the innate potentials with which all people are endowed and which give them the capacity to exercise an infinite variety of ways of being.

We can see these many ways as expressions of the flow of the mysterious subtle energy that animates our lives: *ch'i, prāna, ruach, pneuma.* There are two directions of that flow, as seen from the position of the ego consciousness that perceives the process. From the point on which I stand, I can only feel, know, see, sense energy in two ways—it is going out and it is coming in. It is moving away and it is moving toward. It is not a matter of either/or, because at all times we are functioning in both modes.

Becoming androgynous means more than recognizing the unconscious other within ourselves. Androgyny is the psychological living-out of the harmonious relationship between the greater and the lesser lights. In terms of everyday living it means that men and women pay attention to the subtle fluctuations of energies in themselves and in each other and make space in their lives for these variations on sexual themes to be experienced. Androgyny is a stage in human development when the stereotypical sexual behaviors and habits of thought are being broken down and when efforts are being directed to achieve a condition in which society will impose no limitations upon people specifically because they are members of one sex or the other. Androgyny is a way of breaking down sexism in society. Androgynous child-rearing is a way of starting out young people feeling that being male or being female does not bind them to a certain way of life, it only defines their reproductive structures and capacities. This is not a lesson to be taught. It will only be assimilated if it is practiced in the home where the child grows up.

When finally the solar and the lunar are harmonized in one human being, neither man nor woman feels threatened when they see that the man possesses the virtues of the feminine and the woman the virtues of the masculine. For then it is possible for a man to say: "The more feminine you get, the more masculine you get. That's the paradox. Or is it? The more one leg gets strengthened by exercising it, the more the other is strengthened. It is not a question of masculine and feminine, two separate and opposite qualities, working against each other. We are not 'both masculine and feminine,' we are 'masculine/feminine.' " As a man of forty found himself becoming strong on the feminine side, he could say: "In some settings I am now more assertive, more firm, more of a leader. A man becomes powerful as the feminine power within him comes alive and functioning. He experiences his potency as the feminine power in him is activated. As the masculine becomes potent, the feminine becomes fecund."

Jung had remarked in his essay "The Stages of Life"[3] that by midlife people are usually entrenched in their personal attitudes and social positions. It seems to them as if they had discovered the right course, the right ideas, the right principles of behavior. Yet, at this time of life, statistics show a rise of depression and neurotic complaints, of impulsive sexual escapades and divorce. A change in the psyche is in preparation, and if it is not understood convictions and moral principles are apt to become rigid, and intolerance and fanaticism become a way of life. But if the change can be recognized as the diminution of ego development, and the beginning of the movement toward integration, androgyny can be embraced as a phase in the movement toward the transpersonal.

The transpersonal stage can be entered only after one has experienced the ego stage, and transpersonal sexuality can be experienced only when there has been enough of that sexuality which comes out of the sureness of sexual identity, of knowing who one is, and of feeling strong in one's own power. One cannot give up the power one has never held, nor even the illusion of power if one has never had that illusion. For transpersonal loving there is no predictable scenario. When does it begin? When does it end?

After having firmly established our sense of who we are, we may be free enough from the fear of loss of identity to consider that we are also a concentration of atomic particles with a certain temporary coherence, through which the stuff of the universe is continuously passing. We are utterly permeable troupes of dancing atoms, through which flow air and water, food and drink, music and sunlight and the crying of children, the hum of machinery, the roar of traffic and the dust of stars. In one transcendent moment of sexual union all of this can come together and take fire, like the sun's light focused by a crystal. From such a fire, we were given the gift of life.

That invisible fire remains with us as essence. It has color and heat but no real substance, yet it has the capacity to transmute substances. The fire burns in our loins and in our hearts. We can exclude it from our consciousness, or we can tend it and be warmed by it all through our lives.

What does it mean to tend the fire? It means to commit ourselves to the life-task of harnessing the energies of love, as the generations before us have learned to harness the energies of the physical world. The achievements of the past have been brought about to a great extent through the exercise of the "thinker," the faculty in us which we are schooled to develop as a part of the shaping of the adequate ego. Consciousness has long been associated with the thinking function. It is more than that, but the more has been depreciated in intellectual and scientific circles. The "thinker" values what has been proved, which is to say what has been shown to be true. Consequently, it has petrified knowledge in books and libraries, so that if we want to know how a thing is we can refer back to how the thing was. What we were taught in the old ways of education is out of date by the time we hear about it; it is ancient history in a world of evolving reality, like a still picture of a runner on his course. It is interesting and valuable primarily for providing a context for the present, so that we can better understand what is happening now.

The world of the emerging paradigm already is discovering and creating new tools that are more appropriate for dealing with the living moment-to-moment manifestations of reality. Long-distance telephone calls bouncing off satellites to connect people so that they can communicate with each other in the moment, live television that permits us to see history while it is happening, medical instruments with artificial eyes and ears that penetrate the body and give feedback as to what is happening while it is happening, word processors that move with the speed of the idea and adapt to change as soon as it is conceived, and the burgeoning computer-aided sciences which place unlimited amounts of information at the fingertip's command—all contribute to the possibility of seeing our world whole and its systems as all parts of an interconnected, interlocking web of mutual influence. These tools, and many others, allow us to press beyond the boundaries of ordinary thinking and to develop some other potentialities of ours. This is happening to a large degree without our conscious intent, although awareness can enhance the new developmental process.

An example is the fascination of young people with video games. Whatever criticism may be leveled at them—because they are said to keep children away from "worthwhile" activities—something very interesting is occurring. The games move rapidly, allowing no time for thought. The images move swiftly on the screen and the viewer must observe and react instantaneously. The player indeed becomes part of the action; the player and the game are one. The player, with the computer, experiences in microcosm the feeling of being involved in a mutually influencing activity in which each one is connected with a larger network of systems and has the potentiality of extending its influence even further. The player, becoming practiced and more skilled, learns to anticipate with that lightning-fast perception that belongs to the intuitive function, what the image on the screen will do, and responds not to what has happened, but to what is in the process of happening. The player is learning, while still a child, to engage in consciousness without thought—something that older people must work very hard to achieve because of having been conditioned to value the slow and laborious process of logical-sequential reasoning above any other way of coming to know.

Renée Weber, in analyzing the process which links David Bohm's work in physics with his interest in consciousness, describes the effect of Bohm's capacity for transcending ordinary thought process:

"Atom-smashing can occur only in the present and must occur ever afresh. The analogy of the atom with thought, and with an alleged thinker who authors thought, is crucial. The thinker is like the atom, cohering in time through its binding energy. When the binding energy of the physical atom is released in an accelerator, the resultant energy, staggeringly huge, becomes freed. Analogously huge amounts of binding energy are needed to create and sustain the 'thinker' and to maintain his illusion that he is a stable entity. That energy, being tied up, is unavailable for other purposes, pressed into the service of what Bohm calls 'self-deception' (a phenomenon described in detail by Buddha as ignorance, *avidya*, literally 'not really seeing'). Thought, or what Bohm terms the 3-dimensional mind, mistakenly believing itself autonomous and irreducible, requires and hence squanders vast amounts of cosmic energy on this illusion. Energy thus pre-empted cannot flow into other grooves. The consequence is an unsound cosmic ecology . . ."[4]

Bohm sees this as doubly destructive to the *holomovement* (his term for the dynamic flowing back and forth of consciousness between the unmanifest and the manifest reality, the implicate order and the explicate order—what we have called the *superconscious*). Bohm says that thought can pollute the holomovement so that it misunderstands itself, choosing fiction over fact and thereby enslaving itself. The holomovement also wounds itself by substituting the isolated ego for the consciousness of mankind. He sees the concept of ego as an abstraction "founded on fallacy, enslaving others through its anger, greed, competitiveness and ambition." Bohm's ego concept is equated with the "thinker." This is the one who becomes fixated as residual energy, weighed down by "undigested experience, memory, habit-patterns, identification, desire, aversion, projection and image-making."[5]

The psychologies of the old paradigm were products of the "thinker." Behaviorism treats symptoms, not causes. It can be seen as the enforcement of preselected programs on behavioral processes while reducing the options for free selection. Psychodynamic psychiatry and psychology are concerned with causes more than symptoms. They operate on the principle that the more that can be brought into consciousness concerning the causes of the mental disturbance, the more likely are the symptoms to disappear. Cognitive/developmental psychology is interested in how the thinking process develops over time and how it can be enhanced. Interestingly enough, and not surprising, are the ways each of these psychological approaches deals with sexuality. Behavior modification is the favorite modality of the sexual dysfunction clinics. They use positive reinforcement to bring about desired behaviors and aversive conditioning to extinguish undesired behaviors. Psychoanalysis seeks the causes of sexual dysfunction by reactivating the past and transferring it into the therapeutic situation, seeking to find the basis for present difficulties in the buried parental relationships of a bygone era. And cognitive/developmental psychology observes and reports on developing patterns of sexual behavior over time, in studies which rapidly grow obsolete. There are numerous contemporary psychological schools which adapt the older theories to newer social patterns, or which hybridize the old schools and offer something synthetic which appears different and novel.

If, then, we consider removing the "thinker" from the foreground of consciousness and relegating it to the background where it more properly belongs, where shall we look for a function that heals the wounded holomovement and our wounded selves? It seems to me that the answer lies in *intuition*, the function of insight, which makes things clear "all of a sudden" and, in doing so, changes everything. Thinking is involved with memory; it dredges up the past and sits with it, as with the corpse of an ancient relative. Intuition is involved with re-membering, a vital process of bringing together what has been parted and making it whole again. Intuition means looking into, immediate apprehension, the power or faculty of attaining to direct knowledge without evident rational thought and inference.

Intuition is cultivated by meditation, which opens the person to the influx of that which is beyond ego. Meditation, then, is a way of tending the fire, of keeping alive and active the process of conscious evolution. Meditation has been called "remembrance" or "recollection." It is attention focused inward, enabling the drawing together of energies into a fine flow, concentrating them in one direction and letting go of all that is extraneous. Meditation is being present to what is central in the moment, so that it may be perceived in whatever dimensions the moment chooses to manifest itself.

There are many forms of meditation. Each has its rules of practice designed to liberate the energies that have been locked into ego strivings and bring them into a universal context. The meditative tradition is ancient. It has occupied an important place in many religions, particularly the religions of the East. Taoism, Buddhism, Hinduism, and Islam all make it an important part of their practice. In the West it has not been as central, but it is experienced on some levels in most Jewish and Christian services of worship. I recall in my own growing-up years the silent devotion that was a part of every service I attended, followed by the prayer, "Let the words of my mouth and the meditation of my heart be acceptable in Thy sight, O Lord, my Rock and my Redeemer" (Psalms 19:14). Two things stood out for me: one, that what occurred in the silence of the heart was as important as that which was expressed in the world, and, two, that the meditation period was always too brief.

Ideally, meditation is a spiritual practice to be observed with regularity. It is necessary to set aside certain times to renew the commitment to silence, and to concentrate on the flickering movement of the flame within, burning at all times. Also, one needs to take time to become aware that since we are part and parcel of all that is, the movement within is no different from the movement without. As we train our attentiveness through meditation, we begin to pierce the veils that filter the light of consciousness.

During our daily activities in the world we can also participate in the keen awareness that meditation fosters. To develop the capacity to listen with full attention to another person as one would to the promptings of one's own soul, and to respond with compassion as with the warmth of an inner fire, is a way of being that is well worth cultivating. There is a way of looking at any task that is meditative in nature. One does not judge whether it is good or bad, whether one desires to do it or not. The task is given, or we have taken it upon ourselves—it does not matter which. It lies before us, and we turn our attention toward it, spending the energy that is required without holding back, and staying with it until it is completed. The task must be done carefully and well, whether it is cleaning a house, planting a garden, or establishing a relationship. Attention must be paid to the interaction of all the pieces, so that they may find their place and regenerate, as a new pattern of the whole.

Sexual love, itself, may be experienced as a form of meditation. In this most intimate of relationships, it is possible to open oneself to the other, and to the wider context in which the two exist. Then old patterns and old expectations may be transcended, and each may approach the partner with the same openness and clarity as one would hope to find in quiet moments with the uncluttered mind, in silence. As when we meditate alone, we will have no fixed expectations but will be prepared to accept exactly what is and to perceive it without defending against it or without disguising oneself. So, too, the partner is to be met without fixed expectations, but with great openness. There is no question of succeeding or failing, because there is no goal. There is only what is.

It does not always go so easily, however. Sometimes between two human beings who love each other a cloud of misunderstanding or disappointment is present, or the feeling of not being valued, or any of a hundred other waves of interference between oneself and one's partner. Then there arises a need for the attentiveness which invites dialogue. It is not a matter of clearing the way so that a sexual act can take place. It is, rather, that being sexual is an ongoing process, and every facet of the relationship between the people who are sexually involved is a movement that either draws them together or drives apart the fragments of their being. When two lovers come into each other's presence, the meditative way is for each to attend with all the senses to that other human being with whom deep communion is desired. First, it is necessary to see with soft eyes the other person as a being in space; to take into oneself the totality of the vision of the other, how he or she stands and walks, the message in the movement of the body—whether it is warmly receptive or weary and dispirited. What of the eyes? Are they unclouded, permitting a view into the heart, or defended as though fearful or distrustful? The clothing, what mood does it represent? Remove it, remove everything that is brought in from another place. Begin naked and afresh. Regard the body as an energy body; what sort of energy is the partner sending forth or receiving? Perceive this, not in bits and pieces, but as a totality. One sees the other whole, and takes that vision into one's own depths.

Touch is the elementary way of apprehending another human being. Touch makes the connection that sends the energy coursing through two bodies and filling them with each other's presence. Meditative touching is caressing with care, and with extreme sensitivity to the response of the other. Fingertips discern the subtle nuances of skin and flesh and, more than that, convey the strength and the gentleness that carries the energies of love, though they are capable, too, of callousness and downright cruelty. A touch can say, "I want to be close to you and I will care for you," or "I want to be gratified whether you like it or not." Meditative sexuality allows each the delight of being in tune with the other and experiencing resonance in the relationship. I cannot say it more clearly than that, but once one has felt it, no more need be said.

To hear the voice of the other and understand not only the words but also the tone, the timbre, and the meta-messages that are carried by the voice is a meditative art. Attentiveness is again the key. To allow the person you love to know that in this moment she or he is totally central in your consciousness opens the way for defenseless sharing. To partake of the fullness of the other means also taking in with all senses: to inhale the smells exuded by the other, and to know the taste of all the places to which the mouth and tongue are drawn. To feel the movement of the other's body is to know the other as a total being who has come out of the immensity of space to be a companion, an answer to the insight of a Creator-God who, meditating upon all that he had made, saw that it was not good that man should be alone.

When the obstacles to coming together, if there be some, have been attended to or put aside by mutual consent, and the desire for joining in a sexual embrace is felt, it is time to bring the partner into close touch with your own body and into the sphere of your own meditative attention. With great slowness the energies may be allowed to melt and become fluid, so that they flow, each within each. There is no need to hurry; the prolongation of every sensation increases the sensitivity and the depth of the meditation. It is well to let the fires rise from within in the way that they will, without attempting to "do" anything. Let it happen through you, as the Divine aspects of the Self move through you and your partner, and enter into communion, in perfect resonance with the movement of the physical bodies, which embody the Divine. In this sexual union, orgasm is not deliberately sought; orgasm is not a goal; yet orgasm has a tendency to occur. If it does, it is to be accepted, not as a culmination of the process, but as that which releases the physical tension and allows the spiritual energy to flow even more freely than before. Remain together, then, in deepest quiet for as long as possible. Draw energy from the deep place within yourself to waken the sleeping serpent at the base of the spine, and allow her to rouse herself, if that is her desire, and to spiral upward.

At times there will be no orgasm, and that is because none is needed. Although the presence of the other is perceived by the brain, which then warms and energizes the entire organism, it is not entirely the other's presence that is responsible. Loving brings awareness of a whole world full of potential partners, yet only the partner who is accepted by the mind and heart—as informed by the brain—can be part of this meditation. This one, then, is allowed to awaken the powers within—the powers that are symbolized by the serpent, whose attributes are the ability to penetrate through narrow channels, and to move with lazy slowness or with the speed of lightning.

Resting in the firm and quiet embrace of the other is tantamount to being connected with the rest of the universe; for the "other" represents all that is not yourself, the responsiveness of the rest of the universe to your own being-in-the-world. Being thus enveloped, being touched and held, you sink ever more deeply into the meditative state, the state which leads to a sense of perfect oneness. Give attention to that which flows through the center of your being and follow it, being aware of where it moves and where it pauses, and what is touched when it comes to rest. Allow it to rise in the way that it will without forcing excitement and without inhibiting it. Whatever needs to happen in you will happen, and when the energy is ready to recede it will recede. It has all come about spontaneously, and you have allowed yourself to join with your lover to be a vehicle for the energy of love.

Sexuality does not always require a partner. It can be experienced as inner union. There is a form of celibacy which is highly sexual. By this I mean that the energies of love can be fully experienced by one who is alone. In the alembic of one's own body it is possible to produce a rare and precious substance. This is the result of freely choosing celibacy as a way of life, either for a time or as an ongoing commitment. It is by no means the same as celibacy that is imposed upon one from without, from a source that denies the sexual nature of the human being or else requires that the person transcend his or her sexual nature. Too often this "imposed" celibacy has its origin in a belief system that regards sexuality as an impediment to the full devotion required by the religious life. Imposed celibacy may sometimes be viewed as a burden. But celibacy that is freely chosen may become part of the process of claiming for oneself a close and tender relationship with the Other which is nonmanifest, instead of with the other which is manifest in a human lover.

Alone in meditation, the sense of oneness enters the person as total organism. Not as separate aspects of body, or mind, or spirit, but as a body/mind/spirit totality, one surrenders oneself to the mystery of being. With this surrender of the ego, the opposing energies of the organism are freed to seek each other. The golden forces of masculine energy that radiate outward with the intensity of the sun are taken up by the silver, reflective surface of the moon, and sent forth to shine with a different glow. The creative impulse may then be felt as quietly expanding, and the receptive space is felt as containing it and giving it form. The feeling of oneness does not require a human partner, for all the universe participates in one individual's love for the world as it is. There is something strangely satisfying about this form of celibacy. It allows one great openness to whatever life places on the altar of the spirit. It allows one to walk through life like the Taoist sage who could admire the flecks of dust on the surface of a puddle of muddy water in the street, seeing that they sparkled like diamonds. It allows one to take pleasure in the bite of the wind and the chill of autumn rain. It allows one to smile at a stranger and find a response in the eyes of the other. It allows earth and sky to reveal themselves in their many moods as companions that will never leave you.

The "thinker" is occupied primarily with changing the object—or changing the world. In human relationships, this is translated to mean changing the other person. It does not work, and inevitably leads to conflict with others. To these others, *you* are the object, a part of the world to be changed, and they themselves are the subject. Each works with objects considered to be outside of themselves. Thus the ego continues to labor in the fruitless struggle for personal identity and self-preservation, and finds that a fully loving relationship is antithetical to this endeavor.

By contrast, removing the "thinker" from the position of primacy involves the ego itself, for the ego is the crucial factor in the process. The ego is attempting to transform and is, at the same time, undergoing transformation. Consequently, it becomes essential to replace the "thinker" with the participant-observer. The participant-observer in every experiment is an aspect of the proceedings, and whatever is transformed involves every aspect of the process of transformation. Meditation enables one to "see" with the eye of intuition, the third eye, which looks within and without simultaneously. In the practice of meditation it becomes clear that we are all subject and object, the observer and the observed, the lover and the beloved. There is no separation; there are only different points of view.

This is easy enough to say, but my words are only words and, again, a recapitulation of experience, a commentary after the fact. Therefore I do not wish to press the point. So much of what I have written comes from the "thinker." To place ideas in linear-sequential form has its uses. The word is as functional as the wheel. And so I have made use of a rhythmic sequence of black letters on a white page to communicate with you, the reader. I would have preferred to look into your eyes and see your smile, and to talk with you about your feelings in response to what I have been saying, and to listen to your reflections and take them into my consciousness. Then I would know that in this shared experience we both have been enriched, and in some small measure the entire texture of our consciousness would have been transformed. Our boundaries being permeable, we would have been open to mutual penetration, which on every level is an act of love.

NOTES

S.E. refers to Freud, *The Standard Edition of the Complete Psychological Works of Sigmund Freud* (1953–74). 24 vols. Translated from the German under the General Editorship of James Strachey. In collaboration with Anna Freud. Assisted by Alix Strachey and Alan Tyson. London: Hogarth Press and The Institute of Psycho-Analysis.

C.W. refers to Jung, *The Collected Works of C. G. Jung* (1953–79). Edited by Gerhard Adler, Michael Fordham, and Herbert Read. William McGuire, Executive Editor. Translated by R. F. C. Hull, Bollingen Series XX. Vols. 1, 3–5, 7–12, and 15–17, New York: Pantheon Books, 1953–66; vols. 2, 6, 13–14, and 18, Princeton, N.J.: Princeton University Press, 1967–79; London: Routledge & Kegan Paul.

CHAPTER 1. GREAT KNOWLEDGE AND SMALL KNOWLEDGE

1. *The Book of Thel.* In *The Complete Poetry and Prose of William Blake*, p. 3.
2. Alexander Maven, "The Mystic Union," *Journal of Transpersonal Psychology*, vol. I, 1, Spring 1969.
3. C. G. Jung, *The Practice of Psychotherapy*, C.W. 16, pp. 163–323.
4. Ibid., par. 457; figure 5, p. 249.
5. Alexander Maven, op. cit., pp. 51–55.
6. William Wordsworth, "Ode. Intimations of Immortality from Recollections of Early Childhood (1807)." In Sir Arthur Quiller-Couch, ed., *The Oxford Book of English Verse, 1250–1918*, p. 628.
7. "Soft eyes" was a concept introduced to me by George Leonard in a group workshop. Leonard's writings, especially *The Ultimate Athlete* and *The Silent Pulse*, elaborate this idea.
8. Thomas Merton, *The Way of Chuang Tzu*, pp. 40–41.

CHAPTER 2. MOVING TOWARD MODERNITY

1. Werner Heisenberg, *Physics and Philosophy*, p. 76.
2. Fritjof Capra, *The Tao of Physics*, p. 55.

CHAPTER 3. MODELS OF PSYCHE

1. Franz G. Alexander and Sheldon T. Selesnick, *The History of Psychiatry*, pp. 156–57.

2. *Webster's Third New International Dictionary*, p. 2032.
3. Alexander and Selesnick, ibid.
4. Ibid.
5. Ernest Jones, *The Life and Work of Sigmund Freud*, vol. 1, p. 41.
6. Frank J. Sulloway, *Freud, Biologist of the Mind*, pp. 61–62.
7. Ibid., pp. 62, 131.
8. Sigmund Freud, "Three Essays on the Theory of Sexuality" (1905), *S.E.* 7, pp. 125–243.
9. This case is discussed in Sigmund Freud, "Analysis of a Phobia in a Five-year-old Boy" (1909), *S.E.* 10, pp. 3–147.
10. Karen Horney, "The Flight from Womanhood: the Masculinity Complex in Women as Viewed by Men and Women," *International Journal of Psycho-analysis*, vol. 7, 3/4, pp. 324–29. Cited in Joanna Bunker Rohrbaugh, *Women: Psychology's Puzzle*, p. 111.
11. Ruth Moulton, "The Role of Clara Thompson in the Psycho-analytic Study of Women." In Jean Strouse, ed., *Women and Analysis*, pp. 207–30.
12. Joanna B. Rohrbaugh, *Women: Psychology's Puzzle*, pp. 140 f.
13. G. M. Farkas, "An Ontological Analysis of Behavior Therapy," *American Psychologist*, vol. 35, 4, April 1980, p. 367.
14. B. F. Skinner, *Beyond Freedom and Dignity*, pp. 81–82.
15. Erik H. Erikson, *Childhood and Society* and *Identity: Youth and Crisis*.
16. Lawrence Kohlberg, "The Development of Moral Character and Ideology." In Martin L. and Lois W. Hoffman, eds., *Review of Child Development Research*, vol. 1.
17. Lawrence Kohlberg, "A Cognitive Developmental Analysis of Children's Sex-role Concepts and Attitudes." In Eleanor E. Maccoby, ed., *The Development of Sex Differences*.
18. Jane Loevinger, "The Meaning and Measurement of Ego Development." *American Psychologist*, vol. 21, 3, March 1966, pp. 195–206.
19. Ibid., p. 200.
20. Ibid., citing Abraham Maslow, *Motivation and Personality* (1954) and *Toward a Psychology of Being* (1962).

CHAPTER 4. REBELLION OF THE SELF

1. Charles A. and Mary M. Aldrich, *Babies Are Human Beings*.
2. Allen Wheelis, *The Quest for Identity*, pp. 120 f.
3. M. Esther Harding, *The Way of All Women*, p. 70.

4. Timothy F. Leary, Ralph Metzner, and Richard Alpert, *The Psyche-delic Experience*, p. 13.
5. In *The Complete Poetry and Prose of William Blake*, p. 153.
6. *The I Ching* or *Book of Changes*, the Richard Wilhelm translation rendered into English by Cary F. Baynes, p. 298.
7. Private communication with Ralph Metzner.
8. "The Marriage of Heaven and Hell." In *The Complete Poetry and Prose of William Blake*, p. 39.
9. Ibid., p. 36.

CHAPTER 5. FOUR MEN IN SEARCH OF ENLIGHTENMENT

1. C. G. Jung, *Memories, Dreams, Reflections*, pp. 150, 152.
2. C. G. Jung, "The Spiritual Problem of Modern Man," *Civilization in Transition*, C.W. 10, par. 188.
3. Ibid., par. 190.
4. C. G. Jung, "The Love Problem of a Student," *Civilization in Transition*, C.W. 10, par. 225.
5. Ibid., par. 234.
6. C. G. Jung, *Psychological Types*, C.W. 6, par. 372.
7. Ibid., par. 368, citing Goethe's *Faust*.
8. Ibid., par. 370.
9. Ibid., par. 372.
10. Mary Harrington Hall, "A Conversation with Abraham Maslow," *Psychology Today*, July 1968.
11. Frank G. Goble, *The Third Force: the Psychology of Abraham Maslow*, pp. 19 f.
12. Ibid., pp. 14–19.
13. Abraham H. Maslow, *The Farther Reaches of Human Nature*, p. 45.
14. Ibid., p. 49.
15. Ibid., p. 271.
16. Ibid., pp. 276–77.
17. "The Marriage of Heaven and Hell." In *The Complete Poetry and Prose of William Blake*, p. 35.
18. Alan Watts, *In My Own Way*, p. 355.
19. Alan Watts, *Nature, Man and Woman*, p. 178.
20. Ibid., p. 184.
21. Ibid., p. 196.
22. Ibid., pp. 188–89.
23. Huston Smith, *Forgotten Truth: the Primordial Tradition*, p. 30.

CHAPTER 6. EXPERIMENTING WITH NEW FORMS

1. Allen Wheelis, *The Quest for Identity*, p. 130.
2. Supportive evidence for this is found in the work of the sociobiologists. See Chapter 10.
3. Cited by Martin Heidegger in *The End of Philosophy*, pp. 52–53.
4. Alan Watts, in collaboration with Al Chung-liang Huang, *Tao, the Watercourse Way*, p. 52. Passage is translated by Watts.
5. C. G. Jung, "Foreword to the 'I Ching,'" *Psychology and Religion: West and East*, C.W. 11, par. 1018.
6. *The I Ching* or *Book of Changes*, "Shuo Kua: Discussion of the Trigrams," p. 264.
7. C. G. Jung, "Woman in Europe," *Civilization in Transition*, C.W. 10, par. 275.
8. *Review of Existential Psychology and Psychiatry*, vol. XIV, 1, 2, and 3, 1978–79.
9. Ibid.
10. *The Esalen Catalogue*, January 1981–June 1981.
11. Cited in Hugh Kenner, "Fuller's Follies," a review of R. Buckminster Fuller's *Critical Paths*, in *Saturday Review*, February 1981, pp. 81–82.
12. Edward O. Wilson, *On Human Nature*, p. 129.

CHAPTER 7. OF NARCISSISM, SELF-LOVE, AND
            LIBERATION

1. Sigmund Freud, lecture xxvi, "The Theory of the Libido: Narcissism." In Part III, "General Theory of the Neuroses" (1917), *A General Introduction to Psychoanalysis*.
2. Heinz Kohut, *The Analysis of the Self*.
3. Peter Homans, *Jung in Context*, p. 39.
4. *Quadrant*, Fall 1980, p. 47.
5. Gerd H. Fenchel, "Paternity and the Changing Role of Women." In *Issues in Ego Psychology*, vol. 2, 1, 1979.

CHAPTER 8. SEXUALITY IN THE EMERGING PARADIGM

1. Cited in Fritjof Capra, *The Tao of Physics*, pp. 138–39.
2. Graham Chedd, *The New Biology*, p. 283.
3. Renée Weber, "The Enfolding-Unfolding Universe: a Conversation with David Bohm," *ReVision, a Journal of Consciousness and Change*, vol. I, 3/4, Summer/Fall 1978.
4. Alfred North Whitehead, *Science and the Modern World*, p. 266.

CHAPTER 9. THE JERUSALEM METAPHOR

1. "To the Christians," *Jerusalem*. In *The Complete Poetry and Prose of William Blake*, p. 231.
2. Letter to Thomas Butts, 22 November 1802. In *The Complete Poetry and Prose of William Blake*, p. 722.
3. Rupert Sheldrake, "The Hypothesis of Formative Causation," from *New Scientist*, cited in *Brain/Mind Bulletin*, vol. 6, 2, p. 2.
4. Ken Wilber, "The Pre/trans Fallacy," *ReVision*, Fall 1980, p. 53.

CHAPTER 10. RE-MEMBERING AND FOR-GETTING

1. Edward O. Wilson, *Sociobiology*, the abridged edition, p. 155. Later quotes on pp. 158 and 159.
2. "The Marriage of Heaven and Hell." In *The Complete Poetry and Prose of William Blake*, p. 35.
3. June Singer, *Androgyny: Toward a New Theory of Sexuality*, pp. 225 f.
4. Sam Woolgoodja, *Lalai Dreamtime*. Aboriginal Arts Board, 1975. Cited in *Australian Dreaming*, compiled and edited by Jennifer Isaacs.
5. These stories were told by David Mowaljarli of Mowanjum, Western Australia, and cited in *Australian Dreaming*, pp. 172–73.
6. "General Aspects of Dream Psychology" (1916/1948), *The Structure and Dynamics of the Psyche*, C.W. 8, par. 475.

CHAPTER 11. AWARENESS BETWEEN CONCEPTION AND BIRTH

1. Stanislav Grof, *LSD Psychotherapy*, pp. 46–47.
2. Stanislav Grof, *Realms of the Human Unconscious*, p. 46.
3. C. G. Jung, "A Review of the Complex Theory," *The Structure and Dynamics of the Psyche*, C.W. 8, par. 216.
4. Ibid., par. 210.
5. Ibid., par. 201.
6. Stanislav Grof, *Realms of the Human Unconscious*, p. 94.
7. C. G. Jung, "Marriage as a Psychological Relationship," *The Development of Personality*, C.W. 17, pp. 187–201.
8. Frank Lake, "The Maternal Foetal Distress Syndrome."

CHAPTER 13. THE PRE-PERSONAL STAGE: *Emergence*

1. Milton Diamond, "Biological Foundations for Social Development." In Frank A. Beach, ed., *Human Sexuality in Four Perspectives*, pp. 44–45.

2. "Vala: Night the First," *The Four Zoas*. In *The Complete Poetry and Prose of William Blake*, p. 302.
3. C. G. Jung, "The Stages of Life," *The Structure and Dynamics of the Psyche*, C.W. 8, pp. 387–403.
4. Ibid., par. 750.

CHAPTER 14. THE PERSONAL STAGE: *The Rise of Ego Consciousness*
1. Robert Jay Lifton, *The Broken Connection*, p. 83.
2. Norman Cousins, "Being Healthy Is Not Enough," *Saturday Review*, June 1980, p. 10.

CHAPTER 15. TRANSITION: *From Personal to Transpersonal*
1. C. G. Jung, "The Relations between the Ego and the Unconscious," *Two Essays on Analytical Psychology*, C.W. 7, pp. 121–241.
2. Ibid., par. 254.

CHAPTER 16. THE TRANSPERSONAL STAGE: *Uniting the Fragments*
1. Pierre Teilhard de Chardin, *The Phenomenon of Man*, p. 264.
2. June Singer, *Androgyny: Toward a New Theory of Sexuality*.
3. C. G. Jung, "The Stages of Life," *The Structure and Dynamics of the Psyche*, C.W. 8, pp. 387–403.
4. Renée Weber, "Field Consciousness and Field Ethics." In Ken Wilber, ed., *The Holographic Paradigm and Other Paradoxes*, pp. 36–37.
5. Ibid., p. 37.

REFERENCES

Aldrich, Charles A. and Aldrich, Mary M. *Babies Are Human Beings: an Interpretation of Growth.* New York: The Macmillan Company, second edition, 1954.

Alexander, Franz G. and Selesnick, Sheldon T. *The History of Psychiatry.* New York: Harper & Row, 1966.

Beach, Frank A., ed. *Human Sexuality in Four Perspectives.* Baltimore: The Johns Hopkins University Press, 1977.

Blake, William. *The Complete Poetry and Prose of William Blake,* ed. by David V. Erdman, commentary by Harold Bloom. Garden City, N.Y.: Anchor Press/Doubleday, newly revised edition, 1982.

Bohm, David. *Wholeness and the Implicate Order.* London: Routledge & Kegan Paul, 1980.

Brody, Jane E. "Value of Transsexual Surgery Is Disputed," *The New York Times,* October 2, 1979.

Capra, Fritjof. *The Tao of Physics.* Berkeley, Calif.: Shambhala Publications, 1975.

———. *The Turning Point.* New York: Simon and Schuster, 1982.

Chedd, Graham. *The New Biology.* New York: Basic Books, 1972.

Cousins, Norman. "Being Healthy Is Not Enough," *Saturday Review,* June 1980.

Covenant House Report, January 1980. 460 West 41 Street, New York, N.Y. 10036.

Diamond, Milton. "Biological Foundations for Social Development." In Frank A. Beach, ed., *Human Sexuality in Four Perspectives.* Baltimore: Johns Hopkins University Press, 1977.

Erikson, Erik H. *Childhood and Society.* New York: W. W. Norton & Company, second edition, 1964.

———. *Identity: Youth and Crisis.* New York: W. W. Norton & Company, 1968.

The Esalen Catalogue. January 1981–June 1981.

302   ENERGIES OF LOVE

Farkas, Gary M. "An Ontological Analysis of Behavior Therapy," *American Psychologist*, vol. 35, 4, April 1980.

Fenchel, Gerd H. "Paternity and the Changing Role of Women." In *Issues in Ego Psychology*, vol. 2, 1, 1979. New York: Washington Square Institute.

Ferguson, Marilyn. *The Aquarian Conspiracy*. Los Angeles: J. P. Tarcher, 1980.

——. "Karl Pribram's Changing Reality," *ReVision, a Journal of Consciousness and Change*, vol. 1, 3/4, Summer/Fall 1978.

Freud, Sigmund. "Three Essays on the Theory of Sexuality" (1905), *S.E.* 7.

——. "Analysis of a Phobia in a Five-year-old Boy" (1909), *S.E.* 10.

——. "The Theory of the Libido: Narcissism." In Part III, "General Theory of the Neuroses" (1917), *A General Introduction to Psychoanalysis* (1916–17), translated by Joan Riviere, Garden City, N.Y.: Garden City Publishing Co., 1943.

Goble, Frank G. *The Third Force: The Psychology of Abraham Maslow*. New York: Pocket Books, 1970.

Grof, Stanislav. *LSD Psychotherapy*. Pomona, Calif.: Hunter House, 1980.

——. *Realms of the Human Unconscious*. New York: The Viking Press, 1975.

Haeckel, Ernst. *Die Welträtsel*. Leipzig: Engelmann, 1899.

Hall, Mary Harrington. "A Conversation with Abraham Maslow," *Psychology Today*, July 1968.

Halstead, W. C. and Rucker, W. M. "Memory, a Molecular Maze," *Psychology Today*, vol. 2, 1, p. 40, 1968.

Harding, M. Esther. *The Way of All Women*. New York: G. P. Putnam's Sons, 1970.

Heidegger, Martin. *The End of Philosophy*. Translated by Joan Stambaugh. New York: Harper & Row, 1973.

Heisenberg, Werner. *Physics and Philosophy*. New York: Harper & Brothers, 1958.

Hoffman, Martin L. and Hoffman, Lois W., eds. *Review of Child Development Research*, Vol 1. New York: Russell Sage Foundation, 1964.

Homans, Peter. *Jung in Context.* Chicago: The University of Chicago Press, 1979.

Horney, Karen. "The Flight from Womanhood: the Masculinity Complex in Women as Viewed by Men and Women," *International Journal of Psycho-analysis*, vol. 7, 3/4.

The I Ching or *Book of Changes.* The Richard Wilhelm translation rendered into English by Cary F. Baynes. Bollingen Series XIX. Princeton, N.J.: Princeton University Press, third edition, 1967.

Isaacs, Jennifer, ed. *Australian Dreaming.* Sydney, Australia: Landsdowne Press, 1980.

Jaworski, Margaret. "Interview with Mary Calderone," *Family Circle*, March 11, 1980.

Jones, Ernest. *The Life and Work of Sigmund Freud*, 3 vols. New York: Basic Books, 1953–57.

Jung, C. G. *Memories, Dreams, Reflections.* New York: Pantheon Books, revised edition, 1973.

———. *Psychological Types*, C.W. 6, 1967.

———. "General Aspects of Dream Psychology" (1916/1948). In *The Structure and Dynamics of the Psyche*, C.W. 8, second edition, 1969.

———. "A Review of the Complex Theory" (1934/1948). In C.W. 8, second edition, 1969.

———. "The Stages of Life" (1930/1931). In C.W. 8, second edition, 1969.

———. "The Love Problem of a Student" (1922?). In *Civilization in Transition*, C.W. 10, second edition, 1970.

———. "Woman in Europe" (1927). In C.W. 10, second edition, 1970.

———. "Foreword to the *I Ching*" (1950). In *Psychology and Religion: West and East*, C.W. 11, second edition, 1969.

———. *The Practice of Psychotherapy*, C.W. 16, second edition, 1966.

———. "Marriage as a Psychological Relationship" (1925). In *The Development of Personality*, C. W. 17, 1954.

Kalsched, Donald. "Narcissism and the Search for Interiority," *Quadrant*, Fall 1980.

Kenner, Hugh. "Fuller's Follies." A review of R. Buckminster

Fuller's *Critical Paths*, New York: St. Martin's Press, in *Saturday Review*, February 1981.

Kohlberg, Lawrence. "A Cognitive Developmental Analysis of Children's Sex-role Concepts and Attitudes." In Eleanor E. Maccoby, ed., *The Development of Sex Differences*. Stanford, Calif.: Stanford University Press, 1966.

———. "The Development of Moral Character and Ideology." In Martin L. and Lois W. Hoffman, eds., *Review of Child Development Research*, vol. 1. New York: Russell Sage Foundation, 1964.

Kohut, Heinz. *The Analysis of the Self*. New York: International Universities Press, 1971.

Lake, Frank. "The Maternal Foetal Distress Syndrome," 1980. Unpublished manuscript, used by permission. Frank Lake, Lingdale, Weston Avenue, Nottingham, England NG74BA.

Lao-tzu, *Tao Te Ching*. Translated by Gia-fu Feng and Jane English. New York: Alfred A. Knopf, 1972.

Lasch, Christopher. *The Culture of Narcissism*. New York: W. W. Norton & Company, 1978.

Leary, Timothy F.; Metzner, Ralph; and Alpert, Richard. *The Psychedelic Experience*. New York: University Books, 1964.

Leary, Timothy F.; Alpert, Richard; and Metzner, Ralph. "Rationale of the Mexican Psychedelic Center." In *Utopiates: the Use and Users of LSD-25*, Richard H. Blum, ed. New York: Atherton Press, 1964.

Leonard, George B. *The Silent Pulse*. New York: E. P. Dutton & Co., 1978.

———. *The Ultimate Athlete*. New York: Avon Books, 1977.

Levin, David Michael. "The Opening of Vision: Seeing Through the Veil of Tears," *Review of Existential Psychology and Psychiatry*, vol. XIV, 1, 2, and 3, 1978–79.

Levinson, Daniel J. *The Seasons of a Man's Life*. New York: Random House, 1978.

Lifton, Robert Jay. *The Broken Connection*. New York: Simon and Schuster, 1979.

Loevinger, Jane. "The Meaning and Measurement of Ego Development," *American Psychologist*, vol. 21, 3, March 1966.

Maccoby, Eleanor E., ed. *The Development of Sex Differences*.

Stanford, Calif.: Stanford University Press, 1966.

Maccoby, Eleanor E. and Jacklin, Carol N. *The Psychology of Sex Differences*. Stanford, Calif.: Stanford University Press, 1974.

Maslow, Abraham H. *The Farther Reaches of Human Nature*. New York: The Viking Press, 1971.

——. *Motivation and Personality*. New York: Harper & Row, 1954; second edition, 1970.

——. *Toward a Psychology of Being*. New York: Van Nostrand-Reinhold Co., 1962; second edition, 1968.

Maven, Alexander. "The Mystic Union: a Suggested Biological Interpretation," *Journal of Transpersonal Psychology*, vol. I, 1, Spring 1969.

Merton, Thomas. *The Way of Chuang Tzu*. New York: New Directions, 1965.

Millett, Kate. *Sexual Politics*. Garden City, N.Y.: Doubleday & Company, 1970.

Mischel, Walter. "A Social Learning View of Sex Differences." In Eleanor E. Maccoby, ed., *The Development of Sex Differences*. Stanford, Calif.: Stanford University Press, 1966.

Moore, T. W. "Exclusive Early Mothering and Its Alternatives," *Scandinavian Journal of Psychology*, vol. 16, 1975, as reported in *American Psychologist*, vol. 34, 10, October 1979.

Moulton, Ruth. "The Role of Clara Thompson in the Psychoanalytic Study of Women." In Jean Strouse, ed., *Women and Analysis: Dialogues on Psychoanalytic Views of Femininity*. New York: Grossman Publishers, 1974.

Murti, T. R. V. *The Central Philosophy of Buddhism*. London: George Allen & Unwin, 1955. Cited in Fritjof Capra, *The Tao of Physics*. Berkeley, Calif.: Shambhala Publications, 1975.

Ognitz, Eileen. "Teen Pregnancy: Nation Faces Devastating Problem," Chicago *Tribune*, May 24, 1981.

Pribram, Karl H. *Languages of the Brain*. Englewood Cliffs, N.J.: Prentice-Hall, 1971.

Rank, Otto. *The Trauma of Birth*. New York: Harcourt, Brace & Co., 1929.

Restak, Richard M. *The Brain: the Last Frontier*. Garden City, N.Y.: Doubleday & Company, 1979.

Roberts, E. J. and Holt, S. A. "Parent-child Communication About Sexuality," *SIECUS Report*, vol. VIII, 4, March 1980.

Rohrbaugh, Joanna Bunker. *Women: Psychology's Puzzle.* New York: Basic Books, 1979.

Sagan, Carl. *The Dragons of Eden.* New York: Random House, 1977.

Schlafly, Phyllis. Interview. Chicago *Tribune*, April 28, 1981.

Sheehy, Gail. *Passages.* New York: E. P. Dutton & Co., 1976.

Sheldrake, Rupert. "The Hypothesis of Formative Causation," *New Scientist* 90 (1256), June 18, 1981. Cited in *Brain/Mind Bulletin*, vol. 6, 2, August 3, 1981.

SIECUS Report, March 1980. "Schools: an Essential Component in Good Sex Education."

Singer, June. *Androgyny: Toward a New Theory of Sexuality.* Garden City, N.Y.: Anchor Press/Doubleday, 1976.

———. *The Unholy Bible: a Psychological Interpretation of William Blake.* New York: G. P. Putnam's Sons, 1970.

Skinner, B. F. *Beyond Freedom and Dignity.* New York: Alfred A. Knopf, 1971.

Smith, Huston. *Forgotten Truth: the Primordial Tradition.* New York: Harper & Row, 1976.

———. *The Religions of Man.* New York: Harper and Row, 1958.

Strouse, Jean, ed. *Women and Analysis: Dialogues on Psychoanalytic Views of Femininity.* New York: Grossman Publishers, 1974.

Sulloway, Frank J. *Freud, Biologist of the Mind.* New York: Basic Books, 1979.

Teilhard de Chardin, Pierre. *The Phenomenon of Man.* New York: Harper & Brothers, 1959.

Walsh, Roger. *Towards an Ecology of the Brain.* Jamaica, N.Y.: SP Medical & Scientific Books, 1981.

Watts, Alan. *In My Own Way.* New York: Pantheon Books, 1972.

———. *The Joyous Cosmology.* New York: Pantheon Books, 1962.

———. *Nature, Man and Woman.* New York: Pantheon Books, 1958.

——— and Huang, Al Chung-liang. *Tao, the Watercourse Way.* New York: Pantheon Books, 1975.

Weber, Renée. "Field Consciousness and Field Ethics." In Ken Wilber, ed., *The Holographic Paradigm and Other Paradoxes,* Boulder, Colo.: Shambhala Publications, 1982.

——. "The Enfolding-Unfolding Universe: a Conversation with David Bohm," *ReVision, a Journal of Consciousness and Change,* vol. I, 3/4, Summer/Fall 1978.

Webster's Third New International Dictionary, unabridged. Springfield, Mass.: G. & C. Merriam Company, 1976.

Wheelis, Allen. *The Quest for Identity.* New York: W. W. Norton & Company, 1958.

Whitehead, Alfred North. *Science and the Modern World.* New York: The Macmillan Company, 1948.

Wilber, Ken, ed. *The Holographic Paradigm and Other Paradoxes,* Boulder, Colo.: Shambhala Publications, 1982.

——. "Physics, Mysticism, and the New Holographic Paradigm." In *The Holographic Paradigm and Other Paradoxes,* Boulder, Colo.: Shambhala Publications, 1982.

——. "The Pre-Trans Fallacy," *ReVision, a Journal of Consciousness and Change,* vol. 3, 2, Fall 1980.

Wilson, Edward O. *Sociobiology.* Cambridge, Mass.: The Belknap Press of Harvard University Press, abridged edition, 1980.

——. *On Human Nature.* Cambridge, Mass.: Harvard University Press, 1978.

Wordsworth, William. "Ode. Intimations of Immortality from Recollections of Early Childhood (1807)." In Sir Arthur Quiller-Couch, ed., *The Oxford Book of English Verse, 1250–1918,* Oxford, England: Clarendon Press, 1957.

Zeller, David. *Ruach.* Translation and recording on cassette. Belmont, Calif.: Heartsong Productions, 1981.

INDEX